THE COST
OF TRUTH

Also by Roberta Showalter Kreider

From Wounded Hearts

**Faith Stories of Lesbian, Gay,
Bisexual, and Transgender People
and Those Who Love them**

Together in Love

**Faith Stories of Gay, Lesbian,
Bisexual, and Transgender Couples**

THE COST OF TRUTH:

Faith Stories of Mennonite and Brethren Leaders and Those Who Might Have Been

Roberta Showalter Kreider, Editor

THE COST OF TRUTH:
Faith Stories of Mennonite and Brethren Leaders and Those Who Might Have Been

Copyright © 2004 by Roberta Showalter Kreider

Cover design by Steven Olofson
Pulpit photo by Marilyn Nolt

For orders, information, or reprint permission

kreiders@netcarrier.com

24-B Green Top Road, Sellersville, PA 18960-1223   (215) 257-7322

Also visit our website at:

www.GLBTcoach.com/RobertaKreider

ISBN 0-9664822-3-9

First Printing: September 2004

Library of Congress Cataloging-In-Publication Data

Kreider, Roberta Showalter, 1926-
      The cost of truth: Faith stories of Mennonite and Brethren leaders and those who might have been / Roberta Showalter Kreider
      p. cm.
Includes bibliographical references and resource materials
ISBN 0-9664822-3-9

      1. Gay and Lesbian—Christianity 2. Christian Faith 3. Relationships
      I. Title   II. Kreider, Roberta Showalter

Published in association with:
Strategic Press. P.O. Box 277, Kulpsville, PA 19443   (215) 723-8422

Unless stated otherwise, all Bible quotations are from *The New Revised Standard Version of the Bible,* © 1989 by the Division of Christian Education of the National Council of the Churches of Christ in the USA.

To the People of God

E V E R Y W H E R E

who desire to walk

in the Light of God's Truth

ACKNOWLEDGMENTS

The first copies of the 2003 revised edition of *From Wounded Hearts* arrived on our porch the day before we needed to take them to the University of Pennsylvania in Philadelphia to be entered into the Resource Center for the WOW 2003 (Witness our Welcome) Conference that began on August 14. This was the second ecumenical gathering of gay, lesbian, bisexual, and transgender Christians and their allies (GLBTA) from Canada and the U.S. It felt like a great accomplishment to meet that deadline. It was a relief to feel that my task of compiling and editing faith stories for the GLBTA community was completed.

That very week, I received a challenging phone call from a friend. As we visited together, she said, "I see another book in your future." "Oh, no, Diane," I replied, "You don't know how tired I am." She gently insisted, "But I see another book in your future." With a bit of exasperation, I asked, "Okay, what's it supposed to be about?" Her reply was, "Pastors." I answered, "Well, God will really have to show me on that one." I was sure that a book about pastors was not in *my* future and promptly dismissed it in my mind—at least, I thought I did.

On Saturday morning of the conference, denominational groups met separately. As our BMC group was gathering in our assigned room, Martha Juillerat, creator and director of the Shower of Stoles Project, appeared in the doorway and asked our leader if she could have a few minutes at the beginning of our meeting. Martha has gathered stoles from GLBT people of faith across North America, many of whom are pastors who have lost their credentials because they came out of the closet or because they welcomed GLBT individuals to be members of their congregations. The display that she takes to conventions and other meetings is quite impressive—and sad. (For information about the Shower of Stoles Project, visit www.showerofstoles.org)

Martha said that she is aware that Mennonite and Brethren pastors do not wear stoles, but she wanted their stories to be included in the ever-growing display. She asked if our pastors would send a towel symbolizing servanthood, as in the image of the pitcher, towel, and basin. The towels were to be accompanied by short stories about their defrocking. I raised my hand and asked, "Martha, are you planning to put these stories into a book?" She laughed and replied, "Maybe in my next life." It seemed like a light bulb went on in my head.

Later as we went around the room sharing our stories, we heard from people who felt called by God to leadership positions but were denied that privilege because of their sexual orientation. Throughout the day, I couldn't shake the feeling that these stories needed to be told to the broader church community. But how could I begin the journey with another book when I was so relieved to have just finished the last one?

On the way home that evening the urging became stronger, and the battle raged within. Finally, I silently prayed, "Okay, God, if you really want me to write another book, give me a title." Then I dismissed it from my mind. When I woke up the next morning, I had a main title and the beginning of the subtitle! I was beginning to feel some excitement about it. Now I needed to grapple with how to tell my husband. He had eagerly looked forward to the end of my book publishing journey.

As we worked together preparing breakfast, I carefully broached the subject with a question. "Honey, do you think our marriage could survive another book?" He asked what I had in mind. As I shared the details, he agreed that the stories I would be seeking were tremendously important for the church to hear. It was heartening to see how energized we both felt about it. Thank you, Harold, for all the support and encouragement you have given me on this journey.

Next, I needed to hear from another important person on our team. Rick Alderfer had faithfully worked hours beyond his regular job to help me set up and self-publish the other two books. Would he be willing to begin the journey with another one? Rick was one of the first friends I met on Sunday morning when I entered the building where people were gathering for the last worship service of the convention. When I asked him if he was ready to help me with another book and gave him the title, he laughed heartily and replied, "Of course we'll do it, Roberta." By the end of that day, I had my first author, and I was surprised at how eager I was to begin. Thank you, Rick, for the valuable work you have done on this book in addition to the other two.

We had some personal business to take care of and a trip to my sixtieth high school reunion coming up, so I decided to wait to launch the book until the middle of October. By the middle of December, I had promises for most of the stories I needed.

I am always aware that without people who are willing to take the risk to tell their stories, the books of faith stories would not exist. Though people usually refer to these books as "Roberta's books," it is more accurate to say "our" books because of the many individuals who have made the books possible. Each story is important to the combined witness of the entire GLBTA community of faith. As we came to the final stages of preparing her story for the book, one of the authors sent me this message, "You said you knew it would be difficult for many of us to write, but I had no idea how difficult. The pain is still so fresh."

Thank you, dear friends, for believing that it is important to tell your stories and for working patiently with me as we searched for the right words to express the deep emotions that sometimes seemed too painful to share. Your faith and courage, often in the face of great opposition, continue to be an inspiration to me.

Jesus said, "If you continue in my word, you are truly my disciples, and you will know the truth and the truth will make you free" (John 8:31-32). I hope and pray that the truth that is told within these pages will liberate and empower the truth tellers to live with freedom and joy as God's dear children.

These storytellers are human beings who have needs that are common to all of us. God bears witness with their spirits that they are included in God's family (Romans 8:14-17) and does not deny them the joy of human companionship and intimacy. God calls us all to live responsibly with the emotions and gifts we have each been given. To refuse to hear the stories of people of diverse sexual orientation and to refuse to walk in caring love with them is not loving one another as God has loved us (John 13:34).

Rev. Libby Smith, an ordained minister in the Unitarian Universalist denomination, worships with us at Perkasie Mennonite Church and is a member of one of the small Spiritual Disciplines groups. When I told our small group about my intentions to begin the journey with *The Cost of Truth*, Libby exclaimed, "Roberta, I thought you were going to rest!" Then she added, "If you are going to do it, you need to let us help you."

Libby has given many hours of invaluable help to me as an editorial advisor and proofreader. Thank you, Libby, for helping me see the blind spots of my editing. I am thankful that God brought you into my life "for such a time as this." Your friendship means much to me.

I appreciate the work of my friend Steve Olofson, the graphic artist who prepared the covers for the other two books. Thank you, Steve, for making time in your busy schedule to use your expertise on this book cover also. Thank you to Marilyn Nolt, who provided a photo of our church pulpit for Steve to incorporate into the design.

It was encouraging to receive the good responses in chapter thirty-two from many people in the U.S. and Canada who are willing to be counted as friends of the GLBT community. I thank them for adding their witness to the book.

I am grateful too for all the friends who cheered me on with their gifts to help with expenses, their words of encouragement, and their prayers that God would give strength and wisdom to bring this book to birth. Daily I experience God's answer to their prayers.

I thank God for giving me the opportunity to learn to know the people whose stories are told here. At times, the combined pain of all of them was heavy to bear, but I wouldn't have wanted to miss this journey for anything in the world. To be confident that I am doing the work God has chosen for me enables me to live with joy. My deep desire is that God's kingdom may come and God's will be done on earth as it is in heaven (Matthew 6:10).

TABLE OF CONTENTS

FOREWORD

In Roberta Kreider's first book on sexuality, *From Wounded Hearts* (1st edition), one writer concludes his story with the words, "Does God really want me to spend my life alone, without a satisfying, intimate relationship? Is being gay some kind of unique test that God gives to a small but significant portion of people as some kind of gauge of willpower or faith? I have concluded the answer to these questions is 'no.' But I do not want to do battle with people in the church who disagree." (p. 16).

The Genesis account of creation makes it clear that God does not intend for people to live alone but in relationship to another, others. At the heart of Anabaptist theology, as Mennonites have understood it, is the congregation, the "fellowship of believers." Yet in coping with the issue of those who are lesbian, gay, bisexual or transgender (LGBT), many churches, including many in the new Mennonite Church USA, advocate celibacy for these sisters and brothers in the faith. Some even declare them unwelcome. Let them "repent" or leave. But how can you repent of how God made you?

They are our children, part of our family. We brought them into the world! We are trying, I hope in love, to feel our way in faithfulness to Scripture for those about whom we speak, but we clearly have more biblical, theological, ethical, and especially personal spiritual work to do before we can be at peace. Quoting Bible passages at each other has not solved much thus far.

My first intensive exposure to the issue of homosexuality came in 1968 when a conference on "Christianity and Sexuality" was held at Associated Mennonite Biblical Seminary (AMBS) in Elkhart, Indiana.

This was followed by several sessions of the Mennonite Medical Association during the 1970s. The intention was to articulate a theology of human sexuality. This was likely in response to the loosening of ethical norms during the 1960s, the Vietnam War of the 1960s–70s, and the 1964 "Consultation on Social Ethics" conducted by the World Council of Churches. But it was only in 1981 that the Mennonite Church (MC) and General Conference Mennonite Church (GCMC) conferences appointed a committee to study sexuality. This eventually led to the publication of a study guide entitled *Human Sexuality in the Christian Life.*

In 1986, our congregation in Elkhart, Indiana, asked my wife Wilma and me to lead a discussion group on sexuality in preparation for the tri-annual meetings of the General Conference in Saskatoon, Saskatchewan, using this booklet. It was a sober and challenging experience. We were helped by various resource persons who were invited for specific sessions, including Dr. Willard Krabill, a prominent physician who had studied and written in this field. We also invited two gay men for one class period. Many participants shared later that they had not met a gay person before. This is a crucial point. Until we meet and get to know a person of whom we are afraid or of whom we think negatively and discover that they are just as human as we are, our phobia will not leave us!

This is the great value of the stories shared here. While not a personal meeting, nevertheless, we have the opportunity in reading them to get to know our sisters and brothers in Christ, their struggles, hopes, and aspirations. Some have served in pastoral roles and showed great promise until they shared their sexual identity, which has usually led to termination. This is a tragic loss to the church at a time when pastors are in increasingly short supply. It is also a form of violence against persons who cannot help that their genes are not "straight."

Many wish they were straight, that their struggles might be over, but I would encourage them to find joy and grace in who they are. We need them! Sixteenth century Anabaptism emphasized the importance of the "gathered believers," for it was there that the hunted and persecuted found help and understanding, but in many Brethren and Mennonite churches LGBT individuals are still not welcome. Our congregations are called to be sanctuaries of refuge from the storms of life, a place where the spirit is nurtured and aching wounds find healing. Is your congregation that kind of place?

We owe the individuals who shared their stories here, and Roberta Kreider who published them, a deep, full measure of gratitude for their openness and for making themselves vulnerable. May we, in turn, become their advocates for justice and love in our congregations and in society. *Let us follow the way of Jesus!*

Cornelius J. Dyck
520 Bobwhite Way
Normal, IL 61761
Email: cjwdyck@juno.com

Cornelius (C.J.) Dyck is a historian. For many years, he taught church history and historical theology at Associated Mennonite Biblical Seminary. Earlier he served with Mennonite Central Committee in Europe and South America in relief and refugee work for six years. He served as pastor of a congregation in Kansas for nearly five years, after which he studied at the University of Chicago, receiving his Ph. D. in 1962. From 1961–1973, he was also executive secretary of Mennonite World Conference. Among his more recent publications are Vol. 5 of *Mennonite Encyclopedia* (with Dennis D. Martin), and *Spiritual Life in Anabaptism*. C.J. and Wilma are the parents of three grown children and have two grandchildren.

PROLOGUE

This third book in the series of faith stories from the GLBTA community of faith is more narrow in scope than the other two. (The acronym refers to gay, lesbian, bisexual, transgender, and allies.) *From Wounded Hearts* and *Together in Love* contain stories written by people from mainline churches and synagogues. Because of the need within my own Anabaptist faith tradition, I have chosen to limit the stories in *The Cost of Truth* to Mennonites (specifically MC USA and MC Canada) and to Brethren (Church of the Brethren and Brethren in Christ). These denominations do not have a good track record of listening to people's stories before pronouncing judgment upon them.

The chief priests and Pharisees sent the temple police to arrest Jesus, but the police were captivated by his teaching and returned empty-handed. Harsh words of judgment were doled out on Jesus in absentia, and also on the temple police and the crowds of people who listened to Jesus. Nicodemus was a Pharisee and a member of the elite group of the Sanhedrin. In John 3, we are told that he secretly met with Jesus at night. In the vignette of John 7:45-52, Nicodemus brought judgment on his own head when he courageously asked his colleagues, "Our law does not judge people without first giving them a hearing to find out what they are doing, does it?"

Rich and powerful people dominating and controlling those beneath their status or privilege and turning against colleagues who disagree with them is an age-old phenomenon. It seems to me that it is at the heart of the intensive debate in our day about who can be in and who must be out of the church.

Jesus came to model for us a better way—the way of Love. The following quotes from the New Revised Standard Version of the Bible clearly state his philosophy of life.

If you love me, you will keep my commandments (John 14:15).

I give you a new commandment, that you love one another. Just as I have loved you, you also should love one another (John 13:34).

By this everyone will know that you are my disciples, if you have love for one another (John 13:35).

How sad it is that the church—Jesus' body on earth—has so soon reverted back to the old human way of status and privilege—of judging and condemning.

I was one of the people who felt it was my task as a follower of Jesus (and a member of the "privileged" class) to keep the church pure. Surely, it was Jesus' task to make the church holy and to present it to God without spot, wrinkle, or blemish (Ephesians 5:26-27), but he needed my help to do it. It took almost a lifetime for me to realize that I was usurping Jesus' place! All God asks of me is to love. Now I am finding it true that love is the fulfilling of the law (Romans 13:10).

In the stories that follow, sincere followers of Jesus share their stories of personal struggle and growth. These are not evil people hell-bent on bringing havoc to other people and to the earth that God has created. They are gentle people, seeking to know God and to follow where God's Spirit leads them. These are the sons and daughters of "our" church—the offspring of the body of Christ. Please listen with compassion to the reality of their lives.

I pray that the Spirit of God will lead us all to truth—not my truth—not your truth—but God's truth.

Roberta Showalter Kreider

CHAPTER 1

Mixed Messages

Shannon Neufeldt

I am NOT an activist. I can't be a freedom fighter. That's not who I am. I hate to rock the boat. Yes, I'm attracted to women, but that doesn't mean I have to do anything about it.

These were my words just three and a half years ago. Much of that sentiment still rings true. It is also true that I have had several very strong "calls" in my life, and I've learned to listen to them. This is the story of my calling.

I was nurtured in the faith—Christian and Mennonite—all my life. I was encouraged to be a strong, independent woman—thinking for myself and doing what I believe is right—by parents, teachers, and mentors. I was called and groomed to be a pastor in the Mennonite Church over a period of nearly twenty years.

I began to sense a call to some sort of ministry when I was fourteen. By the next year, I was given opportunities to lead worship several times and to deliver my first sermon in our small Mennonite congregation. I attended a Mennonite high school and found affirmation of my gifts in being elected chair of the Faith and Life Committee. On another occasion, a high school teacher introduced me to a seminary professor by saying that I would be a student of his some day. One Saturday afternoon when I was in grade eleven, I was surprised by a phone call from Associated Mennonite Biblical Seminary (AMBS) in Elkhart, Indiana. Apparently my home pastor had passed on my name as a prospective student without telling them how young I was!

In 1992, at Canadian Mennonite Bible College, I was shoulder-tapped by one of the professors to do a summer pastoral internship. As I finished my degrees in theology and music at CMBC, another professor called me into her office. Of all the graduating students, she felt that I had just the right mix of skills and interests in pastoring and service that were needed to fill a Mennonite Voluntary Service position. So in 1994, I moved to Hamilton, Ontario, to begin what would become nearly three years of service as assistant pastor and community worker at the Welcome Inn Community Centre and Church. By the end of that term of service, I was quite sure pastoral ministry in a congregation was meant to be the long-term vocation of my life.

A year and a half later, after finishing a B.A. in Social Development Studies, I received an unexpected call from someone on the hiring committee for Toronto United Mennonite Church (TUMC), asking if I would consider applying for the new position of associate pastor. After the congregation accepted my application, I was licensed for pastoral ministry and installed as associate pastor on January 31, 1999. Two years later, after the normal review process, my co-pastor, the area pastor, and the pastoral review committee began encouraging me to pursue ordination. Without a doubt, I was called to pastoral ministry.

These influences shaped my public persona, what my congregation knew of me. With much prayer and preparation, I told my congregation more of who I am at the end of the Sunday morning service, April 28, 2002. Here, slightly revised, is part of what I said that day.

*   *   *

I'm into my fourth year at TUMC, and my time with you as a congregation has been rich so far. You have challenged me to grow in my understanding of ministry. You have also affirmed and encouraged me in many ways. Some of you have ministered much more closely with me than others, and I have really appreciated your daily support in countless tasks and emotional and spiritual ways. I say this to let you know that I have come to feel quite at home in this congregation and grateful for our communal Christian walk. However, I haven't always been able to share with you all of my spiritual developments or been able to truly be myself. I would like to do that now so that we can be more open with each other in our Christian fellowship.

Well into my first year as associate pastor, I became troubled by an apparent "stagnation" of my relationship with God. My personal prayer life was drying up. This was not a comfortable state for a pastor, and I felt I would be a particularly bad role model for the youth if I did not do something about it soon. I decided to seek out a spiritual director and found a Mennonite woman who was both comfortable and helpful. Now I could pray with her, and we delved into many spiritual and practical areas of ministry, but I soon began to leave her office with a vague sense that I wasn't getting to the heart of the matter.

I realized that the trouble in my relationship with God was not primarily stagnation, but rather there was something blocking our relationship. Once I noticed and recognized this difference, thoughts from my subconscience slowly came to the surface through each session with my spiritual director. These were unbidden thoughts about my own sexuality. Opening myself up to God was forcing me to admit fears that I might be attracted to women. When I could acknowledge even this possibility, I began to be able to pray again, and my relationship with God slowly began to deepen.

I felt I could not tell my Mennonite spiritual director, so I sought a Christian counselor distant from the Mennonite Church and told him of my concerns. After telling him about my life and history, he assured me that I wasn't homosexual. Good—problem solved in four short weeks. I'm not queer and I can pray again. Thank you very much. In the months that followed, honesty with God continued and the struggles resurfaced. Half a year later, I decided I needed to talk to someone else. I needed to find a new, safe, non-Mennonite counselor.

In the midst of contemplating how I could get a referral to a counselor I could feel more comfortable with, I attended the Mennonite conference in Lethbridge. The issue of homosexuality in the Mennonite Church was on everyone's lips, and it was clear how the church there was deeply divided. In an attempt to present myself as a supportive straight pastor, my emotions broke down. When a friend noticed my distress and offered me a confidential listening ear, I finally disclosed the secret of my sexual orientation.

At first I was relieved, but the next day, I began to fear the repercussions this could have.

For the first time in my life, I could imagine life without my family, my church, and the reputation I have so far enjoyed. These were the things I thought I had built my life around. The thought of losing all this overwhelmed me. And furthermore, I feared rejection from God. But that same morning I heard the "voice" of God as clearly as I ever have, telling me, "Shannon, you are a child of mine and I love you. I will always love you, no matter what else happens." I knew too that I loved God, and my relationship with God was strong enough to withstand whatever might lie ahead.

What followed were months of slow exploration of this new aspect of my identity, a discernment of what an attraction to women really meant to me. I did share with my spiritual director and I did find a new counselor. I began to gather the resources, the language, and the strength to understand myself, my theology, my church, and my culture around sexuality.

A pivotal point in my discernment process came at a youth pastors' retreat last winter. The facilitator led us in a guided meditation using the story of the angel's annunciation to Mary. He asked us what we were being called to bring to birth? I was torn apart by God's nearness in that moment. I thought of all the other youth pastors in the room, dreaming of bringing to birth some new program or energy or spiritual vitality in their youth ministries. I pleaded for that to be my calling that day, but it was not. I was being called to allow the kingdom of God within me to be born into the world through the church. I was being called to be honest about my sexual orientation in the church.

Again there followed a time of slow growth in my life. I found people I could be honest with, people who could pray with me, for me, and for the church. It was a time to share this part of my life with my parents and my brother and his wife. It was a time to look for support within the queer communities, both Mennonite and secular.

This winter at the youth pastors' retreat, the images were different for me. I felt this day drawing near, and I was scared and overwhelmed by the potential repercussions in my faith community. This time the facilitator used Lenten images of light and darkness. A new image for me was that of darkness as being nurturing and necessary, as in the darkness of the soil needed to germinate a seed or the darkness of a womb. In the birthing images, I felt I was no longer being called to bring anything to birth, but to be born. God would do the labor and carry the greater burden of the pain as I and my honest self-expression were being born. I have been nurtured in these many months of darkness, and now it is time for my story to come to light.

As my fellow worshipers each week, as the congregation that has called me here in ministry, as close sisters and brothers in faith, it has been my desire to share with you this deeply personal part of my life and this part of my identity. I find myself created by God with an attraction to women, called by God (and the wider church) into ministry, and called to come out in my church.

I am also happy to share that I am dating a wonderful woman from Danforth Mennonite Church, who shares my faith, who prays with me, who enters many serious conversations with me, but also laughs with me. Her name is Jenn Thiessen.

Many of you are close to me, and I wish I could have talked with you individually. I hope you understand that my silence was not meant to exclude you from my life. I have been on this particular journey for some time now and have spent many hours praying about this day. I invite you now to join me, and others who have gone before me, on this journey. May God walk with us each day and carry us when we stumble. May the Peace of Christ be with us all. Amen.

* * *

That is what I shared with my congregation almost two years ago. Now allow me to backtrack and fill in some details. The years in Hamilton (1994-97) contained my first unknowing steps on a journey about sexual orientation. When one of my friends came out, it spurred me to do some reading and thinking about various sexual orientations. Several years later, a close female friend came out to me and said she thought I was lesbian too. I was shocked and angry at her audacity. I hotly rebuked her, and stated that I might not be a "zero" on the Kinsey scale, but I wasn't a lesbian. I really thought she was wrong, but the height of my indignation could have been a clue.

Now there was a tiny niggling doubt about my sexuality, but I succeeded in burying that thought for over two years while many other issues occupied my mind. I found that I couldn't live in Toronto on a part-time church salary, so soon after beginning my pastoral position at TUMC, I searched for more part-time work. I discovered a great fit as outreach worker at the Danforth Mennonite Church. I worked closely with the Outreach Committee, and this is where I met Jenn Thiessen. Danforth Mennonite was Jenn's home church. She had been out about her sexual orientation at that church for several years, and it had never posed a problem for her. However, long before I recognized her orientation, we connected around common interests and ideals. We compared voluntary service stories, talked about all kinds of issues of justice and spirituality, and had fun together in our work as we planned a Christmas carol-sing or delivered donations to the local food pantry.

As I mentioned above, the annual Mennonite Church Canada conference in 2000 was brutal. The issue of homosexuality was the subject of so much discussion, and I was still utterly alone. After watching me cry throughout a small group discussion on homosexuality, it was Jenn who asked repeatedly if I was all right. I finally let my guard down to her. From there on, we worked at my coming out together. Jenn was someone to whom I could pose all my questions, who listened to all my doubts, and who offered a shoulder on which I could cry.

We went for many long walks that summer. It was to Jenn that I spoke the opening paragraph of this story when I realized that she was attracted to me. The possibility of a romance felt so dangerous. But our relationship already included a strong friendship, a deep spiritual connection, and spending time together almost daily. Late in the fall of that year, I was finally able to admit (to myself and to Jenn) that this was a date—not just time with a friend.

Flush with a new relationship but still plagued with guilt and anxiety, I went to talk to my area pastor. I was relieved to hear that she did not believe I was doing anything inherently wrong. As long as I wanted to keep it a secret, she would not need to do anything about my orientation or the relationship, though she abruptly quit encouraging me to seek ordination. This was the first of a long string of mixed messages.

What confused and frustrated me the most was that, after expressing appreciation for all the work I was doing in the Mennonite Church, that area pastor asked me if I had considered transferring to the United Church of Canada. (It was a known fact that the ordination of gay people was accepted in that denomination.)

I had twenty-one meetings with a variety of local and conference level church leaders to prepare for my public coming out at Toronto United Mennonite Church. This was on top of the regular meetings, events, and work of my two half-time church work jobs. It was a very stressful and taxing time. I wouldn't have made it through all that if it had not been for the support of Jenn and Pam Albrecht, my roommate at the time. They prayed and planned with me, helping me discern who needed to know what, so that the leadership wouldn't be taken by surprise and react out of shock and fear.

By contrast, coming out at Danforth Mennonite Church was not a big deal. They had "done their homework" and were comfortable with gay people in their midst. I had carefully told the pastor and elders ahead of time, but they agreed that nothing more needed to be done to process this event. Thus, I made no public statement and most people heard about my orientation through the grapevine. When my contract came up for renewal several months later, the Church Council decided that they would acknowledge my coming out in the announcement of my new term, but there did not need to be any congregational discussion of the issue.

The relationship between Jenn and me grew in spite of the obstacles that the Mennonite Church kept throwing our way; sometimes it grew because of the bond of adversity. We started the journey to making our commitment permanent when Jenn proposed to me at a Brethren and Mennonite Council for Lesbian, Gay, Bisexual, and Transgender Interests (BMC) retreat that winter. We thought marriage was a natural progression in our relationship, but others were taken by surprise.

We announced our engagement in both our churches and looked to the Danforth congregation for support when we were getting grief at TUMC. That support came only from a few individuals. The pastor and some of the elders at Danforth made things even harder, but we still believed that it wasn't a problem for the congregation. Several months after announcing our engagement, I was checking out the literature table when I found a letter inviting congregants to a series of congregational meetings to discuss Jenn and Shannon's relationship.

We were both aghast. We thought this was a congregation that supported us, not one that would talk about us publicly without even letting us know the meetings were taking place. With the supportive outrage of one friend, the meetings were cancelled, but our trust was broken and subsequent conversations did not allay our worst fears about the lack of understanding. This too was confusing. I could let the church know of my orientation, even of dating a member of their congregation, and they still wanted me to be the prominent face of their outreach program. Yet they could not affirm our choice to be married and make our relationship stable and permanent in the way of common family values.

From the earliest discussions, the vast majority of the meetings were not really about me. They were about those who are afraid of change, those who would no longer feel at home at TUMC or in the conferences if TUMC kept me on staff. The meetings just before I came out and the fourteen months of meetings after I came out were so rarely about homosexuality. Usually they were about how to calm those who are homophobic and keep them in the church.

I and the group I was seen to represent were often perceived as the ones with the advantage. Toronto is a very secular city where there are a number of prominent gay people. Equal rights are slowly being won in the secular sphere. Many of the members and regular attendees at TUMC—a highly-educated, wealthy, liberal church—didn't bother to come to the meetings. They were convinced sexual orientation should not be an issue and certainly wouldn't ultimately affect my employment at the church.

The meetings with congregational or conference leadership were full of nice people. The vast majority of these people still seemed very comfortable with me even after I came out. In those places, nothing nasty or blatantly derogatory was ever said about me or about homosexuality. Nevertheless, the homophobic statement that was repeated over and over again was, "I don't have any problem with homosexuality. It's just that our church will fight, lose members, maybe split... there will be so much conflict, if I advocate publicly for you to stay."

Lots of talking went on around me. Very rarely did anyone think it was important to ask how I felt, nor did they talk to other homosexual people about their orientation. It wasn't about me; it was about the church and whether they could work this conflict out. At TUMC, I joined in the discussions with my fellow pastor, with members of the Human Sexuality Leadership Team, and with the Board, but they all talked to me as a leader in the church, not as an individual who embodies a homosexual orientation and experiences discrimination.

Everyone seemed to like me. I was a good pastor and easy to get along with. It was hard for anyone—least of all, me—to believe that I really was a problem in this situation. I tried very hard to help everyone sort out the problem that frightened them most—that the church would split over this contentious issue.

The congregation could not reach a consensus by the date they had agreed, so the matter of my future employment came to a vote. I was quite prepared to consider an altered covenant; in fact, I was fairly certain I would not retain the pastoral title but equally certain the church would retain me in some form of service. First the option of continuing my original covenant was brought to a vote. It received only forty-eight percent in favor (a two-thirds majority was needed to reaffirm my call). Within minutes, the question of a non-pastoral church worker position was brought to a vote and received sixty-three percent (still shy of two-thirds). Thus, my pastoral employment ended on June 21, 2003.

Now I'm confused and hurt. Many people had said, "Everything's going to be fine. Don't worry." *Fine*? I was fired from a fulfilling position that I felt called to. Sure, I received a severance package; no I'm not destitute or without other options, but still I was *fired*. Hard working, responsible, self-sacrificing, conscientious people who are suited to their positions don't get fired—do they? They especially don't get fired by nice, friendly, reliable employers who say for four years in a row that said employee is doing a good job.

It is now seven months after the church made their final decision, and I'm still confused. No matter how much I tell myself, and others tell me, that it wasn't about me, you can't get fired and not take a blow to your confidence. It's hard not to believe that if I had been a more dynamic youth leader or a more compassionate visitor, people would have fought harder to keep me there. I think, maybe if I had taken on the role of activist, maybe if I had used my power in the congregation more fully—more passionately—people would have listened and understood a little more, enough so that I would still be a pastor. And enough so that people who believe as I believe would still be in the church. It's hard to believe that it isn't about me at all.

Fired or not, I would have lost my license from Mennonite Church Eastern Canada (MCEC). Even if I left Jenn and committed to be celibate for the rest of my life, I would still have lost my license and the chance to pursue ordination because I was now a known homosexual person. This doesn't make any sense to me. MCEC polity calls for celibacy for all people who are not in a heterosexual marriage. Therefore, according to the polity, the issue is celibacy, not homosexual orientation. Yet the MCEC Leadership Commission would not allow me to maintain my license (even if I committed to celibacy) once my orientation was known. Some even admitted that this was a political move to be sympathetic to those within the church who are most opposed to accepting those of homosexual orientation.

In the midst of my coming out, my term came up for renewal on a Mennonite Church Canada conference committee. The committee responsible affirmed the renewal of my position. These ten people wrote individually to confirm that they saw no reason for me not to continue in my current capacity. Then I wrote a letter to those ten people and the staff at MC Canada about publicly coming out to my congregation and accepted the offer of a new term provided they believed, as I did, that my orientation had no bearing on my ability to function on this committee. However, the decision to renew my term was taken out of their hands and given to the General Board to decide. Later that year, I was informed that my sexual orientation did indeed affect my ability to function. I was no longer allowed to serve on that or any other MC Canada committee. Mixed messages again!

Currently, I'm in school again, working on my Master of Divinity, but not at Associated Mennonite Biblical Seminary as I always thought I would be. That esteemed Mennonite seminary would let me study with them, but they will not let a known homosexual graduate. I am still receiving all the brochures and course offerings from the seminary. It must be going on sixteen years now that they have been trying to recruit me. I wonder how many more years it will be until someone like me will be able to graduate from there.

Throughout my life, even after I came out, I have received so much affirmation for my pastoral work and calling. Yet now I have encountered road blocks to ministry in every Mennonite institution of which I am a part. When will our church get beyond these "mixed messages" to a consistent theology and practice of acceptance based on confession of faith?

Shannon Neufeldt, B.Th., B.Ch.M, B.A., was raised in Regina, Saskatchewan, and has made her home in the province of Ontario since 1994. She was legally married to Jenn Thiessen on November 8, 2003. Shannon's parents and 180 supportive friends witnessed the occasion with great rejoicing. The couple lives in Toronto among a vibrant community, enjoying the incredibly diverse arts, culture, and cuisine such a city has to offer. Shannon is currently in her first year of studies towards a Master of Divinity degree at a local, open and affirming seminary—Emmanuel College of the United Church of Canada.

CHAPTER 2

It Is a Joy to Finally Say, "Yes!"

David P. Weaver

How can you tell when the night has ended and the day has begun? It is when you can look on the face of any man or woman and see that it is your sister or brother. Because if you cannot see this, it is still night.

Tales of the Hasidim

During sharing time in a recent Sunday morning service at Germantown Mennonite Church (GMC), I spoke the words I've wanted to say for a long time: "I have a growing sense of peace and excitement about finally deciding to pursue that which I believe has pursued me. It is a joy to finally say, "Yes!" I will take the next step towards congregational ministry, though I don't know where it may lead me."

I cannot remember a time when faith and the church were not a significant part of my life, either by their presence or their absence. Though Islam, Buddhism, Judaism, and a more liturgical strand of Christendom have all held a certain appeal, the faith of my parents and our Mennonite church community—a faith poetic in its living, not in its creeds—has been the primary force for good and for ill in my spiritual life.

My parents' lives were infused with faith, and among their highest priorities was a strong commitment to our rural conservative conference Mennonite church. I think it's safe to say that when the church doors were open, my parents, my six brothers, and I were there, arriving early and staying late. The many services and activities of the congregation were all part of the natural rhythm of our lives. I don't think we ever asked questions such as: "Should we go to the hymn sing tonight?" or "If I have homework to finish, should I skip the youth Bible study?" or "Since we spent all day Saturday canning peaches, can we just sleep in tomorrow morning?"

While some people raised in such a context have chafed at the bit, wanting more freedom, I took from these experiences a sense of belonging, a sense of purpose and vision for life, though I would never have articulated it with these words. Of course, I wished we were allowed to watch television like some of my more liberal schoolmates, and I wondered if people who played the piano really were doing something wrong, as was generally accepted in my church (though my parents did actually buy me the piano I so desired). But I found a safe and nurturing place within my family and within the church community, and it is this sense of trust and belonging that formed the foundation of my early spiritual life.

It was during my junior or senior year of high school when I first felt drawn to leadership and wondered if I might one day be a pastor. I was already a leader in the youth group and often led hymns during worship services and taught Bible school classes. I had no idea how I would become a pastor. Still, I found myself thinking about the possibility from time to time. It was also during high school that I recognized my own sexual attraction to guys, an experience for which I had few words or role models, except the occasional negative locker-room reference to "queers."

At Eastern Mennonite University, I majored in business/secondary education, but took my elective courses in biblical studies and theology. I very much wanted to major in biblical studies and theology, but didn't know how to explain this to my family. No one in my family had ever earned a bachelor's degree, and our pastors were generally called out of the church community; they did not go to college, let alone seminary. As a result, I chose a practical profession—high school business teacher—and took biblical studies classes when I could fit them in.

The fall semester of my junior year I lived in the Middle East, and this had a deep impact on my faith. How could I accept the warm hospitality of Palestinian Arabs—Muslim and Christian alike—and have no answers for why my government supported their oppression? How could I look these people in the eye while knowing that my tax dollars helped maintain the systematic denial of their most basic human rights? I returned to the States with a determination to live out my faith in a way that considered justice as well as peacemaking.

After graduating from college, I spent five years as a high school business teacher, two at Sarasota Christian in Florida and three at Central Christian in Ohio. In Sarasota, I joined Newtown Chapel, an African-American congregation on the north side of town, and was active with the local peace and justice coalition. I returned to Ohio following my father's diagnosis with Alzheimer's to be closer to the family during this difficult time. Soon I found myself involved in many different roles in my home congregation, including worship leader, youth group sponsor, Sunday school teacher, and church council member, and I received much encouragement and affirmation for these activities. While some in the congregation may have had questions about a few of my beliefs, like my five years of war tax resistance, no one doubted my commitment to following Christ and living a life of faith.

During this same time, I was increasingly aware of my sexual orientation and felt very conflicted about it. For a time I explored the possibility of changing my sexual orientation, pleading with God to help me with this. My prayers were answered as I worked with a good therapist who provided a safe place for me to explore all the possible ways of responding to my sexual orientation. Slowly I gained a sense of peace in accepting that being gay was simply a normal part of my identity, though only a handful of close friends knew about this part of my life. I made an initial contact with the Brethren/Mennonite Council for Gay, Lesbian, Bisexual and Transgender Interests and found other gay Mennonites living nearby. It was very helpful to discover others who respected a life of faith and accepted their sexual orientation as well.

In the fall of my fifth year of teaching, while participating in a small Bible study in the church library, I experienced an unmistakable sense of clarity that the time had come for me to attend seminary. In the weeks that followed, I talked about this sense of call with my pastor and several close friends, and they all affirmed my call to pastoral ministry. At the same time, it became increasingly clear to me that God accepted me as a gay Christian. As I continued reading the writings of gay Christians, I came to understand that efforts to change my sexual orientation were as misguided and destructive as using chemicals to change the color of one's skin. But I had no idea how I would be able to integrate my sense of call to pastoral ministry and my sexual orientation. Therefore, after privately discussing my sexual orientation with several seminary professors, I applied to Eastern Mennonite Seminary and was accepted with the tacit understanding that I would not be a "flag-waver" and would remain celibate during my time there.

My home congregation rallied in support of my plans to attend seminary and formed a committee to see how financial assistance might be provided. I experienced an amazing sense of peace and excitement about taking this step, as my call to pastoral ministry was affirmed by the congregation.

Sometime that winter I carelessly told a member of the congregation about my growing acceptance of my sexual orientation—assuming confidentiality—and within several weeks I had been "outed." The response of the congregation was one of overwhelming silence. The financial assistance committee ceased to exist, and it seemed to me that—not knowing what on earth to do—the congregation just held its breath until I left for seminary. I did not speak openly to the congregation about my sexual orientation, and I don't believe anyone from the congregation spoke publicly about it either. What I know clearly is that the congregation loved me and I loved them, and neither of us had any idea how to get over the seemingly insurmountable hurdle of my sexual orientation.

Fortunately, one of my teaching colleagues counseled me to consider other seminaries, predicting that—despite best intentions at Eastern Mennonite Seminary—I would be seen first and foremost as the gay student and little else would matter. So I decided to apply to Princeton Theological Seminary instead. That fall I arrived at Princeton, somewhat shell-shocked from feeling so exposed in my small hometown, but thrilled to finally be preparing full-time for pastoral ministry. On some level I believed I would never really be able to go home again, and I had no idea whether I had any real future in pastoral ministry.

The winter of my first year at Princeton, I realized that I could not simply disappear from the life of the congregation that had nurtured and blessed me in so many ways without any acknowledgement of the loss that we both were experiencing. So with the prayers of my newly found straight and gay Christian friends at Princeton and at Germantown Mennonite Church, I returned one winter Sunday and spoke directly to the congregation during sharing time. After recounting the many ways in which they had blessed and affirmed me prior to knowing about my sexual orientation, I asked the congregation if I was still welcome at the communion table. You could have heard a pin drop. Several weeks later, I received a letter from the pastors and elders detailing the requirements for my continued membership. When my written response was not satisfactory, I was removed from membership.

For the next two and a half years, I threw myself into my studies, reveling in the experience of full-time preparation for pastoral ministry. At the same time, I designed and began quilting a small quilt, as if by doing so I could hold on to my family and church heritage that I felt was slipping away. At some point, I discovered that Princeton and Rutgers had a dual Master of Divinity/Master of Social Work program, and I decided to complete the M.S.W, realizing it would more likely get me a job than the M.Div.

As my senior year drew to a close and many of my friends were interviewing for their first pastoral positions, the reality that I would not now—and likely not ever—be serving the Mennonite Church as a pastor hit me like a ton of bricks. That year I experienced a very painful period of clinical depression. I thank God for providing committed friends and a skilled psychotherapist who helped me to work through this difficult time.

At the same time, I chose to work with a hospice in Philadelphia for my social work internship and discovered that I felt comfortable working with people during this challenging time in their lives. After graduation, I joined my partner in Michigan (we had met in seminary) where he was beginning medical school, and I found a job as a bereavement counselor. I assumed this was as close as I would ever get to pastoral work.

For a time my former partner and I did not attend church, since we were both feeling alienated from our faith communities. Nevertheless, in spite of my grief and anger with the church's response to my sexual orientation, I still felt drawn to finding a faith community. After calling churches at random from the yellow pages to ask if a committed gay couple could participate fully in the life of the congregation, I found First Baptist Church of Birmingham, an American Baptist congregation. Pastor Steve Jones warmly welcomed us, and soon—though the congregation had never had openly gay people attend before—I was singing in the choir, teaching Sunday school, reading Scripture and preaching from time to time. It was such a healing time.

The most powerful experience came when a young girl in the youth group came forward at the end of the service expressing her desire to be baptized and asked if I would be her adult sponsor. It was all I could do to hold it together, standing with her and her parents as the congregation came forward to affirm her decision, and I slipped away after the service to weep in the organ closet at this grace-filled moment. It was such a turn of events to be viewed by this young girl and her family as a role model for a life of faith.

Shortly thereafter, I learned of an available hospice chaplain position and applied for the job—with some anxiety because I wasn't ordained. The interviewer asked directly why I wasn't ordained. When I replied that the church would not ordain openly gay Christians, she said she believed this to be discriminatory, and promptly hired me. I could hardly believe that I was, after all, going to be working in a pastoral role!

Following medical school, we returned to Philadelphia for my former partner's medical residency and joined Germantown Mennonite Church, happily immersing ourselves in the life of this amazing congregation. Not only is the congregation the oldest Mennonite church in North America, established in 1683, but it was also there that my former partner and I had our commitment ceremony after seminary. And as at First Baptist, I found that my spirituality and sexuality were welcomed without reservation.

I continued working with a hospice in Philadelphia and took two additional years of training in pastoral counseling and congregational consulting. As I worked with individuals and with congregations who were experiencing difficult times, I realized that I longed for my congregation's blessing for my pastoral work. It was true that I was working as an employee of two businesses, but I understood my ministries as extensions of the congregation's mission in the world. Since GMC welcomed and affirmed people of all sexual orientations, I wondered if I could be ordained. Perhaps the reason I was not ordained was because I had never asked, believing that I never could be.

Finally, I asked. Though I knew on some level that my ordination could be a "big deal," I wasn't fully prepared for how wonderful and painful the experience would be.

The process of explaining my history and sense of call—first to the congregation's leadership and then to the congregation—reawakened in me all the anticipation and fear associated with putting my spiritual life into a faith community's hands once again. Remembering clearly the pain of being weighed in the balance of the church and found wanting, I had often said I would never allow a group of people to have such power again. Yet here I was, asking for the church's blessing for what I believed to be God's call on my life.

While there was discussion about possible ramifications for the congregation if it took this step, the congregation voiced its resounding affirmation for my ordination. I could not have predicted how meaningful the time of preparation for the service would be. I found myself opening up again to the possibility of receiving a congregation's unqualified blessing for pastoral ministry.

When the letter from Eastern District Conference (EDC) arrived ten days before the ordination, warning the congregation of the grave damage GMC's planned ordination would cause the larger church, it was a bit of a jolt to see such opposition in black and white. And when three days prior to the service, the worship leader called to say her credentials had been threatened if she participated in any way in the service, it felt like a hostile church was closing in on us. I had not intended for my friends and for the congregation to pay such a price for offering their blessing.

At my ordination three days later, I stood to recite Psalm 27:

> [God] is my light and my salvation, whom shall I fear?
> [God] is the stronghold of my life, of whom shall I be afraid?...
> Though an army encamp against me, my heart shall not fear.
> Though war rise up against me, yet I will be confident...

These words spoke the cry and the prayer of my heart, and that chapter has been a part of my daily prayer of faith ever since. I will always cherish the memory of the congregation joyfully singing: "For there is no one to fear, for there is no one to fear, for those who place their confidence in our God!" Celebrating communion, with my mom and my brothers joining my faith family, finally brought all the pieces together into a quilt far more beautiful than any I could have created.

In the months following my ordination, as articles written in the church papers by those who had never spoken with me described me like an insect ("non-celibate homosexual"), and as letters to the editor condemned and supported the congregation's action, a part of me rued the day that I had allowed myself to hope for the church's blessing. It was such a mixed time as one day I felt gratitude for the congregation's courage in ordaining me, and the next I felt ashamed and angry that a part of me wanted to take a sabbatical from church altogether. I wanted to run and hide from the judgment and hatred that many of those letters expressed.

As EDC and GMC selected representatives who would meet to discuss our future relationship, I found it amazing to realize that, in three years, the conference minister had not once worshipped with the congregation. We had to *ask* the EDC representatives to come worship with us prior to beginning the discussion meetings. How can a conference minister truly minister without spending a single hour worshipping with those whom he serves? Yet it was clear to me that he came to those meetings with the intent of expelling us from fellowship if we didn't renounce our welcoming views.

As we discussed our differences regarding Germantown's welcome of gay folk, I found it appalling that the conference president could not articulate even the most basic understanding of Germantown's biblical interpretation. When I asked, he also acknowledged he had not read even a single book that might have helped him understand the congregation's welcome of gay Christians. How can a conference president provide leadership for his flock when, prior to meeting with us, he had not spent time with any of us to hear how we understand the Scriptures, let alone how we've experienced the Spirit's movement in our lives? It seems to me that he came to the table convinced that we must be expelled for our aberrant views.

It is difficult to be hopeful about the future of the church when some in its leadership will not even take the most basic steps to understand their brothers and sisters. Yet I know that God's action in history is not limited by the gifts and blind spots that my Eastern District brothers *and* I possess.

Now three years later, I take the next step about which I recently spoke to the people of Germantown Mennonite:

> In the past year, I have become more and more clear about feeling drawn to working as a pastor in a congregation. In truth, I have always known that serving a congregation was something that I felt called to do. But in the ten years since I graduated from seminary, I haven't really allowed myself to think too much about it, because I couldn't see any realistic possibility for congregational ministry in the Mennonite Church as a person who happens to be gay.
>
> In concrete terms, what I have done is to apply to the United Church of Christ (UCC) for what the UCC calls the "privilege of call." This means that the UCC would recognize my ordination as a Mennonite pastor and ordain me as a UCC pastor as well, with the privilege of seeking a call to a UCC congregation. This allows me to answer the call to pastoral ministry in a congregation now, while leaving open the possibility of pastoring a Mennonite church sometime in the future.
>
> What I know is this: I have a growing sense of peace and excitement about finally deciding to pursue that which I believe

has pursued me. It is such a joy to finally say, "Yes!" I will take the next step towards congregational ministry, though I don't know where it may lead me.

Editor's note: *For many years, Germantown Mennonite Church was affiliated with two denominational conferences, Franconia Mennonite Conference and Eastern District Conference. Because of the congregation's full welcome of gay Christians into the life of the church, it was expelled from FMC in October of 1997. Following a period of discipline, and after David's ordination on September 31, 2001, the congregation was also expelled from EDC in May of 2002.*

David P. Weaver, M.Div., M.S.W., was born and raised in Hartville, Ohio, the fifth of seven sons of Herman and Rachel Weaver. Moving to Philadelphia in 1998, he now lives in a row house in the Germantown section of the city with his two cats Zoe and Ellie. He loves performing with Singing City Choir, which sings at times with the Philadelphia Orchestra and in homeless shelters. He aspires to gourmet cooking with a monthly Diner's Club, and enjoys transplanting starts from his mother's beautiful Ohio gardens. David is completing his fourth year as GMC's congregational chairperson, working full-time as a hospice chaplain with Caring Hospice Services and part-time as a pastoral counselor and congregational consultant with Samaritan Counseling Center.

CHAPTER 3

Living with Integrity: A Journey of Truth Telling

Matthew J. Smucker

Truth-telling is the key to living with integrity. Integrity is a word that describes my approach to life and my journey toward ordained ministry. When I applied to seminary in 1998, I did so with integrity as a gay man who was "out." The second time I was approved for licensed ministry, I described honestly how my spirituality and sexuality informed each other. And when I was ordained to ministry in the Church of the Brethren, I told the whole truth about who I am as a child of God, including my sexual orientation and my love for Jesus and the Church of the Brethren.

My life of integrity did not begin this way. When I left my first licensed ministry in 1992, I did so without telling the truth. I did not see a place for myself as an openly gay man in ministry within the Church of the Brethren. I pursued a career in the collegiate environment, where I could be out and still do valuable work with people, because I felt that I had no hope of working in the church. At the same time, I searched for a worshiping community, and eventually I found a safe, nurturing spiritual home in the United Church of Christ (UCC), my mother's church home.

In 1994, I moved to Kalamazoo, Michigan, where I attended Phoenix Community Church, UCC. At Phoenix Church, I fully participated in congregational life. I saw a new vision of a radically inclusive church where I could be out and pursue God's call as a welcomed member of the church.

This new vision continued to grow when, in January of 1997, I also joined the Skyridge Church of the Brethren in the same city. Skyridge was a publicly welcoming congregation, having joined the Supportive Congregations Network in December of 1995. To my surprise, I was welcomed whole-heartedly into a Brethren congregation, and I eagerly transferred my membership from my childhood congregation. Over the next several years, I led worship, taught Sunday school, and worked with the youth at Skyridge and Phoenix. As my faith expanded and my heart opened, I again heard God's call for service in the church.

God created spiritual communities where I could grow and explore the meaning of faith. However, I felt restless and dissatisfied with my work in higher education and, deep down, I yearned for something more. These feelings became clear in the fall of 1997 when I attended the Brethren Young Adult Conference. That weekend I encountered a new image of ministry and of myself.

With the passing of time, I was more open to reclaiming my call to ministry, envisioning ways I could live out that call within the Church of the Brethren. After six years of running from God's call, I enrolled at Bethany Theological Seminary in Richmond, Indiana. My seminary experience would test my faith and trust in God. My spiritual communities in Kalamazoo were a nurturing haven and leaving them was a huge risk. However, God strengthened me, and I trusted God and stepped forward into the unknown.

I entered seminary as an "out" gay man in September of 1998. My first year was full of loneliness and anxiety as the only "out" person at Bethany. I managed to get through that year by creating circles of support. These circles included a support group of gay men in ministry connected by e-mail, a group of supportive Bethany friends, and regular prayers from both the Phoenix and Skyridge congregations. Most importantly, my partner David moved to join me in Richmond in July of 1999. Each circle was essential to my spiritual and emotional health. In my Moses story, these circles of support were my pillars of clouds that guided me.

My pillars of fire were my ministry experiences. In May of that year (1999), the Michigan District of the Church of the Brethren licensed me to ministry. This decision marked the first time an openly gay man was acknowledged as a person gifted for ministry and called to serve the church. It was an amazing moment for me.

One component of my seminary education took me to a church in Indianapolis, where I served as a student minister, and I focused on worship planning and preaching. This placement was the most challenging part of my journey to that point. Even though some individuals objected to my pastoral leadership, I found a deep passion for congregational ministry. God presented me with a challenge to stand in the midst of conflict. Despite the turmoil, I discovered new gifts for ministry. I found great joy in preaching as well as Bible study and teaching. Through this experience, I discerned that the local church ministry was my calling.

When I reflected on my seminary challenges, I recognized how God had surrounded me with ministers and mentors who nurtured me. They were essential to my emotional and spiritual health. I saw myself surrounded by the mist and mystery of God's love. With each step, a blanket of care protected me and shielded me from the specific details of the weeks and months ahead. If I knew then what I know now, I doubt that I would have chosen to walk the path toward my ordination in the Church of the Brethren. My only consideration was the decision immediately before me, and God's loving voice encouraged me to take another step forward.

As I approached my graduation from Bethany, my call to pastoral ministry grew clearer. While I hoped to serve a Brethren congregation, I realized I would have few opportunities. Nevertheless, feeling as qualified as my classmates, I submitted a pastoral profile for circulation within the Church of the Brethren system. This caused tremendous turmoil within the denominational leadership. When I graduated in May of 2001, church leaders put my profile "on hold" until I could prove that I would be ordained. It was a "catch twenty-two" situation. I could not be ordained until I found a job; however, I could not look for a job until I could prove I would be ordained. Fear seemed to control the process, creating new and unexpected ways to keep me out of church leadership.

I tried to work around the system that blocked me from seeking employment. I attended the summer's Annual Conference in Baltimore, wearing t-shirts that read, "Pastor for Hire." I knew this was an act of civil disobedience, but I hoped to attract a congregation that needed a minister. Very few churches were ready or willing to consider me as a pastoral candidate. By the end of the summer, David and I needed to move out of our seminary apartment. Realizing we could not live in Richmond any longer, we agreed to move to Chicago, where we hoped to find, if nothing else, a quality of life not typically found in smaller Midwestern towns.

During this time, the Ministry Commission in Michigan provided me with tremendous support and encouragement. They approved me for ordained ministry, pending a specific call. When I was hired to work in the Development Office of Chicago Theological Seminary (CTS) that fall, they rejoiced with me and affirmed this position suitable for ordination. Over the next few months, we discussed together how we could best move through this process—"wise as serpents and innocent as doves" (Matthew 10:16). While I doubted ordination would ever come to pass, I knew in my heart I had made a promise to God to walk this path as far as it would go. I was not going to fade away in silence as I had a decade earlier. If I left the Church of the Brethren again, it would not be by my own doing.

To my great surprise and joy, on April 27, 2002, the Michigan District Board recognized my giftedness and my call to ministry. I was the first openly gay man ordained to Christian ministry in the Church of the Brethren. This was not what I had expected. I was prepared for a no, not a yes. As a result, I did not anticipate what would come next.

From that moment, controversy clouded my joy. The Michigan District leadership had followed the standard procedures for candidate review and approval, but voices from within the district and across the denomination objected to the decision. The voices were so loud and angry that my ordination service on June 9, 2002 was nearly cancelled.

I was amazed that, in spite of the protests, I finally stood in front of my friends and family at Skyridge on that morning, reflecting on my ordination vows. It was a moment that I only dared to dream of before. That day, I remembered an inspirational poster in the chapel when I was a student at Manchester College. It read, *"Don't pray for an easy life; pray for strength for the journey."* These words have stayed with me over the years. They provided me with an important vision—crucial images for what I would experience during the year ahead.

I realized how amazing my journey had been. My life had been filled with marvelous surprises. Each day, I sought to remain grounded in my understanding of God's call and faithful to the task that God had presented me. Along the way, I encountered angels, companions, and fellow travelers. I was thankful for the inspiration and encouragement they provided. It was clear to me that my journey was not over. Nevertheless, this was a moment to pause and delight in the abundance of God's love and the fullness of God's grace.

Just a few weeks later, at the 2002 Annual Conference in Louisville, Kentucky, the delegate body passed a query stating, "It is inappropriate to license or ordain to the Christian ministry any persons who are known to be engaging in homosexual practices, and we will not recognize the licensing and ordination of such persons in the Church of the Brethren."

A dark cloud began to surround me. Coming off an unexpected emotional spiritual high, I struggled to claim the joy of my ordination. I was thankful that out of concern for my spiritual well-being, I had earlier decided not to attend the 2002 session of Annual Conference. But the negative vote and the separation from my spiritual family created a sense of isolation and loneliness for me.

My ordination and the decision of Annual Conference delegates attracted the attention of the national media and compounded my sense of isolation. As time progressed, the story felt less and less like my own. When friends from across the country informed me that they had seen the controversy described in their local paper, the breadth of the publicity dumbfounded me, and I felt frustrated by the lack of my personal participation in the process. To my surprise, I have not received any negative correspondence because of this publicity.

In August of 2002, the delegates of the Michigan District discussed the action of the Annual Conference and tabled a petition to affirm the conference action that would invalidate my ordination. Some individuals in the broader Church of the Brethren called for the withdrawal of my ordination; others applauded the district board's bold decision. District leaders, eager to establish common ground, hoped they could establish open lines of communication and affirm their diverse perspectives. They called for a special meeting and gathered together with faithful, discerning spirits.

Unlike the process at Annual Conference, the leaders hoped to provide a space for more dialogue and less knee-jerk action. However, as one side brought a petition to affirm the Annual Conference vote, the other side drafted a query for clarification to send back to Annual Conference. Knowing that this gathering would be both heated and personal, I again decided to stay away to protect my spirit.

As expected, the district gathering was well attended. Virtually every church sent delegates, and Skyridge had nearly twenty members present. Leaders from the national body were there also, including a church parliamentarian and the general secretary. In the business sessions, the conversations and speeches were passionate. The outcome was that the delegates tabled the petition for one year and passed the query asking for more clarification. These two actions allowed time for more dialogue.

That summer should have been a time for joy as a newly ordained minister, but my ordination did not feel like a celebration. I was grateful for the love and support of my family and friends. The Skyridge congregation and the leadership of the Michigan district boldly proclaimed their love and support for me. Emotionally and spiritually, however, I experienced great pain. Those who opposed my ordination often retreated from personal engagement, as they feared my story and me. As a result, they did not see me as an authentically gifted and called servant of God.

At that point, I was still grateful for the opportunity to walk this road less traveled. I prayed for opportunities to share the amazing story of my journey. I hoped for safe places where I could proclaim the ways that God had been present to me; instead, I found myself in the emergency room of the hospital.

By mid-October, each time I had a moment to rest and reflect upon the events of the previous summer, I felt a sharp pain in my chest, and I also had pain in my feet and in my back. For many weeks, I ignored it; I didn't make a connection between these bodily pains and the events of the previous months. When I finally called my doctor, he sent me directly to the emergency room. Thankfully, the doctors found nothing wrong with me physically; however, it was clear that I needed to uncover what was going on emotionally and spiritually.

As I stated, my ordination was a catalyst for hurtful accusations and painful debates. They affected me more than I realized. Throughout the process, I became both an image of change—a poster boy for the progressive church—and a focus of anger and fear for the establishment. I lost my sense of self. The stress and frustration of these events affected me emotionally, physically, and spiritually.

While I tried to remain grounded in the center of this storm, I found myself in an isolated and scary place, and I saw violence and destruction everywhere. I began to discover my own anger about the events of the past year. *"Why did God allow this to happen to me?"* I had not signed up for this public scrutiny and hatred. I had simply vowed to serve God and the church. Not only was I angry with God, I was angry with myself. From where I stood, the future held only more hostility and pain.

Some people proclaimed that I had caused conflict and division within the church. I struggled to understand these accusations, but they did not make sense to me. I knew I had not ordained myself. That was the decision of the District Board. The negative reactions plagued me.

I received a new revelation when my physician referred me to *People of the Lie,* a book by Scott Peck. This book provided me with fundamental insights. In my depression and grief, I realized that what I did was to tell the truth. I told the truth about God's love for me as a gay man. I told the truth about my love for the Church of the Brethren. I told the truth about my desire to serve God and the church as an ordained minister of Jesus Christ. My opponents were angry because I broke the set of rules by which they live. In my endeavor to live with integrity through truth-telling, I created a new reality that they didn't know how to handle. They responded in anger with fearful and hurtful accusations.

This insight allowed me to begin to let go of the stress and pain I had buried within my body. With the help of anti-depressants, massage, counseling, and relaxation techniques, I gained a deeper awareness of how my body, heart, mind, and soul were all connected. I dealt more fully with the painful reality in which I found myself, and I sought out new paths toward healing and wholeness.

In August of 2003, the Michigan District Conference again discussed my ordination. They passed a petition by a vote of forty-two to thirty-eight that directed the district board to comply with the action of the 2002 Annual Conference. While there was further discussion at the November District Board Meeting, I knew there was only a slight possibility of an alternate course of action. The directions given to the delegates to not recognize my ordination passed by a slight majority, as was expected. Interestingly enough, the petition didn't call for the removal of my ordination—only non-recognition. My name would not appear on the official list of ordained ministers.

The message was loud and clear. It was time for me to move on. I knew I could no longer stand in the middle of the storm. It was time for me to find more life-giving venues in which to share my gifts. For my personal health as well as professional opportunities, I transferred my ordination to the United Church of Christ (UCC) in December of 2003. Presently, I am employed as an administrator and fundraiser at Chicago Theological Seminary where I utilize my gifts of ministry to make friends for the seminary and raise funds for theological education.

I found myself in a much healthier place as I began 2004. Nevertheless, this experience left scars on my heart and pain in my soul. Many people ask me if I plan to pastor a congregation in the UCC. It is difficult to know how to respond. For the present, my focus is to rest, heal, and restore joy to my life. I am thankful for the friends, family, and colleagues who supported and encouraged me throughout this time. I fully trust that in the years to come, God will have new ministry possibilities for me as a truth-teller living with integrity. However, I will take my time to discover them.

Matthew J. Smucker, M.Div., is a 1990 graduate of Manchester College in North Manchester, Indiana, where he majored in chemistry education. He also earned a Master of Arts in College Student Personnel (1994) from Bowling Green State University in Ohio. He graduated with a Master of Divinity with distinction in ministry studies from Bethany Theological Seminary, Richmond, Indiana, in May of 2001. Born in Wabash, Indiana, Matthew grew up in Wooster, Ohio. He and his partner David Thompson live in Chicago. They are active members of Epiphany United Church of Christ.

CHAPTER 4

Navigating "Contrary Advocacy"

Kathleen Temple

I became a pastor, in the formal sense at least, fairly late in life. I had committed my life to Jesus Christ in the early 1970s as a teenager, participated actively in several churches over the next couple of decades, and held leadership roles in those congregations. My husband Ted Grimsrud and I first joined the Mennonite Church in 1981, attracted by the Mennonites' dedication to the Bible and to peace. But it wasn't until 1994 that I joined Ted as co-pastor of a Mennonite church in the Midwest. I was ordained in the spring of 1996.

Later in 1996, we moved to Harrisonburg, Virginia, where Ted and I joined the Bible and Religion faculty at Eastern Mennonite University (EMU). In addition to teaching part-time at EMU, I quickly found opportunities to stay involved in pastoral work. We joined one of the Harrisonburg Mennonite churches, and I dove into church life—preaching (in several congregations), leading worship, visiting elderly people, and the like. A year after we moved to Harrisonburg, I began preaching regularly at Shalom Mennonite Congregation, a small congregation that rents meeting space on the EMU campus, and after a few months I was asked to join the pastoral staff.

When Ted and I moved to Harrisonburg, we both transferred our ministerial credentials to the Virginia Mennonite Conference (VMC). Because I did not hold a pastoral position in a congregation at first, VMC placed my ordination credentials in their "special ministries" category, along with chaplains, school administrators, and other professors.

When Shalom called me to be one of their pastors, we all assumed that the transfer of my credentials from the "special ministries" to the "congregational ministries" category would be routine. However....

Not too long before I began working at Shalom, I had joined with several other concerned people in the neighborhood around EMU to form a support group for sexual minorities and their friends. Our intent with this group, which later took the name of "The Open Door," was simply to provide a safe place for discussion and encouragement for people with concerns for the pain the church and society has been causing for many vulnerable people.

To publicize our beginning, we posted numerous fliers in the area, including several on the EMU campus. This is what the fliers said:

> A SUPPORT NETWORK...of neighbors, students, pastors, teachers, friends, parents, and children is forming throughout our Park View neighborhood to provide support and affirmation to people of diverse sexual identities. Are you looking for kindred spirits? Are you searching for supportive resources? Do you want to find out about upcoming events? All calls of inquiry will be kept strictly confidential unless you ask to have your name passed along to others. [Several first names and phone numbers were listed on the flyer.]

My name happened to be one of those listed. This was an almost random choice from within our group, but one that would have significant repercussions. To our surprise, these fliers sparked a major reaction. Immediately, our support network was labeled as an agitating group that was overtly fighting against the Mennonite Church's "official" anti-gay position. Because the phone number we had listed next to my first name was my EMU office phone number, I was quickly identified as the "Kathleen" on the flier.

I faced some pretty strong criticism on campus, but ultimately weathered the storm and continued to teach part-time. Not too long after this controversy, my teaching job at EMU was even upgraded from an adjunct to a half-time salaried position.

On the other hand, things did not go so smoothly in my relationship with Virginia Mennonite Conference officials. Shortly after Shalom requested that my ordination be transferred from the "special ministries" to "congregational ministries" category, I received word that conference officials were deeply concerned about my position on homosexuality.

Over the next few years, I sat in many meetings where this deep concern found expression. At one point, after conference officials made clear that they were reluctant to recognize my status as a congregational minister, a number of representatives from Shalom met with several of these conference officials.

At that meeting, I said I would be willing not to engage in what conference officials had come to call "contrary advocacy." The officials had not spelled out in clear terms what they meant by "contrary advocacy," but we all had a sense that what the phrase meant was to publicly advocate that the Mennonite Church be more inclusive of gay and lesbian Christians. With the full support of the people from Shalom, I stated that I wanted to know precisely what actions would be considered "contrary advocacy" so I could avoid violating the parameters of the expectations of the conference officials. Even though I wanted to pledge to refrain from "contrary advocacy," the conference officials could not identify precisely what behavior(s) would come under that heading.

Several of the conference officials indicated at this meeting that they actually were not only concerned that I not commit "contrary advocacy." Most of them seemed even more concerned that I did not share their anti-gay beliefs, and they expected me to agree that "Scripture condemns homosexuality as sin." We from Shalom argued that to do so would be unreasonable and that nothing in the denominational and conference documents spoke to a requirement about what people believe.

In fact, the conference Faith and Life Commission's statement (October 11, 2000) forbidding "contrary advocacy" stated, "We are not insisting that there be 'full assent of will and intellect' on these issues." It was clear to me, however, that the conference officials with whom I was dealing were appalled that I could not agree with their anti-gay beliefs.

At the end of the meeting with the officials, we from Shalom still had no clear definition of "contrary advocacy." I determined simply to avoid the subject in church and in the classroom, hoping that silence would suffice. At this point, I reduced my work with our Open Door group a great deal, even though our group was not involved in advocating change beyond seeking to foster conversations on the issues.

I had actually been trying to avoid offending conference officials from the time I began working at Shalom. For example, the year before the above meeting, I decided not to add my name to a full-page advertisement in the *Mennonite Weekly Review* that voiced support for the Mennonite Church becoming more inclusive of gay and lesbian Mennonites. I regretted not being able to sign the ad that was signed by over six hundred Mennonite Church members, including eighteen of my colleagues at EMU. I felt that I should not sign it in order to avoid "contrary advocacy."

The conference officials finally determined that they would honor Shalom's request to shift my ordination credentials to the "congregational" category, with the condition that I serve a probationary period for one year. Also, during this year, they required that I meet monthly with the pastor who was the overseer of our area congregations. I was not technically under any official discipline, but they made it clear to me that one of the main purposes of this year of meetings would be that my beliefs should change. The overseer was to make a recommendation to the conference leadership concerning my ongoing status at the end of that year.

We met regularly and had truly congenial and quite frank conversations. It became clear to him fairly soon, though, that I was not likely to change my beliefs. However, he did help me as I continued to try to avoid actions that could have been construed as "contrary advocacy." This was difficult at times because of some problems at EMU, including the summary dismissal of a good friend because of her intimate relationship with another woman. Nevertheless, I did remain behind the scenes when some of the EMU faculty and staff protested this action.

A short time after our friend lost her job, she and her partner honored Ted and me by asking us to officiate in their union ceremony. We told them it would be best for us not to perform their ceremony, but we gladly worked with them in a pastoral manner to help them prepare for the spiritual and practical steps they were taking as they began their life together. We were delighted to learn to know them better and had many hours of great conversation about their relationship and ours.

We believed that it would be problematic for us to perform their ceremony, given the statement in the Membership Guidelines of the newly formed Mennonite Church USA that pastors are not to perform same-sex unions. In planning the ceremony, therefore, our friends included only small roles for us to play. It would be clear that we were not performing the ceremony since we would take no part in their sharing of their vows.

Several events came to a head concerning my relationship with the Virginia Conference early in 2002. The end of the probationary period was drawing near. My overseer recognized that I was not going to change my beliefs, but he communicated to me the hope that he might continue mentoring me for a longer period of time and thereby postpone the need for a final official decision concerning my status.

However, following a meeting where the overseer made this suggestion to members of the Faith and Life Commission of the conference, he passed the word on to me that they seemed very likely to reject his proposal. I had previously told him about my ongoing friendship with the couple who was planning a union ceremony, and at this point I informed him about the manner in which I would be participating so he could rest assured that I was not officiating.

His reaction surprised me. He immediately insisted that, as far as he was concerned, there was no relevant difference between being involved in the ceremony, however minimally, and performing it. He also insisted that I tell my friends that I would have to withdraw from participating in their ceremony in any way. Since I was not willing to do that, the overseer told the other conference officials that I would be participating in a union ceremony.

In short order, not long before the actual ceremony, I was warned that I would be losing my ordination as soon as they could process their decision, probably at the next meeting of conference leadership in late spring.

I was shocked at the speed with which they acted, and I was stunned that the Faith and Life Commission would disregard the work I had done for the previous couple of years to avoid "contrary advocacy." They did not recognize the clear distinction I believed could be made between performing a union ceremony and simply sharing in the ceremony along with many others. The fact that I had declined to perform the ceremony held no weight with them.

As soon as I could, I met with our conference minister. He advised me that if I wanted to avoid the stigma of having my ordination revoked through a disciplinary action, I might want to consider terminating my own ordination first. He expressed confidence that conference officials would accept that arrangement. Reluctantly, I decided (with many tears!) to accept his advice and terminate my ordination.

Ironically, in all the discussions with conference officials, no one questioned the quality of my performance as a pastor in Shalom Congregation. Everyone who communicated with me asserted that they believed I was doing an excellent job as a pastor. They affirmed me in continuing to fill that role in the congregation. Nevertheless, they stated that they could not continue to provide my ordination credentials, even though I was pastoring a congregation that remained in good standing in the conference. It did not seem to matter to them that if I continued to serve Shalom Congregation, but without credentials, the conference would have less power to hold me accountable.

My ordination officially ended on the 31st of August, 2002.

Interestingly, this change is largely symbolic. Of course, this does not mean that it is insignificant. After my ordination ended, I continued to work as one of Shalom's pastors just as before. I also continued to officiate at weddings. As far as the state is concerned, the only requirement for me to perform weddings is that I am serving as a pastor in a congregation. I actually, in theory at least, operate with fewer constraints on my "contrary advocacy" since the conference officials no longer have a formal relationship with me.

However, the past few years have left me quite battered and bruised. I believe the process used by the conference was unjust and disrespectful. That this arm of the Mennonite Church would decide to take away Mennonite Church USA's affirmation of my ministry hurts deeply. I understand my pastoring work to be a fulfillment of the vows I made when I became a member of the Mennonite Church and when I received ordination as a Mennonite pastor—to seek, as best I can, to follow the way of Jesus and to encourage others to do so as well.

Largely as a result of the stresses of living through the experience I have described here—and I have given a significantly condensed version!—I asked Shalom Mennonite Congregation for a leave of absence from my pastoral responsibilities from September of 2003 to May of 2004. As I write this essay in the middle of my leave, I am still discerning my ongoing role in the church. I do know that I have no regrets whatsoever concerning the choices I have made—both to seek to serve the church as a pastor, and to seek to offer whatever support I can to my lesbian and gay sisters and brothers.

* * *

Postscript

The above essay was written in January of 2004. In March of 2004, several more significant changes happened.

I informed my congregation that, though I deeply appreciate their support and their kindness in allowing me to take a leave of absence, I will not be able to return to my pastoral role. I feel sad, yet relieved at the prospect of being out of pastoral ministry.

When I decided not to return to my pastoral responsibilities at Shalom, I did plan to continue to teach in the Bible and Religion Department at Eastern Mennonite University, however. Then, in late March, I made another decision—to leave the life of teaching, as well.

In order to explain my decision to resign from EMU, I wrote the following letter to my friends and sent a copy to the administration of EMU. The note I added to the administration stated that I wanted them to know why I am leaving, and I also wanted them to know what I am saying to other people who ask why I am leaving.

Is It About "the Homosexuality Issue"?

I have been enjoying the privilege of teaching in the Bible and Religion Department here at Eastern Mennonite University for the past eight years. I love to submerge myself in my subjects, Bible and philosophy. I love to work with EMU students and with my colleagues. My eight years in this ministry have been deeply stimulating, engaging, successful, and rewarding. But this semester (spring, 2004) will be my last. I will soon return to my previous profession as a dressmaker and tailor. See me at Ragtime Fabrics in Court Square, downtown Harrisonburg.

I am leaving EMU, and yes, perhaps it does have to do with "the homosexuality issue." The issue, though not always on the surface, has been continually swirling around our community and buffeting many of us. Though I am happily married to an individual who happens to be of the opposite gender (I am therefore not attacked for my own sexual orientation identity), I have been criticized for having the "wrong" opinions about same-sex relationships and for associating with women who love women and men who love men.

Wait. I had better start over with my explanation.

I am leaving EMU, but no, it is *not* about "the homosexuality issue." I could remain on the EMU faculty if it were simply that we have a contentious issue, one on which we have divergent and strongly held opinions. I could stay, maybe for quite a few more years, if it were simply an intellectual or spiritual or ethical issue. If it were just an issue, we would be studying the attendant questions. We would be debating it. We would be asking one another about our experiences and insights and emotions about the subject. I would enjoy exploring and working on "the homosexuality issue" if it were treated as an issue, because we would all be learning and growing and finding out more about one another and our diverse sexualities in the process.

So, no. My resignation is not about the homosexuality issue. No. Rather, it is about disrespect toward women who love women and men who love men and harassment of those of us who want to ally ourselves with our lesbian and gay sisters and brothers. Such treatment toward sexual minorities and their allies is by no means the only discrimination that happens in the EMU community; too often other persons and groups perceived as "different" face hurtful attitudes and actions as well. But who would dare to sanction and defend *those* bigotries? Unkindness toward sexual minorities and allies is unique and constant—it is the one type of discrimination that is condoned by those in power. I no longer want to participate in an institution that continues not only to commit but even to defend harassment, hurt, exclusion, and castigation of people because of their sexuality. I find it difficult to do my work under the dread that another incident against sexual minorities could happen at any moment.

I am not going to list all the cases of this sort of unkindness in the EMU community. I am sure I am aware of only a fraction of them. I will note, however, that there has, to date as far as I know, been no apology for the summary and unfeeling way Sue Blauch was dismissed (though all agreed that she had been a model employee for fifteen years); no apology for the vilification of Ken Roth (though he merely expressed publicly his personal opinion as a personal opinion about same-sex relationships); no apology for the intimidation of EMU employees by the November, 2002 statement by the Board of Trustees; and no apology for the firing of Tom Arbaugh (though he and his partner maintained a celibate relationship). Also, to date, I have seen few serious attempts to defend and walk alongside any student who has come out as lesbian or gay or bisexual. On the contrary, persons who attempt to openly stand with students of diverse sexual identities fear for their own safety. I could go on.

I have remained at EMU as long as I have, not because I did not know what is happening, not because I am tough enough not to be frightened by what I observe, and not because I think the discrimination is waning. I have remained at EMU these eight years because I believe in EMU's mission, because I love the Mennonite Church and her young people, and because I get strong support and encouragement from the myriad of staff, faculty, and students who are working to eradicate discrimination of *all* kinds from our community so that we may truly learn "to do justice, to love kindness, and to walk humbly with God."

But now I am just tired.

I concluded my letter of explanation, dated March 21, 2004, with an expression of gratitude: "I will miss being part of the Bible and Religion Department. I will miss chapel. I will miss teaching and learning with students. I will miss my inspiring colleagues.....I thank you all for the deeply rewarding conversation and companionship."

I feel deep gratitude for the many joys of ministry, both in the congregation and on campus, but I also feel a sense of relief and freedom to be removing myself from what was, for me, a restrictive environment. I will now be free to enjoy my work as a tailor and to be open and honest about my beliefs and, especially, about my support for my gay and lesbian friends.

Kathleen Temple is a teacher, pastor, and tailor who lives in Harrisonburg, Virginia. She grew up in Phoenix, Arizona, and embraced Christianity as a teenager. Upon graduating from high school, she moved in 1972 to Eugene, Oregon, where she studied at Northwest Christian College and the University of Oregon. Kathleen married Ted Grimsrud in 1977 and began to learn to know Mennonites soon afterward when she and Ted studied peace studies and theology at Associated Mennonite Biblical Seminary in Elkhart, Indiana, before studying at the Graduate Theological Union in Berkeley, California.

Over the years, Kathleen and Ted have remained active in various Mennonite communities, ministering in the context of Trinity Mennonite Church in Glendale, Arizona, Eugene Mennonite Church in Eugene, Oregon, Salem Mennonite (South) Church in Freeman, South Dakota, as well as Shalom Mennonite Congregation and Eastern Mennonite University in Harrisonburg, Virginia. Kathleen and Ted have a son Johan Grimsrud and a daughter-in-law Jill Humphrey, recent graduates of Eastern Mennonite University.

CHAPTER 5

My Call to Ministry

John Carter

We do not live to ourselves,
and we do not die to ourselves.
If we live, we live to the Lord,
and if we die, we die to the Lord;
so then, whether we live or whether we die, we are the Lord's.
Romans 14:7-8 (NRSV)

I have been privileged to serve God and the church throughout most of my life. Ministry has been a source of great joy and of great sadness for me, and it has given definition and meaning to my life. For that I will always be thankful.

For God did not give us a Spirit of fear,
but rather a Spirit of power,
of love and of self-control.
Second Timothy 1:7 (author's paraphrase)

My faith and ministerial journey began when I was young, even before I was born. My parents were devout Christians from similar yet not identical backgrounds. My mother is a born and raised Pentecostal, and my father, who died in 1974, was a fundamentalist Baptist. It was through them that I began to sense the call of God on my life. My first memories of my journey began when we attended an Assembly of God mission church on a Navajo reservation in Arizona.

In the summer of 1961, we fellowshipped with a small independent Baptist church in southeastern Kansas while my mother was completing her master's degree in education. I was baptized in that church when I was six years old. In 1964, our family moved from Arizona to western Kansas, where we began to attend another Baptist congregation when I was nine years of age.

In Sunday school, it seemed we always studied the Old Testament stories about the battles of King David and of the Hebrew people. There was not much teaching about Jesus or from the prophets. After a few years, the politics of the congregation began to drive people away. My parents stayed as long as they could, but when they were personally attacked by the leadership, they knew that they could not continue to worship there.

It felt like coming home when we began to attend the local Mennonite Brethren congregation. I discovered a church that talked about Jesus and actually expected us to memorize his teachings, beginning with the beatitudes. After attending for several years, I decided that I needed to join this congregation. I had found it to be a place where my faith was beginning to take flight. I was hearing the call of God and was challenged to learn more of how faith could be lived out in my daily life. I began to read the Bible to listen to Jesus' words and to think about how they should take root in my daily living.

The more I studied, the more I sensed that God was calling me to something greater, and I accepted that call. Over the next few years, as I worked in leadership roles in the youth group, attended ecumenical Bible studies, and as I entered college, I struggled with that call in order to understand where it was that I was to serve. *What did God want from me and how should I fulfill that call?*

After I graduated from Fresno Pacific College, I decided that I needed to do three things. The first was to serve in Volunteer Service, but when I applied to work with Mennonite Central Committee (MCC), they did not have a placement for me. The second was to serve as a youth director or assistant pastor in a congregation, and finally, I was to enter seminary.

Within the year, I accepted a position of assistant pastor/youth director of a Church of the Brethren congregation in California, where I served for two years. During these years, I dated a young Mennonite

Brethren woman and we decided to get married. About four months before our wedding, I realized that I could not marry her. To do so would be unfair and unkind to her because I knew that I could never love her in the way that she deserved. I was beginning to admit that I was gay. I was nowhere near real acceptance of my orientation, but near enough to realize that for me to marry was to live a life that was not honest. I couldn't do that to her or to myself.

What God has made clean, you must not call unclean.

Acts 10:15 & 11:9 (author's paraphrase)

I was planning to enter Bethany Theological Seminary that fall but, instead, I applied to Brethren Volunteer Service and was accepted. During my first year of service, I was asked to lead worship at a Presbyterian congregation that was associated with the campus ministry where I was assigned. That Sunday one of the texts was from Acts 11, and as I read it the pastor's wife noted something. After the service she told me that I read that text as if it really meant something to me, and then she asked what it was that I was feeling. I gave a typical non-committal answer while knowing that I saw myself in that declaration of cleanliness.

It was then that I started to search for an answer, and over the next year I read, studied, and argued with God about life, sexuality, and ministry. I felt that if I accepted being gay, I would be giving up my call. So I made deals with God. I would be celibate and never talk about it. This deal making did not work. I still felt incomplete and shallow in my sense of self-awareness. I began to see that if I could not acknowledge who I am, I would be unable to be a good minister. Therefore, I began to come out. I decided to be celibate but at least to be open about who I am. The calling of God to serve was much more important to me than my individual desires or my sense of loneliness.

After I had been in the process of coming out for several years, my home congregation in California learned that I was gay, and immediately began to take disciplinary actions against me. That time of conversation was mostly one-sided. They never really talked to me about my life and how I expected to live it. They only collected data to prove that I was not fit to be a pastor, and they revoked my credentials for ministry. Of course, I was not surprised, but still I was devastated.

After all, I was celibate, as the rule of the church demanded, but still they revoked my credentials. I decided that I needed to drop out of the Master of Divinity program, and I began to work on a Master of Theology in Peace Studies instead.

I also began to attend a Metropolitan Community Church congregation near the seminary. Here I found a community of faith that accepted me and helped me to hear the gospel again. I also found a denomination that I would not be able to be a part of because of who I am—an Anabaptist radical pietist. They were simply too fundamentalist in their theology for me.

> *In Christ, God was reconciling the world*
> *and has given us the ministry of reconciliation.*
> Second Corinthians 5:19 (author's paraphrase)

It was during my defense of my thesis before the seminary's academic dean, who was also my advisor, that God nudged me again. As I wrote the thesis, I realized that I still felt the call to ministry, and this awareness was reflected in the finished work. During our conversation, the dean mentioned that my thesis/theological reflection was of the quality that he expected from the Master of Divinity students and not from the Master of Theology students. He ended our session with an invitation to return the next year and complete the M. Div. program. A month later, I agreed and re-enrolled in that program. After all of my searching, struggling, and deal making, I was back to where God wanted me.

I graduated from Bethany and accepted a call to serve as an outreach minister with the Night Ministry in Chicago. During that time, I joined Douglas Park Church of the Brethren and accepted a call to be on the church board. When one of the pastors left on vacation, never to return, I accepted the position of interim co-pastor. Three months later, my co-pastor and I were called to serve officially as pastors of the congregation. I served there for ten years before I resigned at the request of the district minister.

The congregation knew that I was gay; however, when it came up for public conversation one year, many claimed that they did not know. In fact, they still to this day make that claim. The problem with their claim was that their teenage children all knew that I was gay and had talked to their parents about it. During the meeting, these young men challenged their parents, and the parents then admitted that they did know about my sexual orientation. Several members within the congregation had struggled with having an openly gay pastor, but all of them accepted my call and seemed to be supportive of my ministry.

During my years at Douglas Park, I attempted to be recredentialed, only to have it tabled for about two years and finally refused. I was celibate and would be during my time of service and I told them so, but the district board felt that I didn't make a strong enough promise of celibacy. I have never quite figured out what that meant. I asked what the refusal to credential me would do to my call at Douglas Park, and they replied, "Nothing." They were happy and pleased with my service to the congregation. What surprised them was that I didn't make a fuss or threaten or storm out angrily. I accepted the decision and was concerned for the congregation. The district minister in charge later told me that he was impressed by my action and response.

As I look back, I must admit I am glad that I was not granted credentials for ministry, because during that year I met my partner. He was supportive of my ministry, and we agreed to a long-distance relationship until my service at Douglas Park would end in 2002.

In retrospect, I am convinced that the district minister asked me to step down for a variety of reasons, from internal Church of the Brethren politics to district politics to a concern for the congregation and a concern for me. I know that one of his private reasons was that he felt that my partner and I should be able to be together. For that I am now thankful.

For Christ is our peace;
in his flesh he has made both groups into one
and has broken down the dividing wall of hostility between us.

Ephesians 2:14 (author's paraphrase)

What the future holds for me, I have no clue. Even though I am not currently in a ministerial position, God continues to call me to use my gifts, education, talents, and training to be a blessing to creation and a glory to God.

There is no longer Jew or Greek,
there is no longer slave or free,
there is no longer male and female;
for all of you are one in Christ Jesus.

Galatians 3:28 (NRSV)

Throughout this brief glimpse of my life story, I have used some scriptural quotations. These texts have always been important to me. They are in many ways my personal credo. When I need to be comforted, challenged, and reminded of God's call on my life, they speak to me of that calling, of God's acceptance of me, and of God's ultimate ministry for me. This also applies to all people of faith. God calls us to be people of reconciliation—to bring people and creation back into right relationship with God and with one another. We are called to be people who see the vision of God's realm that is beyond mere conventionality for what it is—a wondrous place where all are welcomed and all are honored. It is Christ who gives us peace, and it is Christ who calls us to share that peace with the whole of creation. It is a wondrous thing, and it makes all that we go through worthwhile.

But by the grace of God I am what I am,
and [God's] grace toward me
has not been in vain.

First Corinthians 15:10a (NRSV)

John Philip Carter, M.A.Th. Peace Studies, M.Div., currently splits his home between London, England, where he lives with his partner Ashley Jones, and Chanute, Kansas, where he lives with his mother. His membership is still in the Church of the Brethren, but due to the unavailability of a local congregation, he has been worshipping with the Church of England (Episcopal).

He lives out his ministerial calling as a freelance artist and has provided sketches for a walking tour guide for the village of Wimbledon, England, as well as for the Wimbledon Lawn Tennis Museum. He is currently working on some commissioned paintings for a company in northern England. John continues to work on a series of meditative pieces based on Church of the Brethren liturgical practices centering on the Love Feast. He enjoys travel, visiting historic religious sites and cathedrals, art, reading, cooking, photography, and growing orchids.

CHAPTER 6

Haunted by God

Eva O'Diam

All my life, even when I have been trying to run from God, I have known God's presence. Whether I was growing up on the farm in Pleasant Hill, Ohio, or finishing high school in Covington, Ohio, going to college in North Manchester, Indiana, or working as a probation officer in Wabash, Indiana, whether I was following the call to ministry at Bethany Theological Seminary, or pastoring in rural Ohio, or in Long Beach, California, in Dundalk, Maryland, or in Harrisburg, Pennsylvania—I have known God's presence. Sometimes God prods me to learn. Sometimes God waits and wonders why learning takes me so long. At times God dances with me in celebration. Other times God cries out with me. But always, I know the haunting of that Presence and I need not look far! Moreover, I have learned that if I open myself to that Presence, the Spirit will provide every resource that I need and will guide every step!

I always felt that the Church of the Brethren had a right to remove my ordination. That has never been a question for me. But I believe the church had *no* right to remove it on the basis of my being lesbian and *never* with the process that was followed.

I grew up in the Pleasant Hill Church of the Brethren in Ohio, and I attended Manchester College in Indiana where I received a Bachelor of Science degree in Sociology. I worked as a probation officer in Wabash, Indiana, from 1976-77 and then left to attend Bethany Theological Seminary in Chicago in 1977. I was called to the ministry while in college, but gave up the license to minister when I became disillusioned with the church as a "religious institution." Both Robert Blake, who was pastor at Pleasant Hill Church of the Brethren when my mother died, and Phyllis Carter, my pastor at the Wabash Church of the Brethren, had a great influence on me as I reconsidered that call to "set apart ministry." I will always be grateful for the Spirit speaking to me through them.

While attending seminary, I took an extra year to pastor the Olivet Church of the Brethren in Thornville, Ohio, to be sure that my call was to pastoral ministry. I received my Master of Divinity degree from Bethany Theological Seminary in 1981 and was ordained to the set apart ministry in August of 1981 at the Wabash, Indiana, Church of the Brethren. My first pastorate was in Long Beach, California. After that ministry, I moved back across the country to the Dundalk Church of the Brethren in Dundalk, Maryland.

While pastor at Dundalk, I began to come to terms with other issues in my life. As I began to know myself more intimately, I found that I was lesbian. (That is a story all its own!) Suffice it to say, I realized—through the care and concern of friends, a spiritual retreat, some excellent therapy, a woman who challenged me with the words, "Eva, you're a dyke," and a Catholic priest who dared to say that he would treat as a treasure the deepest knowledge of who I am—that I was, am, and always will be a lesbian. I found I loved the Dundalk Church of the Brethren too much to put it in the middle of a denominational fight. (I knew that was where it could lead if I was honest with the church and they decided to ask me to stay.) My decision...to resign.

Was I afraid the Dundalk Church would not want me? Maybe. Fear of abandonment has long been an issue for me. Was I afraid they would want me and the denomination would say no? Definitely! I had no reason to believe that the denomination would support me. I had known leaders who were known to be gay—they had been ostracized. I had known people supportive of gay and lesbian people—but not in public.

The Church of the Brethren was all I had ever known. I was raised in the Church of the Brethren. I went to college at Manchester College and I went to seminary at Bethany Theological Seminary, both Brethren institutions. Where would I go? What would I do? The community of faith called Church of the Brethren defined, in part, who I was. How could I leave that? I have always believed in the call process in the Church of the Brethren. The call to set apart ministry was and continues to be one that leads me to listen to God, but a part of the affirmation of that leading of the Spirit is having that call affirmed by the whole body of Christ. That happened often in my life...not just once, as when Bob Blake, pastor at Pleasant Hill Church of the Brethren, suggested I needed to reconsider my call to set apart ministry, but repeatedly in the local church, the community, the district, and the denomination.

While in Dundalk, I began to work with the People of the Covenant Bible studies. On behalf of the denomination, I traveled to Florida to train People of the Covenant Bible study leaders twice a year for several years. I also served the denomination on the study committee for Annual Conference, writing the position of the Church of the Brethren on the Death Penalty. I authored *Love and Justice*, one of the People of the Covenant Bible studies that was later printed and re-printed. Time after time, I offered my ministry to the local church, the community, and the denomination, and my calling was affirmed and re-affirmed. I have never been more sure of anything in my life! God called me by the set apart ministry to lead the church.

Maybe the Church of the Brethren would simply put up with me if I wasn't a pastor! I could be a chaplain. That way, I would still be in ministry but perhaps the faith community would not be upset about my orientation if I wasn't leading a group within the Church of the Brethren. In fact, my district executive must have agreed to some extent. When I decided to resign from Dundalk Church of the Brethren as pastor, I went to talk with him. I shared that I was lesbian and asked that my sexual orientation not be an issue in my resignation. My sexuality was *not* the reason for my resignation. I resigned because I felt I needed some personal space to know what it meant for me to be lesbian. When you are in a public role as a pastor and living in a parsonage, a few feet from the church, that kind of "space" is not available! My district executive agreed and supported me by naming my work with Prisoner Visitation and Support, an alternative ministry to federal and military prisoners, as my ministry for purposes of keeping my ordination active.

For three years, I worked with Prisoner Visitation and Support. I also began to take more training for chaplaincy. During this time, I continued to work in the district, teaching district classes on worship and prayer, attending district and annual conferences, leading training for People of the Covenant, authoring *Love and Justice*, and working on the Death Penalty Statement. At the end of the three years, I decided it was time to be in one-to-one ministry again. I resigned from Prisoner Visitation and Support and applied to two residency chaplain programs. I was accepted at both. Then the floor dropped out...the funding for *both* programs was lost. Now what was I to do?

I was currently attending the Metropolitan Community Church of Baltimore. On the Sunday after I received this news, the sermon was on the wedding at Cana. The thrust of the sermon was that Jesus was fully prepared for ministry and in this setting was challenged by his mother to simply get on with what God had already prepared him to do. My good friend and former parishioner Janis sat next to me. Elbowing me, she said, "Get the message?" I did. Chaplaincy was what I was prepared to do to satisfy the religious institution called the Church of the Brethren. However, God had called me to pastoral ministry. God called me to walk a long-term spiritual journey with a group of people, not to minister to them in a crisis and perhaps never see them again. I was called to be a pastor—not a chaplain. And it *was* time to *do* what *God* had called me to do.

I again went to see the district executive. I told him that I wanted to put out a profile to be a pastor and that I wanted to be honest and say that I was lesbian. He said he could not allow that. He did allow me to complete a profile for one church in the district—Oakland Mills Uniting—which was tri-affiliated with the United Church of Christ, Disciples of Christ, and the Church of the Brethren. The United Church of Christ was responsible for filling the pastoral slot and they allowed gay and lesbian pastors. I applied for that position but never even received an interview. The church also happened to be my district executive's home church.

I had a choice either to seek out churches on my own and try to fight my way into the Church of the Brethren or to seek a pastorate where I was already accepted. I chose to begin the transfer of my credentials to the Universal Fellowship of Metropolitan Community Churches. In November of 1991, I began to pastor the Metropolitan Community Church of the Spirit in Harrisburg, Pennsylvania. I remained active in the Brethren/Mennonite Council for Gay and Lesbian Concerns (BMC) and still preached occasionally in a Church of the Brethren. My membership remained at Dundalk Church of the Brethren where they have always been very supportive of my journey.

In many ways, the teaching I received in the Church of the Brethren molded and shaped who I am. I learned how important a community is and how it should hold together, even in the midst of differences. When two people could not agree, or when one person felt another had broken relationship, I learned that you were to go to that person and talk. If you could not resolve the issue, then you were to take a brother or sister with you and try to work through the issue. If that did not work, then you took the issue to the larger community (Matthew 18:15-20).

I took to heart that I was to follow Jesus—at all costs. I learned to respect the individual conscience. If someone disagreed with the way I believed, even if that belief was a long-held part of the history of the denomination, I was not to sit in judgment of that person but was to continue to dialogue and to respect them even though they held a belief different from mine. Isn't that what I did in honoring the veterans in my congregations even though, as a pacifist, I did not believe in war? In the very foundation of the Church of the Brethren, I learned that even at the cost of fleeing your homeland, you stand firm in what Christ teaches you by his life and example.

Consequently, when I received a letter one day from the District Ministry Commission, I was not surprised. The letter requested that I attend a meeting to discuss some issues surrounding my ordination in the Church of the Brethren.

I remember that meeting well. When I arrived, the group was in a closed-door session. Shortly thereafter, I was invited into the room. Members of the Ministry Commission were sitting around a conference table. Introductions were made, though I knew most of the people around the table, and I will never forget their first question, "What is it that you would like to share with us?"

That took me by surprise! I looked at them and said, "I wasn't the one who called this meeting. I assume you have some charge or complaint against me. I am here to answer any questions you have and to dialogue about them. You will need to tell me what the meeting is about." They proceeded to lay the responsibility for the gathering on me by saying I had shared that I am lesbian in front of about five hundred people at an Annual Conference. In my memory, that sharing had occurred about a year earlier—why did it only become an issue now? It seems it took that long for people to write letters and complain about it. My question then was, Where were those people? What ever happened to direct dealing? Is it only in civil courts that people have the right to face those who bring charges? However, it seemed that there were no charges—no specific complaints—and we entered an hour and a half dialogue about some of the Commission's "concerns."

They proceeded to write things on newsprint that *might* be concerns. At the end of the hour and a half, they abruptly closed the meeting. It seems that they had already decided on a time frame but failed to mention that time frame to me. As I was invited to leave, I inquired as to what I could expect. The entire group assured me that this was the beginning of the dialogue and they would be in touch. They said that they had not yet decided on their process.

The next word I had from the District Ministry Commission was a letter informing me that they were recommending to the District Board that my ordination be removed because I had admitted I was lesbian. So much for dialogue and conversation! At this point, I sent letters to as many people as I could think of and more through the BMC address list to request letters of support. I will be forever grateful to those who wrote...well over one hundred people. These people became my faith community, my support, my anointing oil.

The fact that I continued to receive royalty checks from Brethren Press, while at the same time receiving negative letters from the district, emphasized the pain of this journey. It felt as though my ministry was being validated as they reprinted the People of the Covenant study, *Love and Justice*, while this same denomination was saying, "But because you are lesbian, you may not have a place at the table. You can lead us in spiritual growth, but you cannot walk the spiritual journey with us." I received the checks at least twice in the course of the removal of my ordination.

The District Ministry Commission notified me that the recommendation to remove my ordination would go to the District Board, and I was invited to address the board for five minutes in closed session. There would be no time for questions, but I could make a statement before they voted. (This is dialogue?)

I did attend the board meeting. My partner Mary went with me; however, she was not allowed in the meeting. I requested at the beginning of my statement that there be dialogue. It was denied. I could only make my statement and leave.

In my statement, I tried to make two points. First: Because of the church's own statement on human sexuality, I do not believe that my ordination can be removed because I am lesbian. The Statement on Human Sexuality recommends that someone not be ordained *if* they are living in a committed relationship. *Never* did the Ministry Commission ask if I were in a committed same-sex relationship. The charge they brought against me was that I was lesbian—not a lesbian in a committed relationship.

Secondly: Even though the Church of the Brethren claims to be a New Testament church that teaches that we should follow Matthew 18, I never had an opportunity to address my accusers. I never even knew who they were until after my ordination was removed, and I went to the district office to see the file kept on me. Those who had complained were listed in that file. In addition, there was no dialogue in the process about the charge itself. The only meeting I had with the District Ministry Commission was one where they admitted they were still trying to decide *if* there was a charge to be made. Once that charge was decided upon, no dialogue ensued. I made my statement and left the room. Very shortly afterward, someone came and shared the decision of the Board. My ordination was revoked.

Thank God, for a partner who supported me. She held me in her arms as I cried—feeling even more like an orphan than I did the day my mother died. Without her support, I could never have survived the process. No one from the District Board came to speak with me. No one offered any visible support at that meeting, but I knew that many in the church supported me because of the letters that I continued to receive. Nevertheless, that day, I knew there was no place for me in the Church of the Brethren. And a piece of my heart ached because of it.

I had the right to appeal the district's decision to the Annual Conference Standing Committee. Eventually, I did—not because I thought anything would change, but because of those who would follow after me. I needed to bring to the attention of the denomination how districts were treating people within the community of faith. I went before the Standing Committee, again in closed door session.

However, this time, I was not alone. I had written to those who were supporting me, and a large crowd waited outside the room where the Standing Committee met. They prayed with me before I entered. When I entered, I requested that the meeting be open—I had nothing to hide. Nevertheless, they denied that request and proceeded with the hearing. A representative of the District Ministry Commission offered their decision. I again objected on the same grounds. I offered copies of over one hundred letters of support. Following the hearing, I emerged into the circle that surrounded me and sang and prayed with me. The Standing Committee felt the process the district used was not proper and "recommended" that they reconsider.

I received a letter a few weeks later stating, without dialogue again, that the district had reconsidered, and the decision stood.

Do I regret the removal of my credentials? My call to minister in God's name has continued in a new denomination with a new people, many of whom have been injured by the same kinds of actions by their denominations. I am still with my partner Mary, whom I continue to love more every day. I thank God for her steadfast love and presence in the midst of that journey. We share ministry now. Through it all, I have never doubted my call to the set apart ministry. God offered the resources we each needed and has blessed us on the journey. It hasn't always been easy, but God has hunted and haunted me, celebrated and cried with me the whole way! The cost of truth can seem too much at times, but I continue to look forward in trust and hope and believe that God will be present to support and surprise us all!

Eva O'Diam was ordained in July of 1993 as a minister in the Universal Fellowship of Metropolitan Community Churches. She is pastor of Metropolitan Community Church of the Spirit in Harrisburg, where God called her in November 1991. She lives in Harrisburg, Pennsylvania, with her life partner Mary Nell Miller Kelly and their dog Sweetie. Eva and Mary have been partners since May 5, 1991. They share ministry; music; a loving family, including six grandchildren; an appreciation of God's creation, especially through hiking, camping, and flowers; and a love of books. They look forward to and work for a time when *all* people will be treated as God's own.

CHAPTER 7

From the Inside Out

Sue Blauch

"Her blood runs Royal Blue" were the words an Eastern Mennonite University cabinet member used to describe me at one point while I was working for my alma mater. It was, I suppose, a fitting description for a variety of reasons, including my six years of involvement with the Lady Royals women's basketball team (four years as a player and two years as an assistant coach). I am privileged to be a member of the 1985 Old Dominion Athletic Conference (ODAC) women's basketball championship team—the first EMU women's basketball team to win a conference title. Or perhaps, and more likely, "Her blood runs Royal Blue" describes the fifteen years of service I gave to Eastern Mennonite University from 1986-2001.

The positions I held during those fifteen years required more than a desire for a job and more than the ability to simply put in a forty-hour workweek. The positions required a personal commitment to the university's mission, dedication to meeting students' needs, and a willingness to give as much time as needed, day or night, to accomplishing the tasks.

After graduating from Eastern Mennonite College (University, since 1994) in 1986 with a B.S. in physical education and a minor in psychology, I knew that Harrisonburg was where I wanted to stay. While I was interviewing for teaching positions in the area, I learned of an opening at EMU for a residence director (RD). I interviewed for the position, was offered the job, and accepted. Additionally, I was offered the opportunity to continue my involvement with the women's basketball team as an assistant coach.

The decision to accept was easy. I loved the EMU community. I loved the idea of working with students and staying involved in campus life. I felt that the EMU community was the best place for me to be. A day or two after I accepted the RD position, I was offered an interview for a teaching position back home in West Virginia at my old junior high school, but I declined. Intuitively, I knew that I was where I was intended to be. If my life were a thousand-piece puzzle, it was like finding the first inside piece just after finishing the border. It was a solid color piece that looked similar to a lot of other pieces. But this one fit perfectly.

I have a deep appreciation for my beginnings as an RD. The experience gained in this position significantly shaped my career direction. Much of the influence came from two women—Peggy H. Landis, Director of Student Life, and the late Erma H. Brunk, Director of Housing—who modeled compassion and professionalism combined with an unending sense of humor. Their mentoring, modeling, and leadership were significant to my personal and professional development, self-confidence, and subsequently, self-acceptance.

After two years as an RD, a full-time position became available as Assistant Director of Admissions. I applied and was offered the job. For the next three and a half years (August 1988 – February 1992), I was a "roadrunner." From Labor Day thru the week prior to Thanksgiving I spent Monday (and sometimes Sunday evenings) thru Friday on the Virginia college fair circuit. Recruiting students for EMU was easy. This was my community, the place where I grew up and was still growing up, the place that received the benefit of my time, energy, and enthusiasm.

I poured a lot of energy into my work at EMU. At the same time, I pursued other interests. I earned my M.Ed. in Counseling while working in Admissions and began a hobby that has since become my livelihood—refereeing women's basketball. After finishing my master's degree, I enrolled at the Virginia School of Massage taking both the beginning and intermediate massage classes. Friends and family greatly enjoyed being the subjects of my practicum hours.

The theme that emerged in this part of my story was "staying busy." While I did not recognize it at the time, staying busy was an important coping strategy for me, because I was uncomfortable with the fact that I was a lesbian. Staying busy was a distraction from *me*. I truly believed that I needed to be fixed and sought freedom through prayer, counsel from my church, my pastors, and close friends.

I knew I was different even as early as elementary school. I was not like the other girls even though I had no understanding of sexual orientation. I recall a brief conversation with my mom when I was very young. I remember that as I walked into the kitchen where Mom was working, my head reached no higher than the countertop. I looked up at her and said, "Mom, when I grow up to be a man...." She stopped me and said, "Susan, you are a girl and you will grow up to be woman. You will never be a man." Whoa—news flash! I do not even recall how I was going to finish my thought. I was probably going to say, "When I grow up to be a man, I want to marry a really nice woman." There are some who would hear this and diagnose me with a gender identity disorder. But for me it is simple. In the core of my being, I felt something very different than other girls. Since we are taught at a very early age that boys marry girls, I assumed I would grow up to be a man. After all, how else could I marry a woman?

My first real crush came during my freshman year at EMU. The feelings I had for this woman and the relationship that developed served as a wellspring of understanding. Finally, I understood all that had been going on within me. I had dated guys before but never did I experience the intense emotional connection or the excitement that comes from being in love. This new understanding of myself brought with it self-condemnation. I had been taught that this was wrong, that something inside me needed to be fixed. I tried to deny these feelings by dating men, but repeatedly I found myself attracted to other women. This battle raged on for years. I prayed for God to heal me and make me normal.

During my last two years of college, I began dating a guy who became my best friend. He was a wonderful person, someone I could talk with, laugh with, and someone with whom I could comfortably hang out. I loved his family too. It seemed like the perfect escape. I could marry him and my problem would be solved. Fortunately, for him and for me, I recognized that this was not the answer. Aside from those in my church and a few close friends, he was the first person to whom I came out. It was very painful for us both. I wanted and needed him to know that this was not about him; it was about me. I was wired in such a way that if it did work, I knew it would only be temporary. One day it would short circuit.

I had experienced the effects of short circuiting already. My life was compartmentalized. When I was with family or in other environments where I felt alone in my struggle, I would experience panic attacks. I recall telling my counselor that I was convinced that I was demon-possessed. After describing the powerful feelings of being overcome with fear and knowing deep in my heart that I was going crazy, along with the cold sweats and lightheadedness, he told me about panic attacks. I felt like I was just hanging on.

As time passed, I learned to manage my life better. I was beginning to accept myself as a lesbian, yet my world was still compartmentalized. My experiences at EMU both as a student and an employee were affirming for me. I found meaning in my work and relationships with co-workers. I was on a journey of self-discovery and acceptance, not knowing where it would lead.

In February of 1992, I made another job transition within the EMU community. Director of Housing and Residence Life was a new position created in the Student Life division. My previous experience in residence life along with a master's in counseling made it easy for Peggy Landis to hire me back to her division and promote me to a department head. I spent the next seven and one-half years directing and supervising the residence life department and programs, hiring and training staff, developing and implementing campus policies, and working with students. It was an easy decision to accept this position—another piece of the puzzle that fit into place perfectly. I was committed to EMU, the community, and the university's mission. I knew I was in the right place.

During these years, I was out to approximately ten or twelve people within the university community. The gay and lesbian Mennonite community was very much closeted and underground. There seemed to be a "don't ask, don't tell" climate at EMU. And believe me, I was not planning on telling anyone. I kept my private life to myself.

In April of 1998, I went through a break up with a woman I had been dating for over five years. Emotionally, it was a very difficult time for me, and I came out to my mother. While there is not a happy ending to my coming out story with my family, it did result in a freedom that I had not experienced before. I did not have to pretend any longer. My immediate family consists of my mom and dad, one sister and brother-in-law and their two children. They were devastated by the news. Even though they had their suspicions, it had not been confirmed. For years I had lived in fear of what my family would do if they knew.

Unfortunately, most of my fears have been realized. Time with my niece and nephew immediately changed. I was not permitted to spend time alone with them. I was also told to be sure that they did not eat or drink after me because my lifestyle made me susceptible to diseases that I could pass on to them. That restriction progressed to not being able to spend time with them at all. Information about their school and church programs and events stopped coming. The message, although not spoken aloud, became clear very quickly—you are a physical and spiritual danger to the family and to the development of the children. Suddenly, I was not the same person to my family that they had known for the past thirty-four years. My journey came from the inside out—a seventeen-year process of discovery and self-acceptance that my family did not know about. Coming out to them was a nightmare that came true.

When I weigh the cost of coming out to my family with the immediate relief and freedom I felt, I have no doubt that it was worth the truth. Intuitively, I knew they would not respond in the positive way that most of my friends experienced when they came out. I do not need everyone I love and care about to agree with me theologically or spiritually.

But I do need to be granted respect for the decisions I make, the partner I have chosen, and my own personal relationship with God. The process of de-compartmentalizing my life required that I stop accommodating and enabling not only my own fears, but the fears of others. It required me to be me and live my life with integrity.

It was not until I met Karen in late summer of 2000 that I would understand my need to completely de-compartmentalize my life. I will never forget that moment when our eyes met for the first time. Ours is a story of love at first sight. I knew I was meeting someone who I was destined to meet and learn to know. There is something miraculous when a lifelong journey and struggle turns into peaceful contentment. I knew in my soul that I had met the woman with whom I would spend the rest of my life. As Karen and I began dating and learning to know each other, our love at first sight grew into a lasting love. Looking back on the events which followed, my faith in God's presence has grown stronger as well.

At the time we met, I was just beginning my second year of yet another new position at EMU. In August of 1999, I made a transition from Director of Housing and Residence Life to Regional Director for Development. Many friends and family wondered how I could possibly think that asking people for money could be an enjoyable job. While I understood their point of view, this was not an issue for me. Considering that I had recruited students and was financially committed to several EMU projects myself, asking others for financial contributions was relatively easy. I was energized by fundraising work and by the many relationships with donors that I developed, primarily in southeast Pennsylvania's Franconia region. I learned to know some very interesting and generous people.

As Karen and I dated and spent time together, it was becoming very clear that we wanted to build a life and home together and as part of that to make a formal commitment to each other. In April of 2001, we hiked Humpback Rocks along the Blue Ridge Parkway, the spot of our first date, and exchanged vows and rings. At this point in time, having a public ceremony did not feel like an option for us. Living our lives together required us to be discrete. That summer, we began combining our households. It was an exciting new chapter of my life.

Toward the end of that summer, I was asked to be one of several speakers at the annual faculty/staff fall conference. The theme was "Stories of Risk, Grace, and Hope." I was asked to share from my experiences because of my longevity at EMU. It was good to reflect on what it was that kept me there. What kept me going was my sense of belonging, my commitment to the mission of EMU, and my love for the community. I also recall sharing that I recognized that EMU was not a completely perfect place—just as I was not perfect, and it is those imperfections that cause us to grow together, prosper, and become a better place for everyone.

Less than a month later, I was on a fundraising trip in southeast Pennsylvania. I was feeling especially energized by one donor meeting in which we mapped out plans for an immediate $100,000 gift to be followed by subsequent donations over time. On Thursday of that week, I was between appointments when I received a phone call from a friend and fellow EMU employee. I learned that when I returned to the office on Friday, my supervisor was planning to ask me about my sexual orientation and my relationship with Karen.

Although Karen and I had discussed how we might deal with this situation hypothetically, we hoped that it would not happen. We were totally unprepared for the pain it would cause us. The more Karen and I talked about how to best deal with this situation, the more we knew in our hearts that the only answer was the truth. I decided to make an appointment with then president Joseph Lapp first thing Friday morning. I somehow managed to make it through my last donor appointment—a dinner meeting—and drove home.

My meeting with the president was brief, especially in light of my fifteen years of service. President Lapp indicated that "an anonymous person in the ministry" from Franconia, Pennsylvania, called my supervisor to let him know that "I was a lesbian living in a committed relationship with Karen Myers." I confirmed that this was true. I was presented with two options—resign or "be terminated." We discussed a severance package, shook hands, and I left. I then met with my supervisor, the Vice President for Advancement, and discussed a timeline for leaving. I spent the afternoon cleaning out my office and went home.

I believe my firing was the result of a tragic combination of fear and ignorance. Leaving EMU was not easy. This was my community, the place where I grew up, the place where I invested my time, energy, and my working years, the place I believed in—the place where I belonged. Suddenly, I became like a bruise in an apple that needed to be cut out and thrown away.

Despite the pain and injustice of that experience, what resulted was amazing. Karen and I received an outpouring of support from her family, some of my extended family, friends, and many EMU faculty, staff, and students. I was out! What I held so closely on the inside for many years was out. The barriers that compartmentalized my life were gone. The fear I carried for so many years was no longer an unknown. While the decline of my immediate family relationships and the loss of my job were painful, I no longer needed to fear the unknown.

Additionally, a lifelong dream of mine came true. My dream was not unlike those of every other living human being—to fall in love and get married. I never believed that this dream would come true, but it did. Karen and I celebrated our lifelong commitment to each other on April 20, 2002, surrounded by over one hundred of our closest family and friends. It was a magical day, full of anticipation, emotion, and excitement. I knew that I had found my soul mate, my lifetime partner, and we were able to celebrate that publicly.

Like most couples planning a wedding, we had a picture of what we wanted our marriage ceremony to be. Our goal was to have a ceremony in a place that provided simple accommodations with an intimate atmosphere. We checked out several locations and decided that Broad Street Mennonite Church would be an ideal setting. After making arrangements to rent the church, we began working on all the details that go into planning a wedding, like printing and sending invitations, meeting with florists, securing a photographer, arranging our reception, and planning the intimate details of our ceremony.

What we had not planned on was dealing with fear and ignorance once again. The Harrisonburg District of the Virginia Mennonite Conference learned that we were renting Broad Street Mennonite Church (a member congregation) and began taking swift actions to prevent our ceremony from taking place there. District leaders threatened to remove Broad Street from membership in the Harrisonburg District and Virginia Mennonite Conference—a threat that they carried out several months after our wedding.

Just two weeks prior to our ceremony, one district leader suggested that perhaps we could just "have our ceremony somewhere else." When Fear and Ignorance hold a committee meeting, they sometimes invite Panic along too. I guess they all forgot what goes into planning a wedding and how logistics would make it impossible to just pick it all up and take it somewhere else and let 130 people from all over the country know about it. We had chosen a setting that was exactly what we wanted for our special day, but the Harrisonburg District leadership took very deliberate steps to create division over our ceremony and politicize the event. In the end we discovered that Broad Street offered us much more than an aesthetically pleasing location; we learned that it housed people of great courage, integrity, and love.

It was very disheartening to once again experience pain and rejection from people who had no interest in hearing our story or our faith journeys. It was also very difficult not to take this personally. The members of Broad Street Mennonite Church were united in acting as a shield for Karen and me as we planned and celebrated our wedding. They surrounded us with love, acceptance, and support. They listened to our journey and were witnesses to our love for each other. Although we offered to make alternate arrangements if it meant disciplinary action against them, they wanted us to stay.

I have always been inspired by the words from a song that was sung at our wedding: "No storm can shake my inmost calm, while to that Rock I'm clinging. Since Love is Lord of Heaven and Earth, how can I keep from singing?" Each step of my coming out experience has brought rejection and pain. Yet each experience has been countered with a more powerful message of unconditional love, acceptance, and inclusion. My relationships with extended family members have been renewed and strengthened; I gained a whole source of love and support from the Myers family and discovered a faith community of which I can now openly be a part.

For many years, I focused a lot of time and emotional energy hiding the truth and compartmentalizing my life. As I began to step back and weigh the cost of truth with the cost of hiding, I saw the paradox that I had created in my life. Now that I am openly out, I know that the greatest cost was living in the closet. Even though I have experienced pain and rejection as the result of living my life with integrity, I have discovered from the inside out that only truth can bring happiness and freedom.

Sue Blauch lives with her partner Karen Myers in Harrisonburg, Virginia. She has been officiating women's collegiate basketball since 1991 and officiating for the Women's National Basketball Association since 1999. She is also certified as an International Basketball Federation official. She would like the ability to call technical fouls and eject people for unsportsmanlike conduct in the real world, as well as in basketball games. Additionally, she works part-time for Blauch Brothers, Inc., a mechanical contracting company owned by her extended family, where she is the Quality Assurance/Service Contracts Coordinator. When she is not blowing the whistle or working her part-time job, she enjoys taking on house projects, landscaping, going for walks with Karen and their dogs Sadie and Milo, and spending time with friends and family.

CHAPTER 8

A Double Life

A Mennonite Pastor

I sometimes feel like a double agent. I have two lives and hold both in a precious balance. I wonder if someday the sometimes stable, sometimes precarious equilibrium will tilt and all that has been so carefully balanced will come crashing down in a thunderous, sonic boom.

You see, I am a pastor in the Mennonite Church. And I am gay. Could there be a better oxymoron? A gay Mennonite pastor? Ah, but you see, most people don't know it. Secrecy is the cost of truth for me. How is it that people don't know, you ask? It's easy—I'm married. Let me tell you my story about the double life I lead.

I grew up an all-American Mennonite boy: two loving, Christian parents, brothers and sisters, a large, extended Mennonite family, involved in sports, music, Mennonite Youth Fellowship, and a part of a rural Mennonite faith community that was tightly knit and had clearly defined values. But secretly I was different. I knew it from the age of childhood. I enjoyed the company of my girl friends much more than the company of my guy friends. I excelled in sports, swimming, fishing, and hunting. I could be mischievous and ornery with the best of my buddies, yet it was in spending time with my grandmother, mother, aunts, sisters, and girl friends that I was truly happy and felt whole.

Within the plain walls and plain floor and plain, hardwood pews of our church, I don't remember ever hearing any sermons condemning homosexuality, most likely because it was already a given. Every good Mennonite knew that it was wrong. The jokes and derogatory remarks about gays and lesbians that I heard in school and among both youth and adult Mennonites were enough for me to realize it was considered a horrible abomination. The whispery gossip at family reunions confirmed it, as rumors revolved around absent cousins and relatives who had "strayed" into "that lifestyle." Fear gripped me as I overheard aunts, uncles, and grandparents murmur phrases with mostly sad, quiet voices. "It's just so wrong...he was kicked out of the house...the wages of sin...I'm afraid for his soul." The cost of truth was made clear in those hushed conversations: rejection, judgment, and disgust.

By junior high, I was already desperately praying for help to God, Jesus, and *anyone* who would listen, including asking pious grandparents and relatives who had "passed on" to put in a good word for me with God. I walked the woods and corn fields crying to Jesus to "take this away from me," "make Satan go away," or "let me die."

In high school, I dated girls because it was expected. I went to prom with a lovely girl, wishing the whole time I was the handsome prom king's date instead. Not once did I confide in another person or talk to my parents or pastor or Sunday school teacher. It was not safe to do so, with generations and generations of tradition, teaching, and heterosexual hegemony firmly rooted within my family and within my Mennonite faith community. I knew the cost of truth.

Even while I was struggling with my sexual orientation in high school, I was sensing a call from God to serve the church. By the time I was fourteen, I was already participating in worship, teaching Sunday school, singing in the choir, and giving leadership in Mennonite Youth Fellowship. I loved the church, and the encouragement and support that I received for using my gifts to serve the church meant a lot to my fragile soul. When the people gathered for worship, for weddings, for funerals, and fellowship meals, I felt included, loved, and a part of something bigger than my immediate family or myself.

In Sunday school, I resonated with the biblical stories of the many outcasts and rejected persons whom Jesus touched, healed, and to whom he extended God's grace and mercy. It was a healing balm to my spirit. Jesus accepted them, and they weren't perfect, so maybe there was hope for me, too? Maybe I could even help others come to know this healing, accepting Jesus? Being baptized and participating in my first communion and foot washing was my own secret coup. I was in! I had been extended the "right hand of fellowship" and had not been struck down or found out. I was called "brother." I felt loved by God and accepted by God's people in every way but one. The cost of acceptance was to stay hidden.

It was in college that I first made friends with gays and lesbians who were "out." I admired them for their courage and strength. I wanted to be like them. I had never been a more complete person than when I was around them. I think most of them knew that I was gay, even if I didn't tell them or even admit it totally to myself. Yet I could not bring myself to confide in them. I was still bound by my strict Mennonite upbringing, and I kept my feelings closely guarded and tightly shut.

It was also in college that I met my wife. We found we had much in common, from our conservative Christian childhoods to our desire to serve God, to our developing, changing, inclusive theology and philosophy of life, to our tastes in music and food. I married her, as many gay men marry, thinking this would finally cure me, take away the "evil, hellish" feelings I had, and force me to stop thinking about men. God would see my desire for holiness and right-living and miraculously slice and dice that evil part out of me, heal me, and send me straight and narrow on my way to heaven.

Please don't think for a moment that I did not or do not love my wife. I do. She is my best friend, soul mate, and wonderful life companion. But, as a gay man, there is a part of my spiritual, emotional, and physical self that will never be fulfilled in being married to a woman. It is not her fault. It is the way God created me. She has been and continues to be for me everything a wife could possibly be.

A year into our marriage, I finally told my wife that I was gay. The cost of truth was devastating. It threatened our very relationship—the covenant we made together. In the beginning, it was incredibly difficult. I read self-help books. I participated wholly in Christian, anti-gay therapy. I considered divorce. Together, we saw marriage counselors and therapists. While she dealt with her feelings of betrayal, acceptance of my orientation, and her part in being married to a gay man, I was finally able to come to terms with my own acceptance of who I was and am—an unconditionally loved and accepted child of God. Throughout those years, we stayed close and kept our lines of communication open. Together, we came through a very dark tunnel, not knowing for certain what we would see at the end. The view has been surprisingly beautiful. And we see it together. Today, my wife is understanding and accepting, and she loves me for who I am, completely. My wife is a remarkable person. I love her deeply.

Being called to pastor a Mennonite church was another time of testing, of struggling to decide if I could balance who I was with what the church teaches and believes about one such as I. The cost of truth has been compromise. There is a deep resonance with the Anabaptist and Mennonite streams of faith that calls to me. I have found it in no other denomination or faith. The ideals of the centrality of Jesus Christ and his call to nonviolent peacemaking, of God's unconditional love and grace to all creation, and the call to extend God's love to others by serving the world within a strong, alternative community of faith— these things keep my faith alive and excited about what God can do in the world.

I love the church. I love the message of the gospel, for Jesus speaks as one who is considered condemned, unrighteous, and unholy. Every time I preach that Jesus came to lift up the downtrodden, to champion the underdogs, to turn upside down the culture that says "you don't belong," I am preaching to myself. And I am preaching for all the lesbian, gay, bisexual, and transgender persons who are rejected and unwelcome within the Mennonite community of faith.

The deep rift that has grown within the Mennonite community over acceptance of homosexual orientation has severely challenged my decision to both pastor and remain in the closet. I have sat through and presided over some heartbreaking church meetings in the last ten years. Some tell me that the vitriolic anger and ungraceful attitudes as people speak their thoughts and beliefs are not a true representation of the church. Others say it is the church finally showing her true colors. As I stand before the congregation and teach what the church believes today about male and female sexual relationships within a Mennonite faith perspective, I am acutely aware of the cost of truth, both for me and for my congregation.

Along the way in my journey of faith, I have confided in close friends, both straight and gay, and have received affirmation, love, and acceptance. It took me ten years to tell my best friend, who is a straight guy, that I was gay. He completely accepted me and was actually hurt that I did not tell him long ago. So you may wonder, why don't I come out? I often ask myself the same question. The questions that form in my mind are also a part of the cost of truth for me. Would coming out do more harm than good to my immediate and extended family? Would my ministry be over? Would I still be able to touch lives and stay in the Mennonite Church? Would it mean one less person who can empathize with the underdogs? Is it hubris or foolishness to think that God can use me more as I am now? Or am I just a coward? I don't have the answers yet.

I am your gay pastor. You see me every Sunday, you hear me preach, you see me with my arm around my wife, sitting with my family, and you don't know. You may never know. Maybe you don't need to know. I will keep shepherding, preaching, teaching, loving, and reaching out to you. And I will continue being my full self to my close friends, my wife, and God. It's a compromise. I love you and feel called to be your pastor, even though I cannot tell you about a completely different part of me. Am I living a lie, you ask? Some people would say that I am, that I am not being true to myself, nor to all those who have come out and are living in the light. Others may say that I am not being honest with the congregation and those I lead.

But when your heart is touched; when God comes to you through my sermon or through the worship service; when, as a result of my ministry, you accept the challenge to live a life imitating Jesus Christ by serving the poor, feeding the hungry, sharing good news of healing and hope, being the hands and feet of God to others; then I know that it is worth it. For now I will keep on being a double agent. I will keep meeting with my gay and lesbian brothers and sisters in Christ. I will keep encouraging them to run the race, to not give up. I will keep telling them we are sons and daughters of God too.

I love who I am. I love my friends, both inner and outer circles. I love my family. I love the Mennonite Church, despite its ups and downs, its imperfections—it is still the place where I find the God I love.

This double life I lead is the cost of truth for me.

CHAPTER 9

Signs of Hope

Ruth E. Wenger

[Jesus] poured water into a basin and began to wash the disciples' feet and to wipe them with the towel . . . "So if I, your Lord and Teacher, have washed your feet, you ought to wash one another's feet." (John 13:5 and 14, NRSV)

On October 5, 2003, I sat in worship with my pew mates celebrating World Communion Sunday. Though I am now a member of a local Presbyterian congregation, my thoughts were drawn to the broader church family—Christians across the world. Most specifically, I thought about my ethnic roots, my family of origin, and my Mennonite Church family. I touched the grief I feel for her. The grief and, yes, the anger over the divide there is on homosexuality.

As I sat there in common with all churches who share communion in remembrance of Christ, the symbol that came to me (and it runs deeply through my spirit) was of the towel and the basin. I was taught that it represents the role of being a servant. I let my thoughts wander and the Spirit be present as I asked, "What would happen if gay and lesbian and supportive folk would be servants to those congregations that are clearly anti-gay and anti-lesbian? By this I mean literally to be of service. A group would go where there were concrete needs to fix, repair, and/or do a "barn raising" as it were.

What if?

I immediately said, "I'm not ready to do this . . . It won't work or make a difference . . . I'm no longer Mennonite, so what do I care or why hope that anything would change . . . I'm tired, don't ask more of me, I have **no more** to give in this effort."

Well, I do care—I can't act like I don't care! I guess the girl can leave the Mennonite Church, but you can't take the Mennonite out of the girl. As you can see, I still have those moments in which I want healing for the Mennonite Church.

As noted, I am now a Presbyterian. The Presbyterians are going through their own process on acceptance of gays and lesbians in leadership. At least their discussions are done in an "orderly" manner. In the Presbyterian Church, it has not become my battle; I'm letting others take the lead. I'll serve at fund-raising dinners; the straight pastors and leaders can fight this battle. In the Presbyterian system, pastors, elders, and deacons are ordained. Since I am a deacon, I have been ordained for that role. In spite of being the coordinator of the deacons, at times I feel rootless.

*   *   *

I would like to step back and briefly look at how I got here.

My parents grew up in the Lancaster County area of Pennsylvania. They were from good Mennonite stock. My father was a teacher and my mother was a secretary with some college education. My grandfather Wenger was progressive and valued education and the church. These values were passed on to my father and through him to me.

My father, as a young man, felt called to be a minister; in fact, he was in a "lot" to be called into the ministry. There were five in the lot. A slip of paper was placed in one of five Bibles that were then placed in random order and brought out to the candidates. When the Bibles were presented, each selected a Bible, apparently picking them in the order in which they were seated. When the Bibles were set up at the front of the worship room, the paper marking the call was showing from one of the Bibles. It was the Bible that would have been my father's. The Bibles were taken back and rearranged, and the lot went to someone else.

Sometime after that, when I was four, my parents moved to Tampa, Florida, as "home (State-side) missionaries." Mom taught kindergarten and Dad was principal of a small Christian school. The school was part of a church planting effort in the local community of Ybor City, a neighborhood where folk of Italian and Cuban heritage came together to work in the cigar industry. Both of my parents were active in this church building effort. They gave me a tremendous gift through this experience; I came to value diversity and appreciate other cultures. They did not shelter us or make us feel superior to our non-Mennonite friends.

I first accepted Christ at the age of nine. The evangelist and my father decided that I had done it out of fear and that it wasn't a real commitment to Christ. I remember hesitantly raising my hand again at eleven, and because I was almost twelve, I was taken seriously. I went through membership class and was baptized at my parents' home congregation in a white cape dress and, of course, the standard head covering. I also took my first communion along with foot washing. In my youth I experienced foot washing and communion as solemn events; we had to be "right" with our brothers and sisters. This meant we had to make sure that we got along with others in the church, and if we did not, we were to confess and ask forgiveness. We also met with the pastor and bishop to make sure we had nothing to confess.

The summer I was baptized, we moved to Virginia where Dad taught at Eastern Mennonite College and Mother became a secretary in the bookstore. At that time, I became much more aware of the Mennonite culture and how exclusive it could be. Since we had moved into a mostly Mennonite area, the diversity I had experienced was gone. I had a difficult time. Messages about sin, forgiveness, being in the world but *not* of it, the peace position, and nonresistance were strongly taught. I took my faith seriously and found it meaningful, though I was plagued with guilt, especially around messages about sexuality. Christ as comforter got me through my teenage years.

As a young adult, I taught young adult Sunday school at my home congregation. The Vietnam War was in full force. I remember defending my peace position on being a conscientious objector in a panel at church. After college, I was also a sponsor of the Wayfarers, the younger version of Mennonite Youth Fellowship. I was actively involved in other ways as well, serving as an elder and also giving several sermons at the congregation that I attended.

After teaching and coaching for five years at Eastern Mennonite High School, I moved to Philadelphia. In Philadelphia, I remember saying to myself, "I am home." I could breathe again! Not because I could *get lost* in the big city, but because I was surrounded by diversity and folk who were different from me. I became involved in a voluntary service assignment where I taught Bible, health, and physical education, and coached the sports teams. After I completed my term, I taught two more years at the Philadelphia Association for Christian Schools.

I continued to be active in a local congregation, served as worship leader, preached, chaired Church Council, and taught young adult Sunday school. I continued this leadership when I began to attend Germantown Mennonite Church, the oldest Mennonite church in America. There I taught adult Sunday school, led worship, served at various times on Worship Committee, Education Committee, Church Council, and on the Vision team. Vision team is somewhat like elders/lay ministers who set vision for the congregation. During the term of an interim pastor, I moved more into a pastoral type role. Because the interim pastor did not have the foundation from which to address a difficult situation with a member, I handled the situation, thereby preventing further disruption within the congregation. I have led memorial services and officiated at commitment ceremonies.

In addition, I worked in a pastoral role while serving on the Philadelphia Mennonite Council (PMC), an organization that brought the leaders of fifteen Philadelphia-based congregations and social service agencies together. A pastor and supervisor at the time described my approach as "a pastor to the pastors." As part of leading PMC, I worshiped with the various Mennonite congregations in the Philadelphia area.

One evening during a revival meeting at one of these congregations, I met the evangelist who had preached the sermon over twenty-five years before when it was decided that I wasn't ready to accept Christ. The evangelist recognized me, and I smiled brightly as I replied to his inquiry about my relationship with God, "Yes, God is good and is working in my life." You see, I had just come out to myself and knew that God indeed did love me and that being a lesbian was not something that would separate me from God; I wasn't a sinner for being gay. Yes! God was at work in my life in a powerful way.

After serving as Coordinator of the Philadelphia Mennonite Council and being groomed for a position within the Mennonite Church, I interviewed with the Mennonite Board of Missions in Elkhart, Indiana, and was offered a position to coordinate the voluntary service programs. At this point, I had come out to myself and felt I could remain celibate; however, I could not enforce this on voluntary service workers, and I could not safely be out in that situation, so I declined.

I also served as a representative of the Brethren and Mennonite Council for Gay and Lesbian Concerns to the Joint Listening Committee on Homosexual Concerns for the Mennonite Church and the General Conference Mennonite Church. In that position, I often felt like a bridge builder between the Listening Committee and the Mennonite constituency. After two years of meeting and dialogue, the Listening Committee submitted a report to the Mennonite governing bodies that was supportive of gay and lesbian participation in the church. To my disappointment, the report was buried and never made available to the broader constituency of the Mennonite churches.

As you see, much of my life was dedicated to the church. It was who I was—my support system, my family, and my community. The natural outgrowth of my involvement in church and faith was that I felt a "call to ministry." I can't pinpoint an exact time when I felt this call; it was a growing awareness that I had pastoral gifts that I believed I was being prompted to use. However, this call ran into several roadblocks. Even though I was raised as a girl to be strong, I was also socialized in traditional Mennonite terms. When I went to college, I didn't know I could pursue religion as a major—I had two choices, nurse or teacher. Seminary certainly was not a possibility for a young woman. Secondly, by the time I realized I had a choice, I had already come out to myself as a lesbian; therefore, I took the wiser course and earned my Master of Social Work degree.

Even after receiving my M.S.W., my friends continued to encourage me to pursue becoming a pastor. With all of my experience, a sense of a call, and their encouragement, I pursued a formal position with a local congregation. However, I did not receive the final call from the congregation. Though folk within the congregation knew my skills, another person was called to be the minister. The fact that the one chosen had seminary training may have been the determining factor in their decision; however, after follow-up discussions with several committee members a number of years later, it was evident that the congregation was not ready to have a pastor who happened to be lesbian.

Since I was an active leader in the congregation and lead member of the Vision Team, I met on a regular basis to support, guide, and provide feedback to the newly developed Pastoral Team. It was painful to regularly interact with the person who got the job I had sought. I must admit, I grieved over the loss; however, I learned early on "to suck it up." With professional counseling and support, I remained a positive leader within the congregation. With this experience, cracks began to appear in what I once believed to be a body that nurtured, supported, and cared for me as I cared for them.

It was during this time that the congregation was in dialogue with the local Mennonite conference about the congregation's support of gay and lesbian members. I became more disillusioned as the dialogue continued. I felt as if the conference leadership process was not one of integrity, and I expressed my concern to those most directly in discussion with the conference leaders.

The result of the dialogue was that the congregation was no longer recognized as an active congregation within the Mennonite Church; however, ties remained to the General Conference Mennonite Church. The Sunday after we were removed from conference, I preached. I spoke about healing and vision for the congregation. I was interviewed by a local television news reporter who asked, "How does it feel?" I replied, "Ouch." What else was there to say?

I had said to myself after coming out, "I know God loves me, my faith is strong, nothing will shake my faith." **Wrong!** Soon after this, my significant relationship of twelve and one-half years ended. The congregation found it hard to be supportive. With so much pain and loss at the hands of the church I had loved, I began to withdraw from my participation in the Mennonite Church and organized religion. It took over three years for me to again walk into a Christian church.

I have continued a spiritual path which has taken me through a Woman's Wisdom course and an appreciation for earth-based religions and finally to the Presbyterian Church; there I have received healing. I have heard the gospel presented with a new voice, one of grace and security. Recently I led an adult education discussion on peacemaking. However, because of the structure of the Presbyterian Church, I do not have the opportunity to preach or lead worship. I wonder if I will ever use these gifts again in a church setting. I miss using my gifts of preaching, teaching, shepherding, and worship leading, but I don't miss the judgment or the emotional and spiritual violence I have experienced at the hands of the organized church.

I have considered the Metropolitan Community Church denomination, the United Church of Christ system, and checked out seminaries— Chicago Theological, Union Theological, and the local Baptist and Lutheran seminaries; however, without a church context to serve as a launching place, I have taken the prudent path and have not pursued a pastorate.

My energy now goes into helping an Elder Care population with mental illness as well as the clients I see for individual counseling. Often part of our interaction and focus is to try to integrate faith, belief, and life experiences. I am reminded that faith, belief, and the sacred are so much more vast than "prescribed" religion and are not limited to those who are called to be a minister in a church. I find I am a servant. It is often this perspective that people respond to, while others don't understand. Someone told me many years ago, "Ruth, you need to let this service thing behind." My response to that is "*No!*" Some folk assume that if one is a servant, one will be taken advantage of. This does not need to be true. I've learned as a therapist to set and maintain boundaries. However, I will do what needs to be done to help clients without enabling dependency. Although I am not a pastor of a formal congregation, I am a minister.

Then on those rare Sunday mornings I find flashes of vision for the Mennonite Church and I wonder . . .

[Jesus] poured water into a basin and began to wash the disciples' feet and to wipe them with the towel.

*   *   *

Postscript:

There probably is a lot more I could say; however, the process of writing this has not been easy. I wanted to be honest, not negative, but to write my faith story means revisiting difficult places of my life. Part of me struggles with the question, "Have I made do?" I am aware of family patterns and history in this. All I know is I don't need negativity in my life. I need to continue to believe in who I am. I respect myself, like myself, like who I have become, and will take care of myself. To that end I release this part of my story to you.

Ruth E. Wenger is a member of a Presbyterian church in the Philadelphia area, where she is ordained and the coordinator of the deacons. She has used her teaching background as a trainer and workshop leader presenting on topics such as: "Anger Management: Hostility Between Staff in a Long Term Care Facility"; "Dementia and the Use of Validation Therapy"; "Sensitivity Training for Staff: Reducing the Negative Impact of Stress on Clients"; "Stress Management for Staff Dealing in the Public Sector"; and "Dealing with the Resistant Client." In her free time, Ruth loves reading mysteries, is an advanced level square dancer, and takes on creative projects—the most recent of which is building a train for the Christmas holidays.

CHAPTER 10

Through a Glass, Darkly

Tom Arbaugh

Even now it remains a vivid memory. I see myself, a young college student, sitting in the office of the church pastor late one afternoon. I have finally found the courage to confess to someone these hidden feelings that the church has taught are so wrong. With trepidation, I say how I struggle with my yearnings for male companionship even though I do not actively pursue my feelings. The sunlight in the pastor's office is becoming dim as I tell him everything about how I am more attracted to males than to females. My story takes more than an hour to tell before I finally stop talking. He says to me, "Let us pray about this matter." After praying, he tells me I have been forgiven and instructs me that I must never do anything to jeopardize what he assures me is this moment of my redemption. He reminds me that I must continue to pray often.

We sit in silence. I am aware that light from the sun is fading even more. He turns on a small desk lamp. Strange and odd-shaped shadows form around the items on his desk. What should now be a moment of self-realization and self-illumination becomes instead a progression toward darkness. I see my sexuality as a demon in these strange shadows. With fear, I ask the pastor to cast out the demons that are doing this to me. At the end of this, his second prayer, there is no natural light left in the room. The small lamp keeps both our faces in the shadows. The absence of natural light leaves us seeing one another through the lamplight that barely suspends darkness.

I believe him when he assures me that the demons in my sexuality are gone. I am assured that I have been set free from the feelings of affection and attraction toward men. I determine that, should they come upon me unexpectedly, I will deny all such feelings. I will never act upon them and by prayer, meditation, and diligence, these feelings will surely fade and never bother me again. Suddenly, I see how the dimming light is an analogy for the fading away of sexual desires. The feelings of same-sex attraction will grow fainter and leave me just as the sunlight left during this time in the pastor's office. My sexual feelings toward men will cease.

Looking back to that day, I know the minister led me to believe that I was at the end of my struggle. I now know that day was but a point on my life map. That little lamp could not send enough light into my mind to keep the shadows out. No matter how I tried, the feelings remained deep within me. The feelings did not simply fade away. I found myself longing more and more for the attention and affection of another man.

Eventually, I would learn that isolation in church settings often accompanies and determines the emotional and spiritual development of many gay youth. The pain caused by the church began early for me. At first the pain had no connection to my gay sexuality. Why was I taught that so many people were excluded from the love of God? Exclusion was the realm of the day. My circle of church friends all knew that certain people were going to hell because they did not believe or worship as we did. It was a chore to remember what all was a sin, what was permissible but not recommended, and what could be done and still allow one to sneak into heaven.

I finally figured out that anything that brought a great deal of pleasure must also have some sin along with it. I was confident that chocolate carried the same potential, but since there were no sermons against chocolate, it was probably something fitting in that middle category—permissible but not recommended. While quite a great comfort, those black and white rules just did not allow a place for a young man who sometimes had a great affection for another man. For me there was no category that would allow internal peace and dissipate the fear of damnation. I sometimes wondered if the man in the pulpit could tell from that distance that I found boys more interesting than girls. I wondered how he could tell and how hard I would have to pray to stop these feelings of attraction.

Following that pastoral conference and for the remainder of my college years, I did my best not to act on my attractions for other young men. I downplayed all male friendships that approached a level of true communication and trust, fearing vulnerability to demons. I fled any comradeships that might cause a male friend to even suspect that I was attracted to him. I absolutely forbade myself to hug another man even when it was quite natural to do so.

Instead, I worked harder on my relationships with women. They enjoyed my company and I made sure I was a good date. I delighted in those times when my female friends and I could laugh and enjoy the moment without thought of long-term relationships. My girlfriends told me what a good boyfriend I was. I was sensitive and caring and never pushed them to do something inappropriate. I really thought I needed to make this girl thing work. It was not an option to be gay, for that was a "do not pass go" ticket straight to hell. I wouldn't let those thoughts stay in my mind.

After college, I continued to fight being gay. I tried to be the good Christian person that I thought God wanted me to be. My grandfather used to tell me of walking uphill in two feet of snow to get to and from school. While there is probably some element of truth in his stories, they could not be quite as bad as Granddad made them out to be. Being gay in a Christian world was all too similar to walking up hill in two feet of snow. It often felt like a cold and lonely world with no one to plow the way or make the path any easier for me.

I once met a deaf guy who said he was eleven years old before he realized he was actually deaf. The other hearing people around me looked at him totally bemused, but I understood what he was saying immediately. It took a long time for me to know I was gay. I knew I was different. I knew that I looked at men the way other men looked at women. Girls did not hold my deep interest.

In later years, my father told me that he had thought I was gay for many years. I wondered aloud why he didn't tell me about myself if it was so clear for him. He said he had indeed told me but I would have no part of hearing it. In my selective deafness, I do not recall any of those conversations. I remember clearly others who tried to tell me about myself, and I would not or could not hear the meaning of their words. I missed so much by my lack of hearing, my lack of wisdom, and my lack of understanding in the attempts that loving people made to ease some of the pain in my life. Consequently, to this day I am determined to make a conscious effort to remain open to painful insights.

I was nearly thirty years old before I fully accepted being a gay man. I became a teacher, and I made certain my mask remained firmly in place. Beneath the facade I was not happy with closing off this important part of myself. It seemed I had no options if I wanted to remain a teacher and a member of social and religious groups. It took the love of someone truly special and important to bring me to the place where I could no longer deny who I am. I remember the specific embrace when I knew everything changed for me. We were holding one another in a way quite similar to how I had held many of the women with whom I tried so hard to be a good date. This moment was different. I felt more complete than I had ever felt before. The feeling was one of being at home in another person's arms, the arms of a man who loved me as I loved him. He declared his love and commitment to me in a way no other male friend had ever done. I knew his words were coming from his heart and our spirits were blending. His words of love were quite simple. Silence spoke loudest. Warmth ran throughout my body in a manner that had never been there with someone of the opposite sex. There was no setting aside the depth of completeness that I felt with this love from another man. I knew a truth that I could no longer refute.

The light from this moment was so strong that I began to weep. I knew I had found a wholeness that brought together the mental, emotional, and spiritual elements in my life. Reciprocated love entered me, piercing through the darkness that I always felt overshadowing me. The dark side no longer needed to be hidden. Darkness was overcome with light. This was the light of self-knowledge and self-assurance that told me I was a complete man.

Teaching and coaching in high schools led me to recognize the value of working with students on an individual basis. It was a joy to see them grow academically, but even more fulfilling for me to watch their personal and emotional growth. After I finished my master's degree in counseling, I began to work as a school counselor. Students' needs were always present, and the days were always too short to meet those needs. I was working on my own issues around being a gay man, and my personal growth kept my counseling alive. I was able to empathize with clients and students as they progressed.

That same wonderful human being who opened up to me a new world of loving myself as a gay man through loving me so freely also sent me quietly on my way. He recognized my talents as a counselor, as a teacher, and as a helper. His confidence in those same talents encouraged me to continue my education and develop the gift of loving and accepting all people. He helped me to recognize this gift in myself. He assured me that I needed to pursue my talents and dreams in teaching and counseling. This man who had taught me so much about love, about myself, and about my abilities as a counselor now gently encouraged me to move on with my life and to finish my doctorate in counseling.

My teaching career at the graduate level led me to a university in Georgia. On a weekend men's retreat, I met a gay couple. One of them was a tall lanky mature gentleman from a strict fundamentalist religious background. His friendly and vibrant partner was a pastor in a church whose ministry was primarily to gay and lesbian Christians. I was intrigued.

The year was 1994, and they invited me to a conference in Atlanta. Little did I know how the Spirit would move me and begin the process of solidifying my faith and reformatting my Christian journey. I sat in an auditorium with a thousand gay Christians, singing from their hearts with voices fully extended, worshiping freely and openly. All the while, they were next to the person of the same sex whom they loved and with whom they could freely express affection, with whom they could share a deep spirituality that was not negated by their sexual orientation.

I was drawn into the singing of the first hymn with a determined focus on notes, rhythms, harmonies—even volume. The next hymn started reaching deep inside me. I was feeling an affirmation that was not dissimilar to the embrace that connected me to my first unifying love with a man. So clear and strong was the connection with this music that hundreds of people were leaving their individual places of hurt and disillusionment and moving with purpose toward God. They no longer felt that God held them in derision or deemed them unworthy to be Christians.

As I sang that second hymn, perfect love began to dissolve fear. I sensed the infusion of a love that included being true to an affection that had long been a part of me. The internal hatred previously required to keep from loving another man was replaced by a love that was greater than the instilled self-hatred and loathing. I cried softly and freely as the fear slowly melted away.

The two kind men with me wrapped their arms and spirits around me to support what they had seen many times. As a long-standing couple, part of their ministry was to walk this path of renewal with young men like myself. The tears rolled quietly off my cheeks and flooded my face as my soul was cleansed of ingrained dogma. I was being washed by the experience of sharing Christian love with hundreds of others together on a journey to spiritual wholeness.

My thoughts, my desires, and my Christianity would no longer be separate elements. I was whole. I would no longer be a man of many pieces—a Christian in one respect, a gay man in another, a counselor in this respect, a teacher in that one. I could love another man and be a whole person. I knew that I did not need to fear God's wrath because of this one part of who I am. Christianity became more than the fear and selected shunning stories designed to keep followers on a prescribed path. That moment brought me closer to understanding wholeness in a completely new light, devoid of demon shadows. From that moment, truth and wholeness in its purest form would direct my life's path.

My mother and my siblings did not comprehend how I could decipher Christianity from this new perspective. It will take years for them to accept the idea of having a Christian gay son and brother. For many years, I thought being true to my orientation would mean that I could not be true to God and to my family. Not being accepted by the family and the church looked for a while like a mountain I could not transverse.

When I decided that indeed I could and would live successfully without their approval, without their understanding, and even without their love, I found a new sense of power and freedom in my life. It was not a trading of sexuality for God and family; it was knowing and being my whole self. It was being who I truly am as a person and accepting myself over and over. As I progressed in my own acceptance, I accepted without hurt or judgment the responses to me that ranged from rejection or vilification to the welcoming that came from gay brothers, sisters, older stewards in the church, and pastors who were loving and supportive of me.

Coming to Eastern Mennonite University (EMU) was another step in accepting who God made me to be. This was a place where I could minister to people with the spirit of Christianity as I taught students the skills of counseling. This was a place where I could be a Christian who worships God and enjoys teaching others. That this was the place for me was confirmed when a student came to me for counseling and shared his angst in struggling with his sexual identify. He said, "I cannot believe that the God of love hates me for who I am." As I progress along this journey of learning how God can love without condemnation, I learn and relearn these lessons. I need to learn again how to love myself when others act in a way toward me that feels so unloving.

When I chose to work at EMU, I was asked to sign a community lifestyle commitment statement (CLC) that included a promise that I would not engage in sex outside of marriage. Even though I am committed to my partner, we are not able to be married and thus my interpretation of this statement meant that I was agreeing to live in my relationship as a celibate man. Restricting love because it is with someone of the same sex made no sense to me. Still it was the rule and I agreed to it. The CLC did not have a restriction on living with another man, only sex outside of marriage. However, I was eventually told that living in a house with another man was the problem. Two gay men living together, even with a commitment to one another and a commitment to celibacy was not an appropriate fit for a Mennonite university.

Over time, I have come to grips with myself, come to terms with my Christianity, and have developed my skills as a counselor and as a teacher. Teaching and counseling allow me to embrace Christianity to the fullest and to help others in their work as Christians in training for counseling. The hard work and emotional endeavor to get to this place was what I thought merited my work in this educational environment. My own growth empowered me to help those I taught to increase their capacity to help others. I thought that my agreement to the CLC rule would be enough to satisfy the requirement to teach at a Mennonite university. However, the administration of EMU asked me to resign from teaching in the graduate counseling program. It seems there was a problem with my loving and sharing a celibate life with someone of my own sex and, in their opinion, I no longer fit within that body of Christ.

Life's lessons around truth and personal growth are not going to stop. I do not want them to stop. I can and I will continue to pay the price for truth as long as there are people in the world who need to hear the truth that two people can love each other. These two do not have to be of opposite genders to love and to serve God. They do not have to sacrifice who they are to be whole. In fact, I cannot be whole while try-ing to sacrifice a part of who I am. I continue to learn lessons of truth and ministry and personal growth. Many of the lessons are painful. My most recent lesson will not be—must not be—the last.

When a male friend touched my hand, it was so much more than when my girlfriend did the same. Never did that change. No praying changed it. No fasting changed it. No pastor changed it. I could not and should not change who I am to mirror what is acceptable to mainstream society with all its components. Finally, I learned that God does not want to change it as I walk humbly before Him and acknowledge Him as my Lord and Savior.

For now we see through a glass, darkly;
but then face to face:
now I know in part;
but then shall I know even as also I am known.
First Corinthians 13:12 (KJV)

Tom Arbaugh, Ph.D., was a teacher, coach, and school counselor in Ohio before moving to Georgia to establish himself as a counseling professor at the university level. His counseling practice has included work with physical, sexual, and substance abuse clients. He has published and presented on a variety of topics around sexuality, counseling supervision, and school counseling. He has traveled to twenty-five different countries and enjoys various cultures and peoples. Presently, Tom is learning sign language and is starting a private counseling practice in his home area of Virginia. He and his partner continue to work toward a stronger personal and spiritual relationship.

CHAPTER 11

Finding Hope

Julia Zacharias

Hope is in part a discipline, I think, and in part a gift. This story is about finding hope.

I knew, coming back to Winnipeg after a semester of doctoral studies, that I wanted to connect to a church. Hope Mennonite had been my church home, although I hadn't participated there for a very long time. I had moved around to pursue my academic education. Still, I knew it had been a good fit when I left for school, and I was hoping that it could be a place for me again. I felt tentative about the connection though. I was feeling a lot of fear of Mennonite church structures, so I wasn't sure I could trust Hope.

I had entered a doctoral studies program in Old Testament at Princeton Theological Seminary in September but left by Christmas for a number of reasons. The easiest way to describe the conglomerate of those reasons is to say that there was personal work I wanted to do, and I wanted to do it without the pressures of academic study hanging over my head. But there are many ways to describe a given. The easiest way to describe something, while often useful for a specific purpose, is sometimes a way of saying something without revealing other relevant pieces of information. Of course, we are sometimes intentional about this; other times, we are conveniently unaware of the biases in the construction of our communication.

As I re-entered life in Winnipeg, after starting and then abruptly ending my doctoral work, there were times when I purposely chose to tell my story using a simple description to explain why I was doing what I was doing. Because people wanted to know why, for God's sake, why when I thought this was what you wanted, why when we were so proud of you, why when you have the potential, why when you've worked so many years toward this? What happened? Why did you leave the doctoral studies program?

Naturally, there are people who are mere acquaintances, to whom it would have been information overload to disclose all the ins and outs of my reasons for coming back to Winnipeg and taking a leave from my study program. In that case, it was a workable answer to say that there were some things going on with my family and myself that I wanted to deal with here. Initially, I even used that answer with those who knew me well. My parents, for example, felt that I hadn't said enough to them to explain my leaving, so when they asked, I repeated something fairly generic and easy—and unsatisfactory from their response. However, at first I wasn't able to say more. It took me another month or so to go visit them and tell them that I was coming out, and that if I looked for a relationship at all, it would be with a woman.

The fact is—I wanted to spend my life partnering with a woman.

This is a fact that makes me suddenly fresh. This fact Sweet Honeys through me with rhythm, color, and vigor. Because I know it, I can dance and sing justice and love my life and my people. It makes me stronger and stranger and hooked on laughter and what is good. This fact makes me who I am.

But here is another fact: I would like to spend my life being active in the Mennonite Church. This fact, too, brings me life and inspiration; it allows me to breathe the divine and to live it in this world. And, just as clearly, this fact makes me who I am. I spent the first ten years of my adult life preparing for and placing myself squarely in the center of Mennonite church structures. I was going to be a teacher of the Bible. Need I say more?

Nevertheless, these two facts together produced the most difficult tension I had ever faced. By coming out and openly being who I really am, I was placing myself, in terms of the Mennonite institutions I knew, into the category of "unhirable"—not fit for human consumption, so to speak. While I live with these two facts, I also live with some chafing and pain. It is pain that sometimes takes the shape of the loneliness of not quite belonging and sometimes the shape of disgust for institutions and sometimes the shape of sorrow for the bright academic who got shunted to the side in all of this. It's pain that takes new shape in different circumstances, and sometimes it includes fear and despair.

So to my reasons for leaving school, I could add fear and despair and the chafing of the boundaries of social structures against my sense of who I am. The strain sometimes overwhelmed me and made me feel very tired and small and undesirable. I do not claim that I was unique among doctoral students in experiencing some feelings of inadequacy and fear, but I do claim that specific to my situation was this tension that I had suddenly been deemed freakish by the very ones who had the power to hire or fire me.

However, although I took the leave from school because I could not function well there, I was not on a journey toward hopelessness. Sometime in those next months, I found a book of poetry in the library in which I came across Frances Densmore's transcription of a Native American "Song of the Thunders." I posted the lines in an obvious spot for myself as a reminder that I might be "pitying myself while I am carried by the wind." I was already conscious that I had seen evidence of the "wind," because I knew that I was most certainly being carried along by the things that give me life.

One thing that gives me life is my connection to the church. It still makes me smile that Hope Mennonite Church has the name it does. I smiled at that the whole year after leaving Princeton, thinking to myself how that was what I was after—hope. It was certainly true. I made it my business to seek out what gave me hope.

Okay, I admit it. What I was also after was fun. Laughter, which did not come easily during the first few months, gradually became one key criterion in determining what I would or would not undertake during that year. And it worked. I was carried by the laughter, and I was indeed moved toward hope.

So I went to Sunday morning worship within a week or two of arriving in Winnipeg and sought out Dori, the pastor of Hope. I wanted to meet with her to ask who I might talk to about the strain and pain I was feeling around leaving Princeton. That meeting itself is still memorable to me, because I was new at coming out to people, and because I was very afraid to talk about sexual orientation—mine, that is—with anyone who belonged to "church." Like many people in our culture, I find sexuality a much safer subject to talk about when it is about generalities rather than about me personally.

It may seem a little corny, but what I remember most vividly from that meeting was when Dori said to me, as she was leaving, "I believe in hugs." Then she reached over to give me one before walking down my front steps. I was surprised, maybe even a little bit shocked, that this Mennonite pastor was offering human touch to me, the untouchable, the perverse one by church standards. I had expected a polite closure to this meeting but not a warm, human gesture. It was a small moment of salvation. Something inside me rearranged itself to a better position, and I began to think that sometime I was going to be fine.

At that meeting, Dori encouraged me to proceed on the assumption that there was a place for me at Hope. And so I did. I intended to participate in Hope's church life and set a date to transfer my church membership there. It felt like a big deal to me to find a church home; when I found out that each person who was joining Hope on that Sunday morning was invited to say something to the congregation, I thought about it carefully. Eventually I asked if the poem, "Ode to My Socks," by Pablo Neruda could be read. The poem is simple and exuberant, a chortling and effusive praise song to a pair of hand-knit socks.

After "Ode to My Socks" was read, I shared my reflections that the socks in this poem have such a tangible effect on the one who receives them, that they seem alive, and that the reaction they invoke is so profuse as to be slightly comical (these *are* just socks, you know) but oddly beautiful. And all of that—the comedy and the odd beauty— reminded me of my own anticipation of joining Hope Mennonite Church. Then I read a list of odes that could have been written to the socks in Neruda's ode—and were my odd and profuse response to the people at Hope as I joined their congregation:

Ode to the things that fit
Ode to the things that keep us warm
Ode to the things that delight
Ode to the things that allow us to continue our everyday work
Ode to the things that make our eyes widen
Ode to the things that call us to check ourselves
Ode to the things that don't let us hoard them or hide them away
Ode to the things we treat with care
Ode to the things that lend softness to the touch.

Joining Hope was an important marker for me, because all along, my journey was not a crisis of faith but a crisis of social structures. The events that surrounded my recognizing my own desire to love and partner with a woman were not for me a reworking of my essential commitment to the God who loves the world and desires its well-being. I was not, because of these events, suddenly unsure of my relationship to the Christian faith. I was, as ever, a lively and active thinker and dreamer and remained on the side of thinking and dreaming and acting in the direction of the good.

At the same time, my faith had thus far been expressed by being active within Mennonite church structures, and I had been placing myself rather centrally within those bounds, so it was most certainly a crisis of belonging and a crisis of location. I was, without having tried to get there, on the edge of things. I was, without having tried to distance myself, no longer worth consideration within broader Mennonite church circles.

In addition, because of the way these pieces of life intersect, it was a crisis of self. Who will I be in order to make this all work? Maybe I could just forget about marriage and intimacy and be a good single Mennonite girl. I would be hirable. On the other hand, maybe I ought to forget about the Mennonite thing and try another denomination or just blink at Mennonite church institutions for a good long while, hoping that the problem will go away. Maybe then I could build a relationship, unencumbered by all my church pain.

As I consider and test these options, I have been finding that I need to give attention to all the pieces that make up my whole. They are what make me tick. Remaining single would make me no less a lesbian, and blinking my eyes at the church would make me no less interested in expressing my faith together with a community of Mennonite believers. To try to abandon what I love on either of these counts has proven unworkable, so I have determined not to go that way.

There is no way that I can say I have entirely smoothed over the stress that I feel from the pull of this tension, but I am resolved— mostly even happily resolved—that both the church and my partnership with a woman will continue to be shaping factors for my life. As for the specifics of my "shaping factors," I feel blessed to name Katharine Wiebe, my partner, and Hope Mennonite Church among them, not to mention a host of good friends and family who choose to stand by me in the middle of diverging pulls.

I met Katharine in 2001, shortly after I became a member at Hope. As I have slowly grown in the trust needed to participate as I wish and as I am able in the life of Hope Mennonite Church, Katharine has joined me there, and the community has become an important part of our lives. I feel that we contribute ourselves and our relationship to each other as a gift to the community, and in return, they celebrate with us and offer themselves to us as friends and fellow justice-seekers.

By the time this story is published, Katharine and I will have celebrated our joy in our relationship and our commitment to each other with a group of family and friends. Since marriage is to me most importantly a celebration of the church, but our relationship is not blessed by the institutional Mennonite church, we are choosing not to be "married" but to gather around us those who will celebrate the joy of creating circles of faithful love for each other as communities and as spouses within our communities.

In the meantime, I choose to live in hope. I choose to live in such a way that there will be a time in the future when a young woman of thoughtful bent and lively faith, who is planning a ceremony to mark how blessed she is by her relationship with her female partner, will not have to ask herself whether she is "in" or "out" when it comes to being Mennonite, that she will not ever have to consider whether she is hirable on the basis of her sexual orientation, and that she will freely teach and live the gospel as she chooses, even in the context of church.

Julia Zacharias studied at a goodly number of Mennonite schools, eventually beginning a doctorate in Hebrew Bible, with the intention of being involved in Mennonite education. For a variety of reasons, including the improbability of being employed by a Mennonite institution while being truthful about her sexual identity, she discontinued her formal studies.

Julia is a baker, a writer and copy editor, a factory laborer, an ESL (English as a Second Language) teacher, a singer, a lover of dogs, and drives a fantastic glider bike with chrome trim and a double kickstand. She lives in Winnipeg, Manitoba, with her partner Katharine Wiebe and their plants.

CHAPTER 12

Okay to be Gay—God Made Me This Way

Bob Life

Growing up on a small farm in Virginia, I always knew that I was different from my friends. I probably didn't comprehend all the ways I was different until I reached adolescence and discovered the word homosexual in the dictionary. I immediately knew that word described me, for I had never felt any physical attraction for the opposite sex. I did believe, however, that it was something that I would outgrow, or could change, especially as I grew spiritually and became a stronger Christian.

As I entered adolescence and began thinking about my future, it seemed a logical choice for me to enter the ministry. I had cousins and uncles who were pastors, many in the Church of the Brethren, the denomination I grew up in. My parents never tried to influence me one way or another, but I knew in the back of my mind that they would be pleased if I pursued a career in pastoral ministry.

When I was twelve, one of my older cousins, who was a well-known COB pastor, was the guest preacher for revival services at our church. He was actually closer in age to my parents than to me, but I had always admired him as a person and as a preacher. He arrived that weekend driving a red convertible, which created quite a stir with some of the older folks who thought that was too sporty and flashy for a preacher. But he had the gift for story-telling, and as he preached that weekend, I felt an affirmation and a calling to be a preacher like him. He was not a "hell-fire and brimstone" type of preacher like many in the church, and he appeared to me to be a "free spirit" who followed his own heart and what God wanted him to do and say.

As I entered my teenage years and began wrestling more with my sexual urges, I became depressed at times and unsure of my faith. During my senior year in high school, I became actively involved in the Youth for Christ ministry. Through this organization, my faith and commitment to Christ grew, and I experienced more inner peace about my life. The stirrings and call for ministry began to increase also, especially for youth ministry. By the time I graduated from college with a degree in sociology, my home congregation affirmed my call to ministry and licensed me. My first job after graduation was a year of intern training with Youth for Christ to be a full-time youth worker.

After that year of training, I discovered that job openings for full-time positions with Youth for Christ were scarce. Therefore, I pursued secular employment for a couple of years as I wrestled with my sexuality and my calling of what God wanted me to do. During this time, a close friend from college, who was attending our denominational seminary, wrote me enthusiastic letters about his life as a seminary student. He was looking for a roommate to share an apartment with him on campus and told me that we could have great fun as roommates. I thought that some theological training and education could help me sort out my sexual orientation and perhaps even help me to overcome my attraction for other men. I still wanted to believe that I could have victory over my homosexual urges if I grew spiritually strong enough. And if not, perhaps I could be a celibate pastor.

Thus I entered seminary, determined to find some answers for my life. While out of town one weekend for a family wedding, I met a married man with whom I had a lot in common. I had planned to spend the weekend with a college friend, but he was called out of town at the last minute. When my new married friend heard this, he invited me to stay at his home since his wife and children were out of town visiting his in-laws. I had no idea that he was bisexual, but that night I had my first sexual experience with a man. After that night, I knew that I could not be a celibate pastor. God had created me to be a sexual being, and I felt alive and whole for the first time in my life.

I continued to wrestle through seminary with my calling and whether I could be a pastor and be gay. I knew that if I could not change my sexual orientation, I would have to be a closeted pastor, and that seemed like a risky game to play. I sought help and guidance from two different pastoral counselors at the seminary. Neither was very helpful, and one insisted that he felt I was not gay at all. I knew in my heart that I was and could not even fathom the thought of ever being married to a woman.

As my last year of seminary began drawing to a close, I knew I had to make some serious decisions about my future. I had not been able to change my sexual orientation through prayer or counseling, nor did I know if that was truly possible. I had spent four years (including an intern year at a local congregation) and several thousand dollars training to be a pastor. I decided that I needed to try pastoring as a closeted gay person to see if I could make it work, even if only for a short while.

As I began interviewing with different Church of the Brethren congregations, it became clear to me that I would not be comfortable pastoring a rural church. Many of those churches seemed concerned with finding me a wife, and most had very few single folks in their congregation like myself, except for elderly widows and a few young adults. One day I received a profile from a small city church in Ohio that was looking for a pastor. Almost half of this congregation of fifty people were single. Their current pastor was serving part-time while working in another full-time job, but the congregation felt they were ready for a full-time pastor to help the congregation grow. After meeting with the pastoral search committee, we mutually agreed that it was the "right fit." They extended the call to me to be their full-time pastor, and I had no hesitancy in believing it was God's will for me.

The last thing that I wanted anyone to know as I began my first pastorate was that I was gay. I reasoned that I could remain closeted for a good while, especially if I was not sexually active. When others asked if I was involved in a relationship, I replied that I was married to the church and that this was my passion and commitment for now.

God, however, has a wonderful sense of humor. He had other things in mind for me, and he wanted me to know that this was where I was supposed to be. Soon after I began my pastoral duties, I arranged to meet with the former pastor, who still had some keys to the parsonage and garage. I met him before when I came for my interview and had learned at that time that he was divorced. As we were seated at my kitchen table in the parsonage one afternoon, I had the strongest sense that he also might be gay. I was curious and wanted to ask him, but did not want him to know that I was gay, especially if I was wrong in my assumption. Finally, I decided to broach the subject. "There's something I want to ask you, but I don't quite know how," I stated. He studied my face and then replied simply, "I am. Are you?" "Yes!" was my quick and surprised response. No other words were needed. It was an affirmation to me that I was in the right place, doing the right thing that God wanted me to do. If this man had been able to function as a closeted gay pastor, perhaps I could too.

Soon afterwards, the former pastor began introducing me to other gay professionals in town, and a couple of those men started attending the church. I also learned that there was a "gay church" in a neighboring town about thirty miles from where I lived. One of the gay men in my congregation and I began attending their Sunday evening services. That congregation was led by two ordained lesbian pastors, and most of the members were gay, lesbian, bisexual, or transgender. It was an awesome experience to be able to worship God as a gay man surrounded by others who were like me. That church believed and taught that God loves us all unconditionally and that God created us as GLBT persons. I no longer thought of myself as a sinner, especially after studying the passages of Scripture in the Bible that talked about homosexuality. I began to fall in love with God again and with myself, as I realized that I could be gay and Christian.

My ministry was going well at the Church of the Brethren congregation, but inside of me a civil war was raging. I knew that my denomination would send me packing if they found out that I was gay. I knew where the church stood on pastors who were gay, and I had no intention of trying to challenge them on the matter. At times, I felt like I was playing Russian roulette by attending a "gay" church on Sunday evenings and socializing with my gay friends, especially the ones attending our church. A few members of my congregation suspected that one of these men might be gay and questioned my social activities with him. Consequently, after two and a half years of pastoring, I decided it was time to leave the pastoral ministry before my sexual orientation was discovered and I was asked to resign. At the same time, I was confused and disheartened about my calling to the ministry and what I should do next.

I moved back to Pennsylvania to the area where I had done a year of pastoral intern training before my last year of seminary. Since our denominational district executive there knew me, he was anxious to place me in another church, but I declined offers to look at profiles of congregations looking for a pastor. However, I found it difficult to find full-time employment.

Eventually I accepted an offer for a part-time interim position at a small church about thirty miles from where I was living. Since it was part-time, I did not have to move to that community which meant I could be a pastor four days a week, but still have a social life as a gay man without being discovered by my congregation. In addition, I learned that there was a Universal Fellowship of Metropolitan Community Churches congregation (UFMCC) near to where I was living. It was similar to the "gay" congregation I had attended in Ohio, so I had a home church to attend on Sunday evenings once again.

After that interim position ended, I took another brief job as an interim pastor, but then I realized that I needed to find a full-time position of some sort in order to survive. I wanted to be more "out" as a gay man, which is hard to do while pastoring in the COB. Friends in UFMCC encouraged me to transfer my credentials to that denomination, but that was a lengthy process, and I didn't feel called at that time to pastor a predominately gay church. In addition, I had discovered the Brethren/Mennonite Council for Lesbian, Gay, Bisexual, and Transgender Interests (BMC). I became involved in some of their local activities and eventually served as a board member for a few years. I felt fortunate to have many exemplary gay Christian friends in my life to continue to enforce the belief that it was okay to be gay and that God made me this way.

The next fifteen years of my life I describe as my wilderness period. I drifted from various secular jobs trying to "find myself" and discover what God wanted me to do with my life. There did not seem to be any place for me at the "table" where God could use me as a gay pastor, unless I pastored in UFMCC. I reached the point of convincing myself that I did not have a calling to pastoral ministry and that God could use my gifts and talents in the secular world just as easily as in the church. I found a Church of the Brethren congregation in the area where I knew the pastor was accepting of gay people, so I started attending and became involved in that church on Sunday mornings, while still attending the UFMCC church on Sunday evenings.

As the years passed, I became increasingly restless and unhappy with my life. I felt that God had something else for me to do, but I did not know what that was or how to discover it. At the same time, the AIDS epidemic was spreading rapidly, and I was watching many close friends and acquaintances die a horrible death. Many of these young men had no one to talk with about their spiritual concerns and needs as they neared the time of death. I longed for some kind of a full-time ministry to persons with AIDS, but I didn't know how to make that happen.

About that time, a job change took me to Harrisburg, Pennsylvania, and fortunately, to another UFMCC congregation. It was no accident that one of my friends from our COB seminary was now pastoring that UFMCC congregation. I became actively involved in this church and once again felt this was where God wanted me to be. One day when talking to my pastor about my dream for ministry with persons with AIDS, she suggested that perhaps I should consider taking a Clinical Pastoral Education (CPE) class. I dismissed that as a possibility for a couple of reasons. I knew the training for CPE was usually in a hospital setting. I have never liked hospitals and have a "weak stomach" when it comes to bodily fluids. I also could not imagine how I could do the CPE training without quitting my job, since it involved some daytime classes. How would I live without an income? Working part-time hours at my current job was not a possibility.

One day a friend who was attending a local seminary told me about the CPE class he was taking. He mentioned that he had found the health care field very accepting of gay clergy. There were in fact a lot of GLBT individuals working in the health care field everywhere. He also told me about a year-long residency program that a local hospital provided for CPE training. The chaplains in that program received a stipend during their training. It wasn't a lot of money, but enough to live on it for a year.

Part of the CPE training included working with terminally ill patients, which had now become my passion. Suddenly I felt I knew where God was calling me. God still wanted me in ministry but not pastoring a church. I would be qualified to do some type of chaplaincy work full-time after taking a year of training. Now my only concern was whether I could handle being in a hospital environment for the training. I knew I had to try.

By this time I was in my mid-forties. I had to figure out soon what God was calling me to do, and I really wanted to be "out" in whatever I did. Finances had always been tight with my secular jobs as most of them did not pay well, and it was hard making ends meet as a single person. Frequently I wrestled with depression and feeling like a failure. If I did not take this leap of faith now, I knew that I probably never would and might regret it the rest of my life. I also knew that if this was God's will, the right doors would open for me.

I applied for the CPE residency and was accepted. For much of the year, I worked on the oncology floor of the hospital with patients who were terminally ill. I felt comfortable with them and continued to feel a calling for some kind of ministry to the terminally ill.

My license with the COB had been inactive for years. I learned that I needed to be ordained with some major denomination in order to do full-time chaplaincy work. It was now clearer than ever that the COB was not accepting of gay clergy, and I was too far out of the closet to go back in to continue my ordination in the COB. I needed to transfer my credentials to another denomination.

There have been so many times throughout my life when God brought people into my life at just the right time. As I was struggling with ordination issues for chaplaincy, my pastor encouraged me to transfer my ministry credentials to UFMCC. I was now willing to do that, but up until that time, UFMCC was only approving ordination for pastoral ministry in a congregation. As it turned out, the chair of the Board of Ordained Ministry that needed to approve my application had done chaplaincy work himself years ago and was a strong advocate for this type of ministry. As chair of the board, he persuaded the other board members to approve my application for chaplaincy ministry after I had completed the additional training that was required by UFMCC. It was not by accident that everything was starting to fall into place. God was working out the details at just the right time. God still had great plans for my life after all!

For the past four years, I have been working full-time as a hospice chaplain and love my job. I feel affirmation each day that this is where God wants me for the time being. I also believe with all my heart that God made me gay, and because of my own emotional pain through the years in struggling with my sexuality and faith issues, I am a better chaplain and have more empathy for the pain of others. I know what it's like to be a "wounded healer" as Henri Nouwen describes the pastoral role. Because I am gay and have been wounded, God can use me to help others who are wounded physically and emotionally.

I have not attended the Church of the Brethren for a number of years now, and I have no desire to be a pastor in that denomination, knowing how they feel about GLBT clergy. I chose to quietly leave the church and not renew my ministerial license rather than to challenge the church on their beliefs and practices about sexual orientation and ordination. I did not leave the church with anger and bitterness. I always knew where the church stood about gay clergy and did not believe that they would change their thinking or policies anytime soon so that I could be an openly gay clergy in the COB and be welcome at Christ's table.

At times I feel a great loss in not being able to pastor in the church and denomination I grew up in. I still strongly adhere to many of their beliefs and practices, and I miss some of their special worship services like the Love Feast and especially the a cappella singing of some of the great hymns of faith. But I believe the church is the greatest loser when they deny talented GLBT people the right to serve in the church as clergy. Perhaps what the church needs now to battle its rapid decline in membership is our gift of healing and our belief that all people who desire to be part of the church should be welcome.

Coming out is a process and a journey for each of us as GLBT individuals. The same is true for our families when they learn of our sexual orientation. As with many families, my family members are at different levels of acceptance of my orientation. My two sisters (my only siblings) have assured me that they are okay with my being gay, and they continue to love me just as I am. Other family members may question why I am publicly sharing my story and not choosing to remain anonymous in this book.

I believe that it is important that other GLBT clergy, either current or future, know that many others have walked the road before them or are walking it now. Names give validity and power to our stories and to the truth. I was always taught to be honest and truthful in all that I do. To continue to be in the closet and nameless is to continue to live a lie. There are times in life when we need to follow our hearts and respond with truth and integrity, even if that truth is hard for others to hear.

One of my favorite hymns is "Blessed Assurance, Jesus is Mine". The refrain states, "This is my story, this is my song, praising my Savior all the day long." For those of you who have been kind enough to listen to my sacred story, I will close by adapting the refrain to my own experience.

> This is my story, this is my song;
> Some may dispute it, and feel that it's wrong.
> Still it's MY story, God made me gay;
> And Jesus walks with me each step of the way.

Bob Life, M.Div., was born in Harrisonburg, Virginia, but has lived in Pennsylvania since 1983. For the past four years, he has lived and worked in Reading, Pennsylvania, as a hospice chaplain. In addition to working with patients who are terminally ill, Bob also leads and facilitates bereavement support groups each spring and fall.

His hobbies include exploring antique and flea markets and collecting clocks and artwork of all kinds. He also enjoys dining in or out with friends. Bob is still looking for "Mr. Right" but would settle for "Mr. Not-Too-Dysfunctional."

CHAPTER 13

The Pain and the Joy of Change

John K. Stoner

I did not grow up with progressive views on "homosexuality" any more than I grew up with a vision of universal reconciliation. What follows is an intellectual and spiritual account of how and why my mind changed.

First, a definition: At the start of this story about my journey to accepting sexual minorities and their right to be and express who they are, I will make a comment on language. In this essay I will put the word "homosexuality" in quotation marks when I use it, because it is a word whose meaning in print and public discourse must always be questioned. Using that word as it stands with no signal that it denotes something highly indefinite and culturally pejorative is in a class with using the word "nigger" with no warning signals around it.

Our cultural situation is rife with instances of bearing false witness by the misuse of language. For example, people often say, "The Bible condemns homosexuality," without saying whether they or the Bible mean "homosexual" orientation or "homosexual" behavior. Even people who are reasonably sensitive and precise when pushed on the issue are frightfully careless about this fundamental distinction. Or one often hears, "Homosexuals are different from other minorities because they choose their minority status," a statement fairly dripping with prejudice and unexamined assumptions, projecting as already answered the whole question which has not yet been seriously asked.

If I am in any way a prophetic type, I am a reluctant one. And the views which I hold at the age of sixty-one are different from those I held at twenty or forty, more because I accepted the pain of change than because I didn't like who I was before I changed.

For most of my life, "homosexuality" was like patriarchy, something that I did not understand. I remember experiences in my late forties when the word patriarchy was used in meetings and conversations, and I really did not know what it meant historically or linguistically. The same was true with "homosexuality."

Growing up in a traditional Brethren in Christ home, my church and family experience conditioned me to believe that the Bible and good Christians viewed "homosexuality" as sin and "homosexuals" as sinners in a class of their own. American culture and German heritage did nothing to contradict the church's exclusion of "homosexual" persons as outside the pale of God's saved and blessed ones.

As a college and seminary graduate with Bible majors, I was seriously engaged in the church's teaching. I was conscientious about knowing and doing the will of God and, of course, taking sin seriously. As a pastor and parent, I was involved in the lives of others, dedicated to understanding and helping people and not just seeking personal adjustment and self-fulfillment. Into this life came voices and possibilities for change.

Working for global peace, racial justice, and women's concerns with the U.S. Peace Section of the Mennonite Central Committee (MCC), I met interesting people. One of them was a peace activist who had made international news with his opposition to the Vietnam War. In a conversation with him, he asked me about MCC's and/or my views on "homosexuality" and "homosexuals." As I recall at the time, I had the impression or information that he was a gay man. I replied something to the effect that I viewed "homosexuality" as a sin, no worse and no better than other sins like killing and war. He expressed surprise that I put same-gender affection in the same category as same-gender homicide. He was obviously appalled, yet his comments were restrained, though without any doubt, deeply felt. That made me think and reflect—at that moment, and for a long time afterward.

This experience moved me toward paying more attention, and seeking to learn by doing some reading. (A response no doubt grounded in my bias toward education, which is rooted in the assumption that there are things still to be learned and that we grow and learn more by effort than by no effort.) One of the books that I read was written by a woman who experienced strong same-gender attractions in her life and who acted on those biological and psychological urges by expressing love for women.

All the while, my biblical and theological reading, studies, and conversations increased my sense that God's saving purposes in history are all-inclusive. I observed in Hebrew and Greek Scriptures a process of God's "chosen people" struggling with and often against the insistent vision of including all of humanity, not just favored parts, and the whole creation in salvation. The building of walls and boundaries to separate the clean from the unclean and the pure from the impure obsessed some parties in Israel's religious establishment and appeared to fail miserably.

I was beginning to see the biblical record and Christian history as a virtually unbroken record of drawing boundaries to exclude some minority, some designated "other" group, only to discover or be forced to conclude that no, they too are included in God's saving purpose. Hittites, women, Babylonians, Greeks, Gentiles, lepers, uncircumcised, and the like—each was in their turn excluded.

The number of excluded groups got smaller, but always there was a new one to be found. Fundamentalist TV evangelists in the United States led the way in the eighties and nineties to make gays the designated enemy and threat as the latest excluded population. Curiously enough, the discovery of the "homosexuals" and the "gay agenda" coincided with the demise of Communism as the popular enemy and provided a new threat around which to raise money.

As a pastor, then church agency administrator, then part-time college teacher, I was not in professional communities that encouraged me to change my views on "homosexuality" or to adopt a more inclusive and welcoming stance. It was quite the opposite. "Homosexuality" was viewed by the church as the place to stanch the encroachments of decadent culture—while unconscionable avarice and consumerism, idolatrous nationalism, vicious militarism, and unbridled nuclear terrorism received almost no attention.

I watched big time evangelists, Bible teachers, and seminarians, who could not see that Jesus plainly taught the way of love and nonviolent response to enemies, as they railed endlessly against "homosexuality" and pontificated earnestly about their undying loyalty to Scripture. While I do not expect perfect consistency from human beings, I found it impossible to pass over this without critique. They have continued for so long straining out gnats and ignoring camels that I claim a right after a while to doubt their eyesight and their integrity.

Yes, there are sincere people, including more than a few Mennonites, who will not criticize those TV evangelists for this betrayal of Jesus' call to love enemies, but will rise up at a moment's notice to strike at the supposed heresy of welcoming gay and lesbian people. In this it appears that, as I suggested a few years ago, Mennonites are approaching a place where they will approve selective homicidal behavior without a blink and condemn selective "homosexual" behavior with steely indignation.

But should a compassionate Christian refuse every impulse to speak critically of those with whom he or she disagrees? It is a truism that nobody can believe or act in ways fundamentally contrary to or beyond their life experience. Thus, we cannot expect people to be or believe other than what they have become because of their experience in life. That should make us patient and humble with other people and how they are different from ourselves. However, it should not blind us (and we hope, not them) to the fact that in very significant ways we are free beings who choose the experiences we have or don't have in life. An observant person can hardly fail to notice that some people shield themselves with exquisite care and great resolve from certain experiences and information that would change them if they were open to new experience and to change.

Here I must speak about the role of reading and of education in my own life. Reading is a freely exercised choice to have one experience rather than another experience. It is thus fundamentally different from the experiences we have because of the children born to us, the people we meet, or the culture in which we live—including, largely, the TV we watch, which is produced almost entirely by greedy corporations, and very little by conscientious authors. Those are given to us and, for the most part, we do not choose them. They shape us profoundly and decisively. But what we read, we choose on the basis of some limited sense of the information and views that a writer offers to us.

As with any subject, a good discussion of the human, moral, biblical and theological issues surrounding same-sex attraction and behavior requires that all discussing parties have a reasonable acquaintance with contrasting points of view. But in the vast majority of American cultural and church situations people are conditioned to hear and know only the condemning view of "homosexuality." Consequently, it takes a deliberate effort of significant proportions to inform one's self adequately to understand alternative views and to have an intelligent discussion of them. A dispassionate observer might conclude that few people make this effort.

My views have changed because of the reading I have done. Some important books have been: *Stranger at the Gate* by Mel White, *Pastor, I Am Gay* by Howard H. Bess, *What Christians Think About Homosexuality* by L.R. Holben, and Walter Wink's edited volume, *Homosexuality and Christian Faith*. There are times when I would like to ask people who disagree with a welcoming view, "Have you read these four books?" I think this an eminently fair question, as fair as an algebra teacher requiring students to have mastered basic math before admittance to the algebra class. Is there any other way to avoid an exchange based on ignorance and ingrained prejudice?

With considerable sadness, I confess that I am repeatedly astonished and disappointed to see the vehemence with which good Christian people, who produce no evidence that they have read a book that disagrees with their childhood view, argue for the condemnation of sexual minorities. It all reminds me of times in history when everybody thought the earth was flat and that the earth is the center of the universe.

I have been influenced also, but less, by experiences from family and other interpersonal relationships. My wife Janet and I have a lesbian daughter, who came out to us more than ten years ago when she was in her twenties. She had tried traditional marriage, which failed after a couple of years. Following her candor with us as parents, our relationship with her improved steadily. We were challenged to seek new understandings. It has been a useful part of our experience. We now have the joy of a very positive relationship with our daughter and her partner of more than ten years. Like a close brush with divorce or cancer, it helped reality to intrude where dogma had previously held full sway.

It is relevant to say here that we humans are tempted to learn too much from our experience as well as too little. We are tempted to take what has happened in our lives, the people and relationships we have known well, and from that presume to know what is right or good for others in general. So from a specific experience we learn too much— too much of one thing—generalizing the whole picture from our limited exposure and experience.

Many times in my life as a peacemaker I have been asked, "Do you have any friends in the military?" or told, "I have friends in the military, and they are some of the best Christians I know." These questions and assertions come from people who believe that they know something more or better than I know because they have firsthand relationships with people who hold a different view. They want me to learn compassion for those who justify war and, more than that, to change my stance of opposition to war.

Some of the same people assume that my view of "homosexuality" has been biased because I have a close relationship with a lesbian person, my daughter. So they would have experience teach me the truth about homicidal violence, but the Bible, presumably, teach me the truth about "homosexuality." You see the problem. In all things, we live in a tension between our experience and other sources of truth. There is no way to avoid this tension, only better and worse ways to live in it.

What has happened to me institutionally and vocationally along the way as a result of my changing views may be of some interest to the reader, so I will summarize that briefly. But all of that is probably less important than the how and why of my changed views, because anybody can allow their views to be affected by reading this, but nobody can have the same life experience that I have had.

I did make decisions to act publicly in keeping with the views I held or was coming to hold. That to me was a straightforward implication of personal integrity. Probably my most important public action took place in 1998 when I initiated in the Mennonite Church what came to be called the "Welcome Letter" (on the internet at www.welcome-committee.org). This was published as the product of an ad hoc committee and appeared as a paid ad in the February 17, 2000 issue of *Mennonite Weekly Review*. More than six hundred signatures were attached to the published letter, although the goal of having a significant number of noted church leaders sign the letter was not realized. We had hoped that, taking courage through the strength of numbers, many leaders, whose private views were considerably more progressive than their public stance, would decide to "come out" together.

The letter affirmed two basic things and, by implication, asked the Mennonite Church to affirm them. First: The letter said, "We believe that affectional orientation is determined very early in an individual's life by a complex mix of biological and environmental factors that are beyond his or her control." Sexual orientation is mostly a biological given, not a choice. Second: It stated, "We believe the church should bless monogamous relationships of same-sex couples and affirm covenant vows between persons who pledge mutual lifelong fidelity and support to one another."

At that time, part of my vocational engagement was teaching a course on faith and society at Messiah College, a Brethren in Christ institution. Parents complained about my support of the Welcome Letter, and I was released by the college from that adjunct teaching role. This move had the effect of freeing all of my time for my passion to work in the church for world peace. With the inspiration and support of others, and out of my engagement in the twenty-five-year history of the historic peace church project known as New Call to Peacemaking, I became coordinator of a movement called Every Church A Peace Church.

The vision and motto of ECAPC is: "The church could turn the world toward peace if every church lived and taught as Jesus lived and taught." This is now my full-time work, and I find it highly rewarding.

One of the continuing joys of my life is to know and work with gay and lesbian people in doing the good works for which, according to the Apostle Paul, we were created. As the Bible stories so often show the outcast and the oppressed being agents of salvation, so now we can see GLBT people doing the will of God. It is a sign of hope, often seen in places of great danger and distress.

To sum up the key ingredients of my changed view, I will share the major tenets of my position. I restate these from an article, "'Homosexuality' and Church Membership: A Model of Power for Unity and Renewal," published in 2001 in the Welcome to Dialogue Series, Booklet #3, *Discerning Church Membership* (available via the website above). The content in the booklet is highly compressed and even more so here.

My views on "homosexuality" are based on other fundamental understandings of historical and theological realities, and to shortchange these is to obscure the substantive rationale for the progressive, welcoming stance that I take. First, I believe that language and culture, both biblical and contemporary, are laced with images of and commitments to dominating male power. This provides the fundamental support for the largest economic and technological enterprise in America, the military industrial complex—a fact with more relevance than might initially appear.

Then I state the obvious, which cannot be said too often or too plainly: A church that fails to critique this ongoing and massive abuse of military power that threatens the world as we know it with imminent destruction most likely will not object to any abuse of power in gender relationships. Heterosexism is an abuse of power in gender relationships, and the church, with small exceptions, is not objecting.

From there, I move to foundational biblical themes. First: Biblical history reveals an expanding circle of salvation and a God who intends to include people whom God's "chosen" people, including more than a few biblical writers, would like to exclude. I maintain that the argument that some people can, will, and should be saved over a finite period of time is no more persuasive than the argument that all people can, will, and should be saved over an infinite period of time. Hence, I espouse universal reconciliation.

Second: The concept of sin is changing. Evolving concepts of sin in the Bible remind us that people's perceptions of sin have changed in the past and will continue to change in the future. This is for the good, and it is not a process that was neatly finished when the canon of Scripture was arbitrarily selected and arbitrarily closed. Jesus said that the Spirit would lead his disciples into truth. On balance, the church finds it hard to believe that.

Third: The biblical themes of justice and liberation for all must include justice and liberation for same-gender attracted people. Moreover, according to Jesus (Matthew 5:6), the human vocation or project is to hunger and thirst to see justice prevail. We are called to liberate those whom culture and power-bound tradition exclude and denigrate

Fourth: Jesus spoke a blessing on peacemakers. Peacemakers work most effectively through the power of nonviolent struggle. Many times those who work courageously for justice and peace are the marginalized groups, such as gay and lesbian people. The church should not overlook or deny their gifts.

Fifth: Scripture regularly counsels us to listen to God's word in creation. Yet, looking over the church's resistance to the observations of science through the centuries shows a sobering record of preferring dogma to truth. This historical tendency to obscure emerging knowledge is still sadly present today. It is evident in the current resistance to seeing diverse gender orientations as a given of creation, and it is present in the widespread judgment that the human expression of those differences is uniformly and irrevocably sinful.

In conclusion, I find that my story of change is far more one of joy than of pain. Why wouldn't it be? I see no better way to find joy than to pursue the truth and to follow it where it leads. But it is a path which many, I suppose, never follow because they fear the bits of pain along the way. From my experience, I can only suggest that this fear exacts too great a price. Better not to give in to it. Better to follow the truth and discover the joy.

John K. Stoner works for world peace from his home in Akron, Pennsylvania, as coordinator of Every Church A Peace Church. He graduated from Messiah College in 1964, the Associated Mennonite Biblical Seminaries in 1967, and is a perpetual student of Christian and other religious traditions. He was pastor of Harrisburg Brethren in Christ Church for eight years and was executive secretary of the Mennonite Central Committee US Peace Section for twelve years. He serves on the boards of Christian Peacemaker Teams (CPT) and KAIROS School of Spiritual Formation. John and his wife Janet have five children (two adopted) and ten grandchildren. He enjoys parenting and grandparenting, reading, bird watching, gardening, hiking, and watching God's purposes unfold in history.

CHAPTER 14

The Person God Made Me to Be

A Former Church of the Brethren Pastor

Have you ever told a lie? Of course, you have. Have you ever told a series of lies to protect the first lie? Of course, you have. We who are spiritual know it is not a pleasant feeling in our hearts when we lie. Have you ever had to live a lie to keep your position in life? Have you ever had to lie just to be accepted by your friends and family?

Have you ever had to say you were someone you were not so that your employer would not fire you because of who you really were? Probably you have not. I know what it is like to lie about my life, my self, my being, and my sexuality just to keep my place in life and to maintain the friendship and respect of those around me. It is not a pleasant experience.

Some of my earliest memories are of being gay and of being different from the other boys around me. My earliest memories are of wanting men to hold me close, to kiss me, to make me their little boy. I wanted to please them, to do what they wanted me to do. I wanted to be good for men. I was good for my father, and I was never happier than when he held me on his lap and hugged me and talked to me. I was happiest when a man or another boy appreciated me or something I did.

When the years of adolescence arrived, and the hormones began raging in my youthful body, nothing changed. There was no magic that made me want to be close to women or girls. Nothing clicked in my head to make me desire to "make out" with girls in the way other boys wanted to. I wanted, as I always had, to be close to boys—mentally,

emotionally, and physically. The magic that made other boys heterosexual in all their desires just never happened to me. It was natural to
me to be a homosexual…to be gay.

One of my earliest memories is of a day in summer when I was
about four years old. We lived in the country, but not on a farm. We
had both a "bread man" and a "milkman" who delivered these bakery
and dairy products to our door. On one particular day, my mother was
hanging clothes outside when the bread man came. He came around to
the backyard and stopped to chat a while with her. I remember how
handsome he was with his moustache and neat uniform. He gave me a
small coloring book that day. After a few minutes he reached down
and, calling me by name, picked me up, held me in his arms, and talked
to me a short while before going on to his next stop. I have never for-
gotten the closeness of that moment and the feelings I experienced for
him. I recall equally well the times he was too busy to stop to play with
a little boy and how disappointed I was if I could not win his attention
for even a brief time.

Other early memories are of the Church of the Brethren. My first is
of the times when the dark blue curtains were drawn in the sanctuary to
divide it into classrooms for Sunday school. (There were only two
rooms to the church then—an entry room about ten feet square and the
sanctuary.) We young scholars would kneel down in front of one of the
benches and be given a picture to color and a Sunday school leaflet
with a story that our teacher would read or tell to us. My teacher was a
kind older woman dressed in her appropriate plain brown dress and
prayer covering, with her hair braided and knotted in a bun just above
her neckline in the back.

Another memory was of communion, the Love Feast. Actually,
part of the memory began the day before the service when members
would gather to scrub the four-inch pine board floor, so it would be
clean for the foot washing service the next evening. On that sacred
night, we small ones did not receive the bread and the cup, but we were
granted the privilege to "partake of the fellowship meal." After the service, we could ask one of the deacons if we might receive a bite of the
unleavened communion bread from one of the eight-inch strips that

might not have been used for the actual service. It took me a long time to understand why the meal was called a "fellowship" meal when the bread and beef and "sop" were consumed in total silence. The a cappella singing during the foot washing service was beautiful, with every voice lifted in harmony as we did as Jesus taught us to do.

When I was but eight years old, we had a two-week series of revival meetings to attract new members from our neighborhood and, indeed, to "revive" our own members in the church. It was during the singing of "Just as I Am" as an altar call that I heard and *felt* Jesus calling me to go to the altar. I first needed to ask my mother if it was all right, and she tearfully gave her consent. I made my way to the front of the church and knelt there, giving my heart and life to God. A few days later, I was the first of some fifteen people to wade into the baptismal waters to be baptized by Trine Immersion, the way of the Brethren. How frightened I was! How happy and proud I was! I was a Christian; I was a member of the Church of the Brethren. Jesus was living in my heart.

Through the years, the church meant so much to me. It became a haven where my personality and talents grew and were appreciated. I was a leader, and by the time I was thirteen, my pastor thought we should have a Church of the Brethren Youth Fellowship. I became the president at that young age and remained president until I graduated from high school and left home to attend a Church of the Brethren college. Being musically inclined, I was chosen to be the song leader of the church and also the director of the first choir the church ever had. We youth had paper drives and donut sales to buy the church's first organ. By the time I entered college, my home congregation had licensed me to the ministry. Some two years after I graduated from college, I was serving a neighboring congregation of the Church of the Brethren as pastor! I had a wife and children and.....and I was gay.

I have had a special feeling for men as long as I can remember. I wanted men to notice me...to pick me up, to hug me, to hold me, just as my daddy did. The *special love* and feelings I had for men came completely naturally to me. Never did I feel I could not pray to God or have Jesus in my heart just because I loved men and had sexual feelings for them. It had been that way all my life. I loved God, sang His praises, did His work, told His story, and felt Him in my heart. When some gay men would ask if I ever felt guilty, I could honestly say that I did not ever feel that my homosexuality kept me from God, from growing spiritually, or from praying to God for daily guidance. It came so naturally to me to be gay; I knew it was as natural as heterosexuality was for others I knew.

It was unnatural for me to make love to a woman, but I felt I had to do that to be accepted by society. I have always felt that the time that I did "that which was unnatural" for me was the time I lived with my wife and pretended to be heterosexual. I had to lie about who I was, what my sexuality was, and what my true feelings were.

What kind of pastor was I over the years as I served several congregations of the Brethren? I was a good, caring, loving pastor. I ached with my people when they ached, I buried their loved ones, I married them, dedicated their children, and I baptized them. I can honestly say that the members of the congregations I served were totally at peace with one another while I served them. My messages were timely and spoke to their hearts as well as to my own. I always made it a practice to make the sermon one that spoke to my own heart, and with the help of God, the sermons spoke to the hearts of others also. I worked well with my congregants in the Church of the Brethren, and we were at peace with one another and in love and fellowship with one another. Did I ever make mistakes as a Brethren pastor? Of course, I am certain that I did. Was I ever called on the carpet by a ministerial commission or a church board because of some serious problem between the church and me? No. Was I gay during each of my pastorates? Yes. Am I still the same today? Yes.

I am totally convinced that I was born gay. I never had a thought that said, "I think I will try out the gay lifestyle," or "I think I'll *choose* to be gay." How ridiculous! Why would anyone in his/her right mind decide to be gay in the United States where gays and lesbians are scorned, ridiculed, and told that God hates them? Being gay was being myself....it always was me, and it is me today. There was no thought or desire or decision on my part to be gay. It was who I was as far back as

I can remember. Oh, many were the hours that I spent praying, thinking, wondering why I was gay, and trying not to be gay. Can the leopard change its spots? I wonder, if the tables were reversed, how many heterosexuals could deny their heterosexuality and *decide* to be gay, to deny that which is truly a part of their inner being and to do what is unnatural for them?

I attempted to come back to the active ministry several years after I was divorced, but someone told the district executive that I was gay. When he asked me if I was gay, I told him the truth. Naturally, the next step was an interview with the District Ministerial Board. They postponed the meeting as long as they could. Finally, they held the interview, and I had to wait weeks for their decision. They refused me employment, even though the local church was willing to hire me with the knowledge that I was gay. The District Ministerial Board gave me another excuse for why I could not be employed by the church, other than my homosexuality. But they know and I know that the real reason they denied me employment was because I was gay. I was devastated, as was at least half of the congregation.

Today, I still cannot be completely out in the open about myself. This is evidenced by the fact that I need to be anonymous in writing this story. Sometimes, I still need to lie about my self, my being, and my sexuality to shield some of my family members and friends who remain Brethren. I still preach the good news of the Scriptures in a church that accepts my homosexuality, but I am not able to be God's messenger in the denomination I grew to love over a long period of years.

Do I ever miss the foot washing service, my days of Brethren fellowship and membership, and lifting my voice in song with hundreds of other Brethren at Annual Conference? Yes, I do. But being true to the person God made me to be is a deeper reward than having a ministry in the Church of the Brethren and needing to lie to keep that ministry.

CHAPTER 15

Conference-Minded: A Rainbow Thread
in the Mennonite Church

Doug Basinger

Mission-minded

It was a dark and stormy night. Our family was enroute to First Mennonite Church, Lima, Ohio, to hear a missionary speak. Was it because our own church, First Mennonite, Bluffton, Ohio, did not particularly favor a strong evangelical approach to church work? Was it because my folks wanted to support a church they had attended for a few years when they lived in Lima as newly-weds? Was it because they were a bit more conservative than other First Mennonite, Bluffton congregants? I never knew.

I did know that as I listened to this man speak about his calling to minister in Africa and convert the natives, my heart skipped and sank with anxiety. To speak of a calling was not in my church vocabulary, but I knew exactly what he meant. Was I being called to become a missionary in Africa when I grew up? I did not want to go.

When the service ended after a long, pleading prayer, the missionary strode down the aisle, wrapped his arm around me (I had the misfortune of sitting next to the aisle), looked deep in my eyes, and asked "Are you saved?" "Yes," I stammered, my face red with embarrassment and my heart beating far faster than normal. I knew I should have avoided eye contact with him during the service. As I responded, I wondered if he knew that I had not yet gone through the two years of catechism our church required prior to baptism and membership. I was unwilling to engage him in further conversation; "yes" was the only response I could think of.

This early memory captures one of my first glimmers of call to church work. Was I called to be a minister? I didn't think so. Certainly no one else in my family had ever gone to seminary. My family came from a rural Swiss Mennonite community that supported higher education (Bluffton College), but most Mennonite clergy seemed to come from elsewhere.

Conference-minded

First Mennonite of Bluffton was deeply involved in conference. From the early Witmarsum Theological Seminary and Bluffton College to Central District to Camp Friedenswald, many in the congregation were part of the larger church. These professors and church workers were my Sunday school teachers, my parents' friends, and part of my local church community There was never any clear way in my mind to separate congregation and conference. Not until many years later, when I met people for whom conference was incidental, did I realize that not everyone connected the two so closely.

Goshen College

Goshen was my introduction to the (Old) Mennonite Church. My friends at Bluffton assumed that I wanted to become a minister since I was going to this "Bible school" instead of Bluffton, Bethel, or some of the Quaker schools such as Earlham, where students from our congregation usually attended. Although my mother had been from the Illinois Conference (Amish Mennonite), and I knew vaguely about prayer coverings and churches with small, unimpressive, or no organs, I was startled to see a clerical collar on one of the faculty during my first semester at Goshen College in Indiana. I thought perhaps Goshen was more ecumenical than those of us at Bluffton had believed. I learned the professor's name was J.C. Wenger. I had no idea that some Mennonites dressed in such a fashion. In 1969, at the height of the Vietnam War, I quickly participated in civil protests in Washington, D.C., along with many other Mennonite students, including several cousins from various Mennonite colleges.

Mennonite Central Committee

Disillusioned with school in the midst of such goings on, I applied to Mennonite Central Committee (MCC) as a part of my conscientious objector alternative service. Although I was younger than the average, MCC accepted me and assigned me to metropolitan Vancouver, British Columbia, on Canada's west coast, far from my Midwest roots. Here I had my first introduction to "Russian" Mennonites and my first experience of exclusion. With a name like Basinger, they assumed I was not Mennonite, and most congregations hardly knew what to do with me. Since then, I have always been keenly sensitive to congregational newcomers, especially those who are not from Mennonite background.

In the early 1970s, while I was in Vancouver, the Jesus Movement and charismatic expressions of faith swept the west coast. While in MCC, I found Killarney Park Mennonite Brethren Church and several Anglican churches more open to this emotional expression of faith than the General Conference churches I visited. I was also introduced, for the first time, to gay people at my place of work. While I did not identify with them at all, it was clear that they saw a kindred spirit in me. Being a soul who was always wanting to please people, I accepted their friendships but was not yet self-aware enough to understand that I, too, was one of them.

School and Beyond

Following two years in British Columbia and several months in rural Quebec with MCC, I returned to Goshen to finish my studies. I selected English as a major, partly because my father taught English in high school and partly because I saw that major as the strongest at Goshen of those I was interested in. I also took various Bible and Christian faith courses. As I considered various career paths that I might choose, I was drawn to English and communication, because effective writing and editing would be especially helpful to making good administrative decisions.

Nearing the end of my undergraduate studies, I pondered my next move. MCC had contacted me about working in Washington D.C., to edit a publication supporting Native American history and law, but there was also an editing position at *Mennonite Weekly Review* that interested me. I consulted with Mary Bender, one of my professors, who advised going to Washington. "You have your whole life to work for Mennonites," she said. What neither of us knew at the time was that, as I became aware of my gay identity, I would not have my whole life to work for Mennonites in the way we both imagined; there would be precious little room for gay people in the Mennonite Church.

I had begun toying with the idea that I would like to work in church administration, probably at the denominational level, which meant in Newton, Kansas. However, this idea took a back seat as I went off to Washington, D.C., and spent two years with MCC and a total of three years working with Native American concerns. It was during this three-year period that I came out to myself and a few friends.

Needing to make a longer term decision about whether to remain in Washington, D.C., or to move to the Pacific Northwest to be near Vancouver, which I had found to be a lovely place to live before, I visited San Francisco and was offered two part-time jobs. Considering this the Lord's leading, although this was not language I was prone to use, I drove to San Francisco, figuring it was as close to Vancouver as I could get.

Out in the Church

In San Francisco, I attended Haight-Ashbury Mennonite Fellowship, the only Mennonite congregation in town. I was not especially attracted to the intentional community aspects of this rather closed community; it felt heavy-handed in style. I was cautious about my initial involvement but was eventually asked out to lunch by Ken Reed, one of the leaders. Over lunch in Union Square, the commercial hub of San Francisco, Ken asked me point-blank if I were gay. I have always been a private person (because I am gay?), but I was so startled by the question that I responded affirmatively. We quickly concluded that we understood the issue very differently from one another, but I continued to attend the church with reservations.

During this time, I had written to Stan Bohn, my pastor when I was in high school. Stan now served in Newton, Kansas, as the conference minister for the General Conference Mennonite Church. I timidly expressed my interest in working for the church in some capacity and also mentioned that I was gay. Immediately upon receiving my letter, Stan called to express support and concern. Was I comfortable with being gay? Did my parents know? Could he recommend a support group for them? Grateful for his support, I returned to Haight-Ashbury Mennonite Fellowship with a renewed sense of identity.

Less than a year after moving to San Francisco, I was invited to work for the Mennonite Church's Mennonite Board of Missions (MBM) as a regional director for their Voluntary Service and Student and Young Adult Services programs. Stan was very happy for me, but Ken wondered if MBM knew I was gay.

I accepted the assignment and opened a small office in San Francisco, along with a part-time regional director Lois Janzen (Preheim), who was also part-time pastor of the church. One of the VSers provided administrative support. For three years, I reveled in this position. I was able to combine my experience with various non-profit organizations for placing volunteers. Having lived in various parts of North America, I could identify with the feelings of estrangement that both VSers and young adults felt. Best of all, I got to meet with pastors at the various VS locations and attended many church conferences. For me this was an ideal job, combining my interest in well-developed and well-administered church programs, social outreach through volunteers (by this time I had spent nearly four and a half years as a volunteer through MCC), and connecting with Mennonite young adults, especially in urban areas where there were few Mennonite congregations or none at all.

As I served in this way, I felt that there would come a time when being gay would get in the way of serving the broader church. I was pragmatic enough about institutions, even godly church institutions, to know that no matter how effective or well-liked I might be, if I did not fit an appropriate category—out I would go. But even with my pragmatism, I was appalled at the particulars that conspired to end my MBM term.

Here's the short version, slightly convoluted because I'm using only pronouns, not names: One of the San Francisco VSers was gay; he was one of the household leaders, so I worked with him more closely than the others. He had a close gay college friend, working at a Mennonite institution, who wanted to be in relationship with him and envied his friend's friendship with me. While visiting his home community, this youthful college administrator spoke with his childhood pastor about how best to manage his feelings toward his friend and the friendship that existed between his friend and me. While one might naturally assume that such a pastoral counseling visit would be confidential, the following day the pastor called the head of MBM and objected strenuously to having a gay person working for MBM. During my ensuing discussions with MBM personnel that took place during the week I was leading a VS orientation in Elkhart, Indiana, we agreed that I would finish out my third year of service, which was some six months away. This decision was communicated back to the pastor.

A month later, I had a chance to visit this pastor (now deceased) in the course of my work. His affectionate physical touch while he prayed for me following our conversation led me to wonder nervously just what his strong interest in gay issues was all about.

During the next weeks, I advised all seven VS households for which I was responsible that I would be leaving and shared with each household leader the reason. This was an extremely painful thing for me to do for several reasons. For one, I have always been a private person. For another, everyone was shocked that I was leaving because they knew that I enjoyed my work immensely. After learning the reason why I was leaving, some were supportive and some were confused; I disliked putting them in that uncomfortable position.

During the last six months of my service, I became romantically involved with the San Francisco VS household leader (a different one than the one mentioned above). John and I recently celebrated our twentieth anniversary of being together.

The Next Twenty Years

After three years of service for MBM and a total of nearly seven and a half years of church work, I now had to sort out a different direction, because I had imagined that I might continue in church administrative work for a number of years. Through a series of temporary happenstances, I ended up in the biotech industry where I have worked for nearly twenty years.

I remained actively involved in First Mennonite Church of San Francisco, as the Haight-Ashbury Mennonite Fellowship came to be called. The congregation, no longer a heavy-handed, closed community, was both outraged and supportive following the loss of my job. I have served as treasurer of the congregation and editor of the newsletter. I have also been chair of the congregation and have served on nearly every church committee, including being chair of the Steering and Worship Committees. Being forced out of my job plus conversations with our conference about the role of gay people in lay leadership seemed to be the impetus the congregation needed to become an intentionally welcoming community of faith. They continued to be supportive of gay members and attendees, and eventually we joined the Supportive Communities Network of BMC (Brethren/Mennonite Council for Lesbian, Gay, Bisexual and Transgender Interests).

Our congregation has made an intentional decision to be conference-minded. Over the years, individuals from First Mennonite have served in our local districts (first Southwest Mennonite Conference and Pacific District, then later, the merged Pacific Southwest Mennonite Conference) as newsletter editor, treasurer, and on various committees. The congregation has hosted the annual district conference more than once, most recently in 2003.

In addition to leadership participation in my local congregation, I have continued with my own understanding of Christian faith and community as one that must be conference-minded, including as much denominational participation as I can. I have attended district and denominational conferences, often as a congregational delegate, and I was invited by the broader Mennonite Church to participate on a Listening Committee for Homosexual Concerns. Unfortunately, even though we listened well and reported our findings, the report was shelved. I have also participated in other churchwide activities, special events, and meetings when invited. Even though San Francisco may be on the edge of the Mennonite world (in many ways), church leaders who have passed through our city have worshipped with our church, and many have been guests in our home. I also served for many years as a board member of BMC.

Anno Domino

We are each called to be faithful as salt and light in different ways. I have always felt called to remain affiliated with the Mennonite Church. Since the door of church employment is closed (how I would have loved to be part of the staff working on the recent merger to create Mennonite Church USA), until gay Christians are less threatening to more people in the church, I find I can contribute best by being an example of a Mennonite Christian who remains more interested and passionate than the average person about church history and polity. In spite of my frustration with the pace of institutional inclusion, I am thankful for all the quiet (sometimes too quiet!) advocates who I know have supported and defended me to others within the broader church that has been less understanding and supportive. Thanks be to God!

Doug Basinger lives in San Francisco with John Flickinger, his partner of twenty years. Both are active in First Mennonite Church of San Francisco and enjoy spending time at their weekend cottage in Sonoma County, near the redwoods, the seaside, and wine country. They ponder together how to support their parents with the issues they face in their aging years.

CHAPTER 16

You Can't Teach Here Anymore!

Ronald E. Brunk

To be asked to abandon one's call in order to be true to oneself is a painful and life altering experience, especially when the request comes from the very church that nurtured you in the Christian life and called you to the ministry that was so intensely satisfying to you.

My life began in a small farming community in McPherson County, Kansas, northwest of the town of Inman. Born in 1944, the third child and second son of my parents, I joined my family who for the seven years before I was born was a small unit of four. Two years later, my younger sister was born to complete our family. We lived one mile as the crow flies from my paternal grandparents and two and one-half miles from my maternal grandparents on an eighty-acre farm of which my father and mother were sharecroppers.

Family and church were intertwined during the first seven years of my life. Four sets of aunts and uncles and numerous other cousins and relatives lived inside a three-mile radius from the Mennonite church we attended. Our minister was my mother's first cousin. Church and family gatherings blur together in my recollections of those early years. From as early as I can remember, we attended church twice on Sunday and again on Wednesday night. We spent Sunday afternoons, if not occupied by a potluck dinner at the church, at one of my two grandparents' homes, having dinner with extended family and playing with my cousins.

Religious activities were an important ingredient in my life. Daily Scripture reading and prayer preceded every family breakfast. All adult women in the church wore the devotional prayer covering; my mother wore hers every day. Bedside prayers were expected when we were tucked in at night. As soon as I was old enough, I attended annual summer Bible school.

A Mennonite church sponsored education was important to my parents. When my oldest brother was ready for high school, they arranged for him to attend our church-related high school at Hesston, Kansas, a boarding school about thirty-five miles from our home. Later, my parents moved our family to a 160-acre farm that was located three and one-half miles from Hesston so that my two older siblings could attend Hesston Academy without the added cost of boarding. With the absence of extended family, the Mennonite congregation located on the campus of the academy and related junior college became our spiritual home.

During my elementary and high school days, I attended many evangelistic revival meetings conducted by George R. Brunk (Yes, he is a distant relative!) and later by Myron Augsburger, both staunch evangelists of the Mennonite Church. Although I had affirmed my faith by joining the church when I was ten years old, I was always moved to contrition and recommitment of my life to Christ by these revival meetings.

Much of my life was devoted to the church. I regularly attended activities sponsored by the youth fellowship. When it was time to register for the draft, I turned to my pastor for assistance in registering as a conscientious objector.

I received the intellectual tools I needed to refine and fine-tune my faith through my education at Mennonite institutions, and my commitment to the Mennonite Church grew. Anxious to learn more and have a deeper commitment of faith, I memorized the New Testament book of Philippians for a Mennonite Youth Fellowship convention in Pennsylvania and participated on our church's quiz team. Singing in high school and college choirs also served to strengthen my faith.

Easter morning in Kidron, Ohio, was a memorable date during my senior year at Goshen College in Indiana. I was on tour with the college choir that spring. On that morning, I made my own adult personal commitment to God. I promised I would spend my life serving him in whatever way he called me.

On choir trips, we were guests in community homes and often slept in double beds. This presented a problem because to sleep in a bed with another man caused sexual arousal for me, and I would have strong feelings of guilt. As a result of these experiences, I began to question my sexual identity.

After graduation, I accepted a position in the accounting office at Goshen College. Suddenly, however, my future became very uncertain. My number was called up by the armed forces draft. Marriage would have exempted me, but I had earlier broken off an engagement, so that was not my option. After my physical, I received a IV-F classification because of a bout with rheumatic fever that I had as a child. Consequently, I was able to honor my commitment to the college.

When I moved to Goshen, Indiana, to finish my college education, my best friend from my junior college years at Hesston College invited me to his church in nearby Elkhart. It was the mid-sixties, and issues of race and the disenfranchisement of the lower social classes were the hot topics of the day. The pastor, who was very socially conscious, was eloquent about our responsibilities as Christians to be compassionate and involved with those regarded by American society as subhuman. Because I identified with and adopted these concerns as my own, I made this my home church.

As I became more conscious of a desire to fulfill my commitment to God in the best way possible, I began considering full-time pastoral ministry. I received strong encouragement from the pastor and the congregation, and I began attending seminary in 1969 to prepare for full-time pastoral ministry.

At the seminary, I was exposed to effective teaching of the Mennonite Church's position of peace and justice for everyone, and I adopted that position as my own. I vowed to be an advocate of these causes for the rest of my life. Involvement with organizations that procured better housing opportunities for the disenfranchised and providing leadership to a Boys' Club from the "project" area of Elkhart were ways in which I pursued these causes. A summer in Chicago under the

Urban Ministries Program for seminarians opened my eyes more fully to the needs of the disenfranchised in our society.

I returned to my home congregation in Hesston, Kansas, to complete my seminary education as a pastoral intern. I was involved in all aspects of the pastoral ministry at Hesston Mennonite Church. The year included training in Clinical Pastoral Education (CPE) at Prairie View Mental Health Center in nearby Newton, Kansas.

It was a critical year for me. Discussions with my intern instructors and my CPE director helped me to determine that I was uncomfortable with the requirements of becoming a pastor. As a result, I did not return to seminary for my final semester. I was a seminary dropout at age twenty-seven. Nevertheless, the pastor at Hesston Mennonite encouraged me to continue my involvement as a layperson. During the next several years, I participated in planning worship, youth leadership, the formation of small groups, and other activities.

I entered the business world with a job at Hesston Corporation. The controller of the corporation recognized my abilities and encouraged me to pursue a graduate degree in accounting. Heeding his advice I became a full-time student at Wichita State University in 1977. During that year, I learned of an opening for controller at Bethel College in nearby Newton, Kansas. I applied for the job and was accepted to begin work in 1978. This turned out to be the opening of the next door for what was to become my "call to ministry" in the church.

In the fall of 1979, I was asked to teach intermediate accounting for the next academic year at Bethel. I had never thought of myself as a teacher but discovered a task that was enjoyable and personally satisfying. In 1980, I completed my M.B.A. program, sat for and passed the CPA exam, and began a fifteen-year career of teaching accounting in Mennonite colleges. Six of those years were at Bethel College and the last nine at my alma mater Goshen College.

Teaching came naturally for me. Given the gift of an excellent theoretical understanding of the accounting discipline, it was challenging to explain the intricacies of accounting to college students and to concentrate on improving my communication skills. At both Bethel and Goshen, I developed a program for accounting students who were interested in pursuing careers in public accounting as well as accounting for private companies. I mentored accounting students to understand their options after graduation and was able to steer those who were not interested in public accounting to options that suited their personality and skills. Most of all, I was able to convey my concerns for peace and justice in the world and my commitment to the Mennonite Church through my life and interaction with my students. My student evaluations showed that my students appreciated my teaching skills and my desire to find new and exciting ways to communicate with them and to challenge them.

At Goshen College, I developed an accounting internship program, assisted students with their resumes, and helped them develop skills for job interviews. This provided a springboard that allowed me to keep in touch with them and to continue to show interest in their lives. Many times graduates would come back to ask for guidance or to share their successes and failures with me.

I had found my "call to ministry" in teaching at a church-related college. For the first time in my life, I was content with my job and expected to continue my teaching career until retirement.

* * *

Now I need to backtrack to pick up another thread of my story. During the first year following graduation from Goshen College, I invited three of my friends to share an apartment with me for the second semester of that year. Needing to share a bed with another man caused frustration for both of us, and my bedmate chose to sleep on the couch in the living room. (An interesting side note to this story is that three of the four of us from that house have since come out as gay men, including the friend who shared my bed!)

At that time I was engaged, and I shared my concerns about my sexual identity with my fiancée, who was very understanding and supportive. We were able to come to the resolution that I was bisexual, and we continued our plans for marriage. We were married on August 6, 1966, and our two sons were born in the years that followed. Marriage, however, did not change the feelings and situations that made me question my sexual identity. The most critical of these experiences was a friendship with another married man. We became very close friends and did many things together, sometimes without our wives, who became jealous of our friendship. I gradually became aware that my feelings for this man were more than just friendship. The friendship was so important to me, however, that I would not risk discussing my feelings with him. He was very much in love with his wife, and his friendship was more important to me than my sexual feelings for him.

That experience heightened my awareness of my sexual identity, and I began coming out to myself. During this time, my wife's sister and her husband separated because he was gay. My wife and I were the only ones in her family who continued to be supportive of the ex-husband as he explored a new life. I began reading more about homosexuality but was always afraid someone would find out what I was thinking.

In the late seventies, I was one of our church's delegates to the Mennonite Church Assembly in Bowling Green, Ohio. Our assignment was to observe the discussions that resulted in the formation of the Task Force on Human Sexuality of the Mennonite Church. I also attended a workshop on homosexuality where a pastor from Pennsylvania who was working with an ex-gay ministry and two men from the Brethren/Mennonite Council for Lesbian and Gay Concerns (BMC) shared their views. (The name has been changed to Brethren/Mennonite Council for Lesbian, Gay, Bisexual, and Transgender Interests to reflect the expanded vision of the organization.)

As I left the workshop, I covertly picked up the BMC brochure. For the first time, I read that homosexuality was not just about physical sexual experience but also included one's feelings and attractions. At that moment, I knew that I was gay. But it would still be years before I would be able to come out fully. I wrote to both of the men from the BMC workshop and appreciated the support they gave me. However, I was not ready for that degree of involvement and did not continue these contacts.

While teaching at Bethel College, I became interested in the discussions that were emerging between my (Old) Mennonite denomination and the General Conference Mennonites. I decided to attend the first joint conference held in Bethlehem, Pennsylvania, in 1983. Of course, part of my interest was piqued by the discussion of human sexuality that was on the agenda.

In the BMC workshop, a young gay man, who had attended Goshen College, shared his story in a room packed full of people. I talked with the young man after the workshop, and he invited me to the BMC booth. There I met more people who were involved with BMC. Later, I had dinner with the coordinator and attended a meeting of the BMC Board members. All of this was done with an eye over my shoulder, afraid that someone I knew would see me and "report" my activities.

In 1984, I entered the Ph.D. program in accounting at the University of Texas in Austin. That fall, I lived in Austin by myself because of my wife's job in Kansas and because of the ages of our two children. The plan was for me to do this temporarily until they could move to be with me.

While alone in Austin, I was able to explore my sexuality, and I became involved with a gay support group. The Ph.D. program, however, was a disappointment, and I moved back to Kansas at the end of the first semester. I had managed to open the door of the closet a wee bit, but now I was completely back in it.

In 1986, I accepted a teaching position at Goshen College, and we moved our family there. Our oldest son was just entering high school, so we felt it was a good time to make the move. During the next seven years, while our sons completed their high school years, much of my time was consumed with their extra-curricular activities and with my involvement in the church and college. Nevertheless, I kept in touch with the BMC coordinator on an infrequent basis, and I began to provide financial support to the organization.

The fall that our youngest son left the nest to attend college, I suddenly began thinking about the rest of my life. I became increasingly convinced that continuing in the marriage would result in both my wife and I living in an unhappy situation for the rest of our lives. My wife was concerned about my "impotency" and began suggesting that I see a doctor about it.

In January of 1994, I came out for the first time to a female friend who I knew from community theatre involvement. She was supportive, and as a result I was able later that month to come out to my wife and suggest that we would both be happier living separate lives. At first she was devastated; however, she came to see the wisdom of that decision and supported me in it. She has since remarried and is very happy.

We needed to share what was happening between us with our sons. Therefore, my wife and I took a trip together to visit them at the colleges they were attending. I appreciate much that they are both supportive of me, and we continue to have a good relationship.

Now, I had to deal with my job. I knew the position of the Mennonite Church on homosexuality and was quite certain that if I came out publicly, I would be asked to leave my teaching position at Goshen College. Therefore, I asked my wife and sons to keep the reason for the separation quiet so that I could continue my teaching job. I was very careful to whom I came out and how much I shared. Through my involvement in community theatre, I began gradually to explore what it would mean to be out.

In the fall of 1994, I met my future partner, who lived in Atlanta at the time. By Thanksgiving, we decided that we wanted to be together for life. I assumed that continuing at Goshen College was not an option under these circumstances, so I submitted my resignation and made plans to move to Atlanta after the school year ended. I still did not tell anyone at the college my reason for resigning for fear that my job would be terminated immediately if they found out.

My partner Charles and I traveled back and forth between Goshen and Atlanta on a more and more frequent basis. He would sometimes visit me for more than just a weekend. On those occasions, he would accompany me to the college, most of the time sitting in my classroom as a guest.

On the weekend of the college's Christmas vespers, Charles sat with me in the front row of the balcony. I had been asked to read

Scripture from that location. Inadvertently, I had come out in the eyes of some of my colleagues. Without discussing it with me, one of them proceeded to "out" me to the rest of the faculty.

I did not find out that I had been "outed" until several weeks before the end of the term. When my department had difficulty filling my position, I had some second thoughts. After discussing it with Charles, I presented the possibility to the department that I could continue to teach for another year. At that time, I decided that I needed to share with my colleagues the reason I had resigned. To my surprise, I discovered that they already knew! They also told me that some of my students were asking questions about my "friend" and me.

The department chair told me that, even though I was one of the best teachers at the college and students appreciated my teaching skills, he did not agree with my "choice" of lifestyle. If I wanted to stay on, he would need to discuss it with the administration of the college. I did not want to be the subject of such a discussion when I was quite certain what the outcome would be, so I decided to let my resignation stand.

We moved to Atlanta and attended church at the Atlanta Mennonite Fellowship there. We became involved in the life of the church and, when I was asked to participate in the leadership of the congregation, we asked if we would be allowed to become members. The support we received from that congregation was more than negated by the efforts of the district conference to disenfranchise the congregation because they had accepted us into membership. We have since moved to Minneapolis, Minnesota, where we have distanced ourselves from the Mennonite Church and are reluctant to become involved with any church.

What happened to the many relationships I had made in the Mennonite Church during my lifetime? It is very painful for me to report that it feels like I am a "non-person" in the Mennonite Church. There has been support from former colleagues at both Goshen and Bethel on an individual basis, but no continuing contact with either former colleagues or students. After moving to Atlanta, I explored some job openings in the teaching field at Bluffton, Goshen, and Bethel Colleges, as well as McPherson College, a Church of the Brethren college in Kansas, but it became clear that I would not be considered for a faculty position because of my sexual orientation.

Before our move to Minnesota, a friend asked me if I would be interested in a financial management position at a Mennonite institution, and I affirmed my interest in the job. Later my friend reported that I was perceived as an "activist," and the gossip line stated that, being unwilling to leave my position at Goshen College, I had put up a lot of resistance. Anyone who really knows me is aware that such a way of acting is not my style. Although my contact person wanted me to further consider the position, I withdrew my name from the pool of applicants because of the false rumors about my departure from Goshen College.

I want to share a very positive experience that I had the day before I left Goshen College for Atlanta. I needed to submit some paperwork to an administrative assistant for a course that I taught the previous semester. She invited me to sit down. Then she told me that because of me she had to change her thinking about homosexuality. She was not Mennonite, but had grown up in a similar church environment. Over the months that she knew about my sexual orientation, she realized that I was still the same person that she knew before she found out that I was gay. This caused her to make some changes in her attitude toward gay people.

I am sad that I can no longer continue doing the one thing that was extremely satisfying to me, both in terms of job and Christian calling. The church that nourished me and helped me grow in my Christian faith told me that, because of who I am, I could not continue my call to ministry.

I have moved on, but I continue to hope and pray that the Mennonite Church will some day allow justice to roll down for its lesbian and gay members.

Ronald E. Brunk, CPA, M.B.A., lives in Minneapolis, Minnesota, with his partner Charles Parker. Since their commitment to each other on June 3, 1995, they have celebrated nine years of life together. Ron was a member of the BMC Board of Directors for four and a half years and served as treasurer for three of those years. He still keeps the account books for BMC. Ron and Charles have been active in the lesbian and gay community, both in Atlanta and Minneapolis.

In Minneapolis, Ron was a member of the One Voice Mixed Chorus, and he currently sings with the Twin Cities Gay Men's Chorus. He served two years as treasurer on the Board of Directors of Quorum, the GLBT Chamber of Commerce organization in the Twin Cities and as treasurer for Headwaters Fund, a foundation that funds grassroots organizations involved in social change. Ron has been actively involved with Outward Spiral Theatre Company, a GLBT theatre group, and Rainbow Families, an organization supporting lesbians and gays with children. Charles is part of the Minnesota Freedom Band.

CHAPTER 17

The Craziest of Second Comings

Anita Fast

Christ climbed down
from His bare tree
this year
and softly stole away into
some anonymous Mary's womb again
where in the darkest night
of everybody's anonymous soul
he awaits again
an unimaginable and impossibly
Immaculate Reconception
the very craziest
of Second Comings
～ From "Christ Climbed Down," by Lawrence Ferlinghetti *

When I was a little girl, I remember wondering how God was going to bring Jesus back again. I must have been unfamiliar with the biblical texts describing the trumpets sounding and Jesus appearing on great clouds in grandeur and pomp, as I expected that God would likely bring Jesus back in a similar manner to his first coming—as a baby born of a virgin. With childlike sincerity and longing to be available to do whatever God might ask of me, I assured God that should it be time for Jesus to return and should God be looking for a willing virgin, I was most keen to be chosen for the task. Like Mary, I wanted to give my whole self—spirit, mind, and body—to do God's will, whatever that might be. Perhaps I also knew that should I decide to get pregnant it would have to occur in an untraditional manner!

I was raised by Mennonite parents in a Mennonite church in London, Ontario, Canada. I remember the love and faith I had in the church—its projects, its institutions, its community. I was taught that being Christian made a difference in the way one lived life, and that difference was centered around a commitment to nonviolence, peace, justice, and service to others. At age seventeen, I stood in front of my congregation and spoke of my faith and commitment to God and the Body of Christ and was baptized into the life of the church. I was dedicated to being a Christian in the world, seeking peace and justice, living with compassion and an open heart, choosing simplicity and service as my way of life. As my parents cupped their hands over my bowed head, and the pastor poured the baptismal water into them, I was filled with a profound sense of belonging and love.

Yet not even five years later, I sat in the midst of the same community and struggled to hold back my tears as I passed the communion bread to my mother beside me, without partaking myself. I was discovering a different side of "my people" who I had thought could do no wrong, and I felt betrayed. When I looked at the church buildings, read Scripture, or heard hymn singing, I no longer felt empowered by the community of God. Instead, I saw the pain of the masses of people trampled over by the skeletons of church history—women burned as witches, indigenous people ripped from their lands, African people dragged onto ships and sold into slavery, millions of Jews and other social undesirables tortured in concentration camps and gassed in the ovens of Auschwitz. All of this, and more, was justified by many in their own time as the will of God. So I concluded that the Bible was a dangerous book used as often to fuel hatred and oppression as to hold up promise and love. The Christian church quickly became for me a place devoid of the presence of God.

Around this same time, I began to acknowledge and act upon my attraction to women. I had the good fortune of having wonderfully supportive parents who unquestionably and immediately embraced me and loved me unconditionally. I am aware that had this not been the case, the rest of my story would be fundamentally altered. As it was, beginning to identify as lesbian was a joyful process for me, one of new possibilities and an open future. I did not have many struggles with self-acceptance. Being outside of the church helped. I had already rejected it, so it was relatively unimportant that it was rejecting me. It was irrelevant to me at the time that the Mennonite Church taught that I was committing a grave sin. The church's own bloody history seriously called into question for me its role as an authority in determining what sin was. In fact, its condemnation of same-gender relationships was only further proof to me that the church's defining feature was closed-mindedness and oppression, regardless of what it claimed to stand for. This was the year that Christ climbed down from the branches of the Christian church for me.

Still drawn to the spiritual, I committed myself to the study of other religious and spiritual traditions. I explored pagan, aboriginal, and other earth-based spiritualities. I read books on Buddhism, Taoism, and mystical traditions from a variety of perspectives. I found a religious community within the Unitarian Church, which encouraged the exploration of many different approaches to understanding God and the Spirit. With passion, I engaged new ideas and spiritual paths, yet something remained unsettled within me. Even as I got more and more involved in the Unitarian Church, delighted at their acceptance and celebration of my gifts of leadership and preaching as well as my sexuality, I could not come to call myself a Unitarian. When people introduced me as such, I felt compelled to correct them and say that I was a Mennonite, even though I remained alienated from the Mennonite Church and the Christian tradition.

In spite of my uncertainty as to which religious community I was called to be part of, it was becoming increasingly obvious that I was called to some sort of religious or spiritual ministry. In 1996, I entered seminary at Vancouver School of Theology, unsure of where the path would lead but certain that this was the path I must take. It was with a fair amount of trepidation that I even considered going close to a Christian community again, let alone beginning a three-year course of study in one. I decided, however, that I was going to be "out" from the very beginning and not let my re-entry into a Christian context scare me back into the closet. What I found at VST was a faculty, staff, and student body made up of predominately supportive people, as well as a few other gays and lesbians studying to be ministers in their respective denominations. In fact, the United Church of Canada, one of the major Canadian denominations that sponsors Vancouver School of Theology, had voted as early as 1988 to ordain gay and lesbian Christians without requiring celibacy.

Even so, with several doors of ministry open to me as an "out" lesbian—either the Unitarian Church or the United Church of Canada—I knew from the beginning that, should I begin to find life again from within the biblical texts and the Christian worship and community that engages them, I was and always would be Mennonite. And sure enough, as I studied the Bible, church history, and theology, those texts and songs and liturgies set on fire a part of my being that had not been touched for many years. It became more and more evident that God was calling me to travel down a road I had thought I would never set foot on again.

My partner Kelly and I began to attend a local Quaker meeting, as it was both a supportive community and a place where the silence of worship allowed for my own journey and approach to the Holy. Its strong commitment to social justice and peacemaking also helped me feel at home. In the silence, I often prayed over and over again, "Not my will, but yours, O God." I listened and waited for guidance. I hoped that the word I would receive would be a call to become a Quaker and join this new community in which I had found comfort and solace. That call never came. Finding a place in this Quaker community only awakened a deeper longing to find that place among the people of my roots.

I had left the Mennonite Church before I could be kicked out, but now I suddenly cared about belonging. I began, slowly and tentatively, to attend a local Mennonite church that I had been told was the most liberal in Vancouver. Afraid of rejection and the pain of having the door closed on all that I wanted to share, I remained silent about my relationship with Kelly. I came out to a few people with whom I felt safe, but I told myself that it was better to become part of the community first and then come out as lesbian. I figured that this way they would know me and value my contributions and have a harder time rejecting me once they discovered my "secret."

There were some payoffs to this tactic. I was invited to preach a number of times and my gifts were well received. The downside was the sweaty panic that would break over me whenever the topic of homosexuality came up, and I was tossed into the mental torture of trying to decide whether this was the time to tell people I was lesbian. Too afraid of having to face those potentially empty, uncomfortable moments when people shift uneasily, clear their throats, and don't look me in the eye, not to mention the loss of a community I was just beginning to establish, I invariably allowed the moment to pass.

It was becoming more and more obvious to me that I would never be a full member, or even a full participant, as long as I could not speak freely about the things that might reveal I was lesbian. When a close friend was terminally diagnosed with leukemia, I felt comfortable asking for prayers for her, but never for her female partner. When Kelly and I were going through tough times in our own relationship, I didn't feel comfortable going to my church community for support and insight. Even when I was speaking casually about my day to day activities, it took effort to edit out any reference to "my partner and I." Most of the time, my presence in the church was cloaked in subtle unrest and fear. Nevertheless, for a few years I attended the church in this manner, never feeling fully comfortable, always remaining somewhere on the edge of community life. I wasn't sure whether this was simply a case of not finding the right "fit," or whether I was preventing my own welcome in the community by not giving the community a chance to welcome all of me.

Although Vancouver School of Theology was somewhat of a haven, my choices of a course of study were affected by my knowledge that certain doors of opportunity were closed to me. Rather than pursuing a Master of Divinity in preparation for pastoral ministry, I chose to graduate with a Master of Theological Studies. When I was encouraged to consider publishing some of my papers incorporating Anabaptist themes and approaches, I felt discouraged and never took the advice, thinking that any of my challenges and insights into Anabaptist hermeneutics or theology could easily be discredited and ignored because I was gay. When I was considering pursuing a Ph.D., and my cousin, who teaches at Canadian Mennonite University, told me that they were looking for more women to teach on their faculty, I didn't even allow myself to think that one of those women might be me. Whatever I produced, whatever gifts I developed, I was constantly haunted by the possibility that they would not be received by the community to which I deeply desired to offer them.

I am grateful that God does not give up as easily as I am inclined to do and, in spite of the numerous dead ends I saw in all directions, God gave me a stubborn heart and a strong will. I refused to change my track. With passion and enthusiasm, I continued my studies at Vancouver School of Theology, bringing my Anabaptist tradition and my lesbian sexuality into conversation with theological ideas and biblical texts. I encountered a gospel that consistently reveals that God's wisdom and power is found in the foolish, a foolishness exemplified by the weak and despised Jew, Jesus of Nazareth, hanging upon the cross.

In Jesus, I found that the dualities we so often live by become blurred: male/female, law/gospel, insider/outsider, friend/enemy. The apostle Paul helped me to see that categories that defined, separated, and often oppressed people in the ancient world—Jew and Greek, slave and free, male and female—were broken apart and deemed to be of no consequence in God's kingdom. In the biblical stories, I encountered a vast array of situations in which God was present and active in places where a human, ever-changing morality found the people and activities unacceptable. I found an understanding of family that differed over time and place and that ultimately was at risk of becoming an idol that could usurp the place of Christ in our lives.

I recognized new life in the apostle Paul's proclamation that in Christ's death and resurrection there began the in-breaking of a new creation, a creation in which we are all called to question the powers of our day, to be fools for Christ, to be open to God's unsettling ways and amazing grace. The Anabaptist emphasis on the church as a counter-cultural community lifted up for me the vision of a church organized along entirely different lines than those the wider culture defines for us. All of this burst open a whole new world for me, and I began to understand my call from God as including and involving my lesbianism. My call from God was a call to be queer—in all senses of the term. Perhaps the greatest gift I could give to the church was my queerness, my place on the margins, my sexuality that challenged our human tendency to want to cling to worldly identities of gender.

All of this theological and biblical discovery only made me more committed to the Mennonite Church and more certain that God was calling me to minister to and with it. Even if I would have to work, teach, and preach in other Christian communities and institutions, I was not going to give up on the people to whom I belonged. I knew from the depths of my being that God's love and commitment to me did not rise or fall based on the gender of my life partner, and because of this assurance and trust in God's faithfulness, I figured I would be given the grace to persevere for the length of time it would take for the Spirit to open up for the church new ways of relating and new possibilities for community.

God indeed blessed me abundantly. After I graduated from Vancouver School of Theology, I decided to postpone any pursuit of further education in order to explore and deepen my understanding of peace, justice, and Christian discipleship. I wanted to put my theology and faith into action. In true Mennonite fashion, I began to look for an organization for which I could volunteer. I looked with the most interest at Christian Peacemaker Teams (CPT) and Mennonite Central Committee (MCC). Both had programs of nonviolent peacemaking that I respected. My choice of CPT rather than MCC was at least in part because CPT did not discriminate on the basis of sexual orientation. CPT was the only Mennonite organization that would offer me a place where I could live out with integrity and honesty my commitments to what I considered some of the foundations of my faith—nonviolent peacemaking and sacrificial love.

My Christian Peacemaker Team in Hebron, Palestine, became my first experience of a predominately Mennonite community where being lesbian was not seen as inhibiting my ability to be a disciple of Christ. I could struggle with the questions that nonviolent commitments in a violent, unjust world thrust upon a believer in Christ. I could test the limits of my ability to love my enemy even when angry eyes and loaded guns came my way. I could risk dying to my self over and over again and taste the sweet promise of a different sort of living together each time faith led me to the edge of hell and asked that I still believe in the overwhelming power of life. I could love God and love my neighbor and love myself—no one needed to be left out.

Discovering for the first time since my childhood the profundity of belonging as a full member of a Christian community, I returned to Vancouver with the resolution to come out as lesbian to the Mennonite Church there that had supported my work with CPT. I asked a few trusted friends in the congregation to set up a meeting with a larger group of congregants—mostly, but not entirely, people who I thought would be more or less supportive. For the first time ever, I publicly shared my journey as a lesbian Mennonite and my hope of becoming a more central part of the life of the congregation.

I don't remember much of that evening, other than mixed feelings of relief that my "secret" was out in the open, surprise at how many people assured me they were glad I was a part of the church and respected my commitment to Christ, and a gnawing sense of unease that, even so, this was not going to change my overall discomfort with the congregation.

I sincerely believed that what I needed was not a congregation to unequivocally embrace me as a lesbian, but rather a congregation that was willing to walk with the Holy Spirit and me, guided by possibility rather than fear. Rightly or wrongly, I did not sense that this was the place. Even though there continued to be a core of people who sincerely valued my presence at the church, before long I was hearing word that others were disgruntled about the way I had "come out" to such a large group of people and about what this might mean for the church's relationship with the conservative British Columbia Mennonite Conference. Other people were relieved that I wasn't asking to become a member of the congregation. I was not surprised that the step I had taken did not end up taking me through a doorway into a greater sense of belonging. Even fewer people spoke with me at coffee time, and my invitations to preach dried up.

On the other hand, I was getting invitations to preach and speak all over Vancouver's Lower Mainland, even in some of the most conservative evangelical Mennonite Brethren congregations. I was invited to preach and teach about my experiences in Palestine and Israel with Christian Peacemaker Teams. For the most part, I welcomed the opportunities to speak about my journey in nonviolent, active peacemaking, and enjoyed the irony of knowing that a lesbian was preaching and teaching people who would swear that people like me have been abandoned by God.

Although at times I wondered when the "shoe would drop" and whether people would think that I had deceived them by accepting invitations without "confessing" that I was lesbian, I ultimately decided not to silence an important message of peacemaking, discipleship, and faithfulness because of other people's misconceptions. To do so seemed to me like giving power to a force that I do not believe comes from God.

Through the extensive network I created due to my teaching and preaching, I soon got hooked up with other Mennonite people in the Vancouver area who were committed to peace and justice. Doors began to open, and before long I was invited to be part of a gathering of people that we decided to call "The Gathering." These were mostly Mennonites, although not exclusively, who all felt somewhat on the fringe of the church and yet wanted to gather together to discuss topics of depth and Spirit. Both my partner and I were welcome, and in the openness of a common search, we found a community where we could connect and grow. That group continues to be the cornerstone of my Mennonite connection and an undeniable blessing in my life.

By this time, I had almost stopped attending the Mennonite congregation in Vancouver, although I continued to hope that I might be able to find a congregation in which to worship. Then I got another sort of invitation. A Sunday school class from a Mennonite church in Langley, British Columbia (thirty minutes east of Vancouver), invited me to speak to them about being a lesbian Mennonite. The church was one I had kept my eye on for a while and had considered attending. Some of my friends from The Gathering were part of that congregation. I knew they were involved in many social justice projects locally and globally. In fact, I had preached one of my first sermons about my work with

CPT from their pulpit. My previous tactic of becoming part of a congregation before coming out had not assured my acceptance, so I figured that beginning this relationship with the truth might actually be a better way forward. I accepted the invitation.

My years in Palestine had taught me much humility when it comes to conflicts between people of competing truths. In Palestine and Israel, many different groups, including Christian Peacemaker Teams, were doing what they were doing in the name of God. Lives were risked and people were martyred as witnesses to each irreconcilable vision of what God was doing in the world and how we must respond.

Who was right? Where was God in all of this? How could any one of us know with certainty that we had chosen the right path in the face of such competing truth claims? All these questions led not to answers or certainty but to a complete reliance on God's faithfulness, love, and mercy to us all—an ultimate trust that God could and would find a way towards reconciliation, using our fallible attempts at faithfulness to do the unimaginable and impossible. I discovered that disagreement about important matters of truth need not divide, but could be the very things that draw us together into a greater dependency on God's faithfulness and mercy.

This is what I tried to emphasize that day as I shared my story with Langley Mennonite Fellowship. God's gift to us in Christ was the breaking down of the barriers that divide us into warring parties. We could love our enemies not because we no longer had any, but because what divides us is no longer as important as what unites us. If in all faithfulness I could not call something sinful that I experienced to be holy, I was only asking that others trust my commitment to God and God's commitment to me. In return, I would also work on trusting that God's faithfulness to the Body of Christ would result in a coming together in unimaginable ways with those with whom I also thoroughly disagreed and thought to have a faulty theology and biblical perspective. I was ready to be part of a Mennonite community in which there were competing truth claims as long as we could all trust God's faithfulness to one another and to the church.

That kind of faith makes its demands—whether it is in the middle of a war-zone as I experienced in Hebron or in the middle of a divided church as I continued to encounter at home. It demands a re-conception of expectation, a redefinition of success, a reliance not on numbers or positions of power but on forbearance, forgiveness, a commitment to truth, and a willingness to suffer. The greatest test to my faith may turn out not to have been the peacemaking I strove to do in a community a world away, but the peacemaking I must do in the community that is my own future. Here my passport will not protect me. Here the wounds I may receive cut far beneath the surface. Here I have nothing but the strength of my own vulnerable self, my convictions, and my faith that with God all things are possible.

As I look into an uncertain future, I pray that God will make the pathway clear with each step I take. I continue to be afraid of rejection and the pain of being silenced, shut out, and judged unfairly, yet I am comforted by the knowledge that even in my darkest nights there has always been light to be seen and companionship to be found. God has never failed to provide such beacons on my journey.

My greatest joy was sharing my vows of love and life commitment in a chapel full of friends and family, including Mennonites from nearly all of the various Christian communities with whom I have walked throughout my lifetime, and having them pronounce my partner Kelly and I married—in true Anabaptist style—without needing to wait for the authorities, be they from the world or from the church, to share in the blessing.

God is good. The future is open. And the very craziest of second comings is yet to occur.

---

* Lawrence Ferlinghetti, "Christ Climbed Down," *A Coney Island of the Mind: Poems by Lawrence Ferlinghetti. (New York: New Directions Publishing, 1958) 69-70.*

Anita Fast, M.T.S., lives with her partner Kelly and two other housemates in a community in Vancouver, British Columbia. She is the Coordinator of Admissions and Academic Planning at the Vancouver School of Theology. Anita enjoys reading, writing, deep conversations, playing soccer, and dancing to ABBA.

CHAPTER 18

When the Truth Is Told, Who Will Be There to Listen?

Amy Short

Preface

In the spring of 2002, I was contacted by Vange Thiessen for help to solicit authors for a Mennonite Central Committee (MCC) Women's Concerns publication about women who have left the church. She was looking for a lesbian or bisexual perspective and wanted to know if I had any suggestions for potential writers. I contacted a number of Mennonite and Church of the Brethren women I knew, but the lackluster response I received told me there was a strong sense of ambivalence from these women.

Wanting to have this perspective present, I considered writing something myself, but I felt a little out of place doing so. Not only was I an active participant in a local Mennonite congregation, but I was also employed as Executive Director of the Brethren Mennonite Council for Lesbian, Gay, Bisexual, and Transgender Interests (BMC)—an organization engaged in confronting the life and workings of the institutional church. When speaking with Vange, I told her I would be happy to put some thoughts together, but the reality for many GLBT individuals is not the sense that we have left the church but that the church has left us. She agreed that I could write the piece from that perspective, and I quickly went to work. I submitted the following article in June of 2002.

MCC Women's Concerns Report—How the Church Left Me

Some of my earliest childhood memories revolve around church and the feeling of comfort I experienced there. My father, who was a pastor, would travel from church to church on Sunday mornings, and my sister and I were often left to ourselves during the service. Many times, I found myself on the lap of one of the white-haired women in the front pews. I was warm from the heat of their bodies and from the enduring love of the Spirit. Often if I was acting up during a sermon, I would feel a gentle hand on my shoulder and hear a soft voice whisper, "I don't think your father would like you doing that." On the rare Sunday that my mother wasn't working at the hospital or singing in the choir, I would find myself cuddled up next to her, gleefully singing alto to her crystal soprano voice. I found myself comforted in the warm embrace of the church.

In high school, I found church took on a new meaning for me. It was the beginning of the Gulf War, and I needed a place to explore my pacifist beliefs and a deeper spiritual connection, so I attended the local Brethren in Christ congregation. Both of my parents were attending there as well, and they eventually became members. Through the years, the people in the BIC Church became my friends, my companions, and my community. I fondly remember producing Christmas pageants, serving as an usher and an acolyte, singing with my mother during special music, and reading Scripture from the pulpit. My gifts were called out and affirmed, and I was grateful to have an opportunity to serve my Creator and my community in these ways.

Then I came out of the closet as a lesbian. I wouldn't say that I faced active rejection from anyone from that community, but it was clear to me that there would be no future for me in leadership, either within the congregation, or in the broader BIC denomination.

During a women's Bible study class, my mother shared with her classmates that I was a lesbian. Many of the women shared with my mother that they supported her and me, but others made it clear that, while they loved me as a person, they could not recognize my relationship with another woman and would not affirm my membership in the congregation. As more and more people within the congregation learned about my orientation, smiles became forced, conversations became trite, and invitations to participate in the life of the church became less and less frequent. The warm embrace of the church was beginning to feel more like a cold shoulder.

As this was developing, I began to learn about the struggles in other denominations as well. The injustices that were taking place in the Presbyterian, American Baptist, Church of the Brethren, Mennonite, and other denominations did not resonate with my understanding of the central message of the Gospels. These churches and denominations were forgetting about Jesus' ministry with the outcast, the poor, and the marginalized. These institutions were so busy drawing a line in the sand that they were forgetting Jesus' embodied actions of God's reign—an open table where all were invited to eat and drink of the Spirit. The warm embrace of the church had let me go to wander in the wilderness. I made a promise to myself to never again be part of a church that actively participated in homophobia and heterosexism without first calling it to accountability for those actions.

I left angry and bitter and cold. In college, I continued to wander for a while but found myself missing that community and that communal experience of worship. I explored other faiths and visited Protestant denominations who would accept my gifts. I made contact with the Brethren Mennonite Council for Lesbian and Gay Concerns (BMC) and became acquainted with people who shared my experience. BMC gave the communal experience I desired. Sometime later I relocated to Minnesota to serve BMC as a voluntary service worker and eventually as the executive director.

I became involved in the Saint Paul Mennonite Fellowship (SPMF), a publicly affirming member of the Supportive Congregations Network (SCN) and was eventually re-baptized at age twenty-six. I found a community in SPMF that welcomed and affirmed my gifts for ministry, and I can't imagine my life without the support of this congregation. My basic needs of fellowship, support, and a community of like-minded peacemakers are met as I continue to be confronted with obstacles in the Brethren and Mennonite denominations. At the end of every worship service, we hold hands and pray together the Lord's Prayer. Each Sunday, I am warmed and comforted by this embrace. I forget from time to time about the troubles in the broader church and the fact that the larger Mennonite denomination would not acknowledge my call to Christian ministry.

I was harshly reminded of that the summer I served as a delegate to the Nashville 2001 Assembly. After the gathered body strongly affirmed membership guidelines that actively promote heterosexism and infer discipline of leaders who participate in same-sex unions, the delegates heard a pleading cry for future leaders. We listened to staggering statistics of a shortage of pastors, and I found myself in tears, knowing that my gifts were needed but were not welcomed in this denomination.

As I sat in tears, I felt a hand on my shoulder. It belonged to the woman next to me at the table. The others in my table group knew why I was crying, and a man from Lancaster Conference asked what they, as a group, could do to support me. He then asked the woman with her hand on my shoulder to lead us in a time of prayer. As the rest of the delegate body sang a hymn and moved on to the next item of business, my table sat in prayer for me, my gifts, and the denomination. It was a glimpse of hope for me. I don't know what the others at the table shared with their congregations about that experience, but for a brief moment I felt the warm embrace of the church once again.

I felt that same warmth in June as I witnessed the first ordination of an openly gay man in the Church of the Brethren. As the gathered body of credentialed leaders laid their hands on Matt and prayed over him, I imagined the warmth he must have felt, not just from their hands, but also from the affirmation of his gifts of ministry. I don't know if it is a warmth I will ever feel, but I live in the hope that one day the church will open her doors to all whom God chooses to send.

I often think of how I felt when the church first left me behind. I still have feelings of bitterness, anger, and coldness, but from time to time, I see glimpses of hope as I did in June. There are days like today when I feel like the church is looking over her shoulder at me and gesturing for me to come back into her arms. I do long for that holy embrace once again.

Postscript

It feels like a lifetime since I wrote that article. At the time I was impressed with MCC's willingness to seek out this perspective. I was prepared to reconsider my choice not to support them financially, and I was prepared to compliment MCC for taking a pretty big step toward furthering the conversation on LGBT issues in the church.

Luckily, I didn't waste a lot of time in my preparations.

I submitted the article to Vange in June. In September, I received a letter from the editor, a check for my work, and a copy of the publication that did not contain my article. The editor offered her personal apology for not printing my story. The Executive Director of MCC felt the topic was "too controversial" for many within MCC's constituency. The editor did mention in her introduction to the issue the intent to include a lesbian perspective, but this is the first time this piece has seen general readership.

At the time, I was disappointed but not terribly surprised. In my head, I had drafted my response to MCC, telling them that I had donated my honorarium to BMC (which I had), because it is an organization that wasn't afraid of creating a little controversy in order to make room for tolerance. I was going to tell them that I felt the printed issue was dishonest and that it was disingenuous to publish an issue on this topic without giving voice to a large group of women for whom this experience rings true. Instead, I put the article aside for a time when I felt it could be used.

That time is now. A year and a half has passed since I wrote the original piece and much has changed. The Church of the Brethren voted against recognizing the ordination of openly GLBT individuals. Matt Smucker has transferred his ordination to the United Church of Christ, and I have resigned as Executive Director of BMC to pursue other endeavors. I spent the last four months studying theology and the arts at United Theological Seminary of the Twin Cities, but I find an even greater distance growing between me and the institutional church. While I remain active in my local congregation, I find myself in a state of righteous ambivalence toward the broader denomination and toward ordination in particular.

Over the last six months, I participated in a number of ecumenical ventures. I am finding more and more that ordination is being used less as an instrument of calling out and affirming the gifts of those who seek to serve the church and more as an instrument of systematic oppression.

In a small group discussion at seminary last fall, one of my class-mates mentioned her support of GLBT individuals and her uncertainty of ordination if she is honest about this. She struggles with how she can affect change within the denomination if she can't have access to the denomination. I can't recall how we discussed this at the time, but I think the way I would respond to her question now is to ask the follow-ing question: When does the cost of silence outweigh the cost of truth?

For me, the cost of remaining silent has been far greater than the cost of telling the truth. I no longer wait for the broader church to em-brace me once again. I have found solace and encouragement from my participation in the Saint Paul Mennonite Fellowship. I am in awe of this congregation's ability to turn tragedy into resurrection again and again. I continue to be amazed at how I feel my sense of call satisfied in lay leadership of a congregation that truly lives into the vision of a priesthood of all believers. Today I understand my call to embody the spirit of the early Anabaptists, participating in an anomalous commu-nity of dissent that calls the greater church to accountability. I am for-tunate that I have found a community that allows me to fulfill that call. For this, I give thanks again and again. Amen.

Amy Short spent four and a half years with the Brethren Mennonite Council for Lesbian, Gay, Bisexual, and Transgender Interests, serving as executive director from 2000 to 2003. Amy and her partner Rachel live in Minneapolis, Minnesota, with their nine-year-old cat Fruvous.

CHAPTER 19

An Exciting Journey

Ken Roth

I was raised in a loving Christian family. My father was a Mennonite minister in a small country church in southern Ohio. My mother was a very important part of Dad's ministry throughout their lives together, until the Lord welcomed her home in June of 2003. She was the most loving person I have ever known. I am the youngest of four children, with two sisters and a brother. My childhood was generally wonderful, a realization that becomes increasingly cherished when I think about kids who are raised in abusive or dysfunctional homes. I have been truly blessed, and I regret that I have often taken that fact for granted.

My parents consistently modeled an attitude of acceptance of others, regardless of race, differing religious views, socioeconomic status, or past indiscretions. Dad was the chaplain at a local branch of the Ohio Penitentiary, and he often expressed his sadness that the inmates were not treated with the respect that should be afforded to all human beings. Of course he disapproved of their crimes, which in some cases included rape and murder, but he saw the inmates as men with great potential to do good.

Everyone in the area knew what kind of people my parents were. I remember many times that people who were in need of something or other were referred to my parents, because everyone knew that my parents would do whatever they could to help them. I recall a time when two teenage boys ended up at our house after they had wrecked their car. (The driver was charged with DUI.) Fortunately they weren't seriously injured, but they needed a place to stay until someone could travel some distance to pick them up.

Mom was about to drive into town to get some groceries, and she asked them if they needed anything. One of the boys asked if she would get a pack of cigarettes for him. Much to my surprise, she did! I'm sure the poor kid had to endure her anti-smoking sermonette, but he got his cigarettes. I would have loved to have been a fly on the wall to see how self-conscious she was when she bought them. Incidentally, even though my parents strongly disapproved of smoking, they always kept an ash tray handy for visitors who felt they needed to smoke. This was just who my parents were.

My sexual identity was clear to me at least by first grade. I am definitely a heterosexual. My sexual fantasies have always been about females. The closest I have ever come to a homosexual experience was when my childhood friend taught me how to masturbate. We never actually touched each other...he just showed me how to do it. I don't remember ever having to deal with the topic of homosexuality during my childhood. I vaguely knew what it was and had a basic understanding that it was sinful, but I was never directly confronted with it. I now imagine that some of my school friends were probably gay, but I just did not know it.

My first realization that I actually knew a gay person came after I graduated from Eastern Mennonite College in 1979. During my final year, I had lived in an off-campus house with five other males. The summer after graduation, one of my housemates came out of the closet. I was stunned! I felt betrayed, deceived, embarrassed and incredibly stupid, all at the same time. This was hard to take. He was my friend—more like a brother—and he was gay. How could this be? He didn't *look* gay. I will have to admit, my immediate fear was that he had seen me naked at some time and had entertained wicked thoughts about me. There was something very emasculating about imagining that a gay guy had fantasized about me. The thought was simply disgusting.

About a year later, we had a reunion of all the guys from the house, including the gay housemate. Understandably, there were some uncomfortable silences. Finally, he asked us if we had any questions.

That was the start of what has become a fascinating and continuing journey for me. We spent the next hour or two asking him things people don't normally ask each other. One of the guys asked him if he had ever been attracted to any of us. When he answered, "No," my reaction was one of genuine disappointment. I was honestly upset. Then I realized that I had, in an instant, gone from being horrified that a gay housemate may have *looked* at me to being hurt that he had not. It was an eye-opening moment.

Our painfully honest question and answer session made me think that maybe this whole issue isn't so black-and-white after all. I was confused. This didn't fit with my upbringing, it was tough for me to deal with, and I didn't know what to do. I wondered what Jesus would have done. Since then I have become aware of other homosexual friends and have had some enlightening discussions with them as well. This was just the beginning of a personal search for God's truth for me, a journey that continues today, many years later.

I am now an Associate Professor of Biology at Eastern Mennonite University. Shortly after coming to EMU, I learned of a group of people who were preparing to publish a "Welcoming Open Letter on Homosexuality" in the February 17, 2000 issue of the *Mennonite Weekly Review*. My wife Terri and I read the letter and decided to add our signatures to it. (The letter can be found at www.welcome-committee. org/openletter.html.)

Several other faculty and staff at EMU also signed the letter, but because I had signed it a little late in the process, I didn't receive the letter of reprimand that our university president felt compelled to send to the signers. (I later requested a copy from his secretary.) There was some concern among this group that their employment might be terminated for this public show of support, but I never felt directly threatened at that time. In time, it seemed that the dust had cleared a bit, and people were becoming a little more relaxed. My brief experience with social activism had apparently ended.

In 2001, a sixteen-year employee of EMU was forced to resign because it was discovered that she was in a committed, same-sex relationship. I was acquainted with her, but I did not know her well. I had thought she was a lesbian; however, I wasn't absolutely sure. It really wasn't any of my business anyway. Nevertheless, her removal bothered me deeply, because the way she was forced to resign did not seem very Christ-like to me. It seemed too judgmental and violent. To have a sixteen-year career ended so suddenly must have been very painful for her.

I am aware of the official Mennonite stance on homosexuality, and I am sure it is based on prayerful interpretations of various biblical passages. I think it is very important for the church to have written accounts of our beliefs and principles, such as the *Confession of Faith in a Mennonite Perspective,*[1] the Saskatoon statement of 1986,[2] and the Purdue statement of 1987.[3] I appreciate the amount of prayer and dialogue that must have gone into the creation of those documents. However, I think we must also recognize that human beings are not infallible, and our search for clarity is a dynamic process that requires periodic review. When I witness what I believe to be a judgmental and violent act that is based upon the church's position, I find myself experiencing an inner conflict that compels me to review my position.

When the EMU employee was dismissed, I could understand on one level why the administration thought they had to take this action, but it still made me angry. I know that many people, including my parents, believe that the Bible tells us that homosexual activity is sinful. I used to feel the same way until I began to discover that some of my Christian friends were gay. (I used to think the term "gay Christian" was nonsense.) This prompted me to study the Bible more to try to resolve this conflict. The result of my study has been more confusion. I am really not sure what the Bible is saying. Does the Bible condemn homosexuality flat out, or is it talking more about sexual promiscuity, or gang rape, or other forms of sexual abuse? It depends on how you look at it.

When I encounter this kind of ambiguity, I must resort to prayerfully attempting to discern what is "right." When I look at the EMU employee, I see a good person who did positive things for EMU during her sixteen years there. It does not seem right that she was asked to leave because she *loved* someone. It seems a bit ironic.

By way of response, I wrote an article for the EMU student newspaper, *The Weather Vane,* that was entitled "Ken's Coming Out" (September 26, 2002). In this article, I expressed my convictions in the form of the following three confessions: (1) I, Ken Roth, believe that a person can be homosexual and a Christian at the same time; (2) I don't believe homosexuality is a choice people make, and I don't think the Bible condemns it as sin; and (3) I support covenanted unions (weddings) of homosexual couples.

As one might imagine, these statements were not well-received by every reader. I had expected that some would be concerned, but I did not anticipate the scope of the responses. I am happy to say that I received many e-mails, letters, and phone calls from people who were very supportive and grateful. I also received, to a lesser degree, feedback from those who were troubled by my confessions. The following are a few examples:

Late one evening, I got a phone call from an EMU supporter and father of a student. He had obtained my home phone number from the university president. Our conversation, which lasted over two hours, was never hostile or angry, for which I am thankful. He was concerned that I was causing great harm to EMU and to the church as a whole. I assured him that this was never my intent, and that I was deeply saddened that anyone would ever think that it was. I had a generally positive feeling about our conversation.

I also got a personal visit from a former EMU president who told me that if I felt this way, I should resign. After talking with him for a few minutes, I think he began to understand that I was responding to my own conscience, and that my intent was not malicious. We parted with a friendly handshake.

Perhaps the most devastating response was a letter written by a dear friend expressing his deep disappointment in me. Although the affirming, supportive letters I have received number nearly one hundred, this is the one that keeps popping into my head. I pray for healing.

Many of the responses were not sent to me directly, but were in the form of letters or articles published in *The Weather Vane.* I responded to some of these by writing additional articles and letters in an effort to explain how my journey had brought me to this place. I tried to write these in a tone that was confessional, rather than judgmental, but some readers saw my articles and letters as attacks, describing them as "cowboyish" and "in-your-face." I regret that I wasn't more careful with my writing. Tact has always been a growth area for me.

A culmination of this flurry of varied perspectives appearing in the *Weather Vane*, which is circulated not only on campus but to many constituents as well, was an action passed by the EMU Board of Trustees on November 9, 2002, which states that "persons who publicly advocate positions contrary to EMU's Philosophy, Mission Statement, Community Lifestyle Commitment, and *Confession of Faith in a Mennonite Perspective* are not abiding by their commitment and thereby jeopardize their positions as employees of the university."

I do not know if my story in this book will be viewed by the board as "public advocacy" or not. Their statements, like so many things, are subject to varied interpretations. I do feel comfortable publicly expressing that I wish things were different. I wish the official position of the Mennonite Church was different. I pray that we, as a church, will continue to search for God's truth together, and that we will arrive at a place where our official positions are in harmony with that truth. Perhaps, after much prayer and dialogue, our positions will remain as they are. Perhaps God will move us to change them.

Although I have not been directly threatened by authorities of the church or of EMU, I sense a need to "watch my step" in order to keep my job. I recently became eligible for a five-year contract renewal, the closest thing we have to tenure. At contract renewal time, a faculty member is evaluated based upon students' course evaluations, input from peers, and self-evaluation and other information supplied by the faculty member.

The undergraduate dean reviews the material and makes a recommendation to the Faculty Status Committee, which then accepts or rejects her recommendation. In my case, the dean recommended a three-year contract. Her reasons for the shorter contract included concerns that my "courses are lacking in rigor." This came as a surprise to me because, up to that point, I had not been aware of any concerns about my teaching effectiveness. In fact, the feedback I had been getting from students and administration were mostly positive.

My skills have generally been affirmed by course evaluations that are completed by students at the end of each semester. Their responses are organized into categories such as "overall quality of course" and "overall quality of instruction." In these two categories, I have consistently scored well above the EMU mean. This is very affirming for me. In a separate category designated "course was challenging" I have consistently scored at or near the university mean. I feel pretty good about this also. I think we have a very talented group of people on our faculty, and it is an affirmation to me that my course evaluations suggest that I am walking stride-for-stride with the majority of them in this respect.

My personal feeling was that my lesser contract was due to my public confessions concerning homosexuality rather than my teaching, so I sent a letter of appeal to the university president. However, before the Faculty Status Committee was able to reconvene to consider my appeal, I withdrew it. I had been told by colleagues that the Board of Trustees "would not be pleased" if it got to them. I perceived this to be a threat of dismissal. It just wasn't worth taking that risk.

If this is the worst that happens to me, then I am indeed blessed. I have been allowed to continue my ministry at EMU, and have made a lot of wonderful new friends—many of whom are gay. Sadly though, I have lost some friends as well, and it grieves me deeply. I will continue to seek God's truth and the wisdom to know when to speak and when to remain silent. It has been an exciting journey that will surely continue. I pray that God will continue to nudge us into ongoing loving dialogue so that one day the church will be one that truly welcomes and loves all of God's children. How wonderful if it would happen in my lifetime!

---

[1] A con-joint statement, published in 1995, of the tenets of faith of two Mennonite groups in North America, the Mennonite Church and the General Conference Mennonite Church. These

two groups merged to form the Mennonite Church Canada in 1999 and Mennonite Church USA in 2001.

[2] The "Resolution on Human Homosexuality" was adopted at the 1986 meeting of the triennial session of the General Conference Mennonite Church meeting in Saskatoon, Saskatchewan.

[3] "A Call to Affirmation, Confession, and Covenant Regarding Human Sexuality" was a resolution adopted by the Mennonite Church Assembly in 1987 in its biennial session held at Purdue University, Lafayette, Indiana.

Ken Roth, Ph.D., is an Associate Professor of Biology at Eastern Mennonite University in Harrisonburg, Virginia. His wife Terri is a full-time homemaker and is also a homeschool teacher to their three wonderful sons: Benjamin, Joseph, and Daniel.

CHAPTER 20

Searching for Integrity

Pat Spaulding

"Are you a lesbian?" "No, of course not!" I barked back at my mother. I couldn't believe she had asked me that. My young adult life was filled with enough turmoil in the late sixties and early seventies. My number one passion was being a peace activist. I wanted to be part of bringing justice and peace to a world of war and pollution. But the Vietnam War wasn't the only conflict I was aware of at the time. Within me another war raged. I felt like a casualty of that war every day as I tried to understand my own sexuality.

Thinking back, something happened somewhere between elementary school and junior high. One minute my best friends were boys. We had so much fun together—basketball, baseball, experimenting with our science kits, building forts—and then, wham! We couldn't be friends like that any more. We were growing up and it was time for me to start hanging out with girls. And life began to get complicated.

Why do teenagers have to be so class-conscious? I don't mean geography class either. I'm talking about the "in-group" and the "out-group," the "college preps" and "other" students. I'm sure the fact that my school put kids into numbered sections did not help. We were in groups from the "ones" to the "twelves." I was in the threes, not a bad group. It seemed that the most popular kids were in the first four groups. They set the standards for "popular." It was really hard to feel good about yourself at that age and being liked by others made all the difference.

My home economics class was unusually diverse with a mixture of all the numbered groups. All the girls had to take it, whether they were going to college or not, so it just got scrambled. One day a girl asked for someone to scratch her back. She was not in one of the first four groups. She was not popular; she was actually a little weird. None of the girls I knew wanted anything to do with her. Their response to her was, "What are you, a lezzie or something?" I whispered to one of them, "What's a lezzie?" That's when I found out that *it* was about the worst thing you could be called. *It* was the very opposite of popular.

A "lezzie"—oh, no. Could that be what I am? Oh, no. Please, no. So I went along with the games. I dressed the way popular kids dressed and hung out with them. I learned about the kind of music they liked and went to all the school dances. I hoped the popular boys would like me and ask me to dance. That was a real sign to everyone that you were "cool."

But it wasn't me. I was hiding very deep inside, just peeking out of my eyes, watching, waiting, holding my breath. No one could know my secret. No one could know that I would rather be dancing with a girl. No one could know that my clothes, my make-up, all of it felt so phony. It wasn't me, but it had to be. It was like playing a game, and I had to make every effort to win. There was no one to talk to. I ached for someone to know and accept the real me, but I could never let anyone know.

One summer at Cape Cod, I found myself "adopted" by a wonderful family, the Zieglers. They had a daughter my age, and I consider her my first genuine friend. I felt like I could really trust her. We stayed up all night talking about everything—almost everything. We drank fancy teas and burned incense while listening to her Baroque and my Joni Mitchell music. Then we watched the sunrise from a cliff over the ocean near the lighthouse. It was a wonderful summer and my self-control was working a double shift, but I could not risk the wonderful relationship. She never knew about the real me; that was one thing I could not share. She did not know how I felt about her. She did not know how much it hurt to have feelings for her that I knew could never be returned, to fear that, if she were aware of them, she might completely reject my friendship.

My attraction to girls and disinterest in boys continued through high school. I was pretty popular, though, and had lots of dates. Occasionally I even went steady. That was a real sign of success. The only one who seemed to notice my discomfort was my mother. If I was happy when I came in the door after a date, it meant there was no good-night kiss. If I was miserable, she knew things had gotten mushy. When I graduated, the yearbook statement under my photo read, "There's something about her that sets her apart." If they only knew!

I wondered, "What is wrong with me? Why can't I be like the other girls?" There were some really nice boys, and I loved having them as friends, but as soon as things got the least bit intimate, I had to fly. On the other hand, about the time the other girls began getting crushes on boys, I began to get crushes on girls. Why couldn't I have a date with one of them? Never!

I spent the summer after my graduation alone, roaming around Europe. My parents had just divorced and life felt even more confusing. It was more than a travel adventure—I was searching for answers. I became friends with a Buddhist and asked him a steady stream of questions. Maybe, I hoped, some belief system would hold the answers to understanding myself. I visited great cathedrals, and at one I was impressed by all the crutches and canes that were left behind by those who had been healed. Maybe even Christianity held the answer. And then, one night, a group of German students invited me to a tent revival. If it had not been held in the German language, I probably would have answered the altar call.

I returned home from my adventure and went off to college as an art major. Between my passion for peace and the turmoil of my sexuality confusion, my ability to stick to my studies was not very good. I quit school in an all-out effort to maintain my sanity. A friend and I rented a house together. We really hit it off, and one night I could not stand it any longer. I told her I was in love with her. I couldn't believe it—she didn't reject me!

We lived together off and on for about three years. During that time, we shared an affectionate relationship. I thought I could have committed myself to her forever, but she was not a lesbian and continued her search for the right man. She encouraged me to do the same and I tried. She would say, "He's such a great guy and you have so much in common." And I would think, "Yeah, that's true, but I just can't—I don't feel the same way toward him as he feels toward me. I don't feel the same for him as I do for her." It was hard and after three years I had to leave.

I headed up to Maine in my VW bus to look for land. Maybe I should become a hermit. I wandered and looked and thought and cried. At Baxter State Park, I started up Mt. Katahdin for a day of hiking. It was a beautiful day and it felt good walking up the trail. I had left later in the day than I should have to hike all the way to the top, but I kept going and going. I had passed the tree line long ago and was hopping from rock to rock, getting closer and closer to the summit. Finally, I reached it. What a view! It was lonely, but it was also very beautiful— just me, the large rocks, the vast sky, and the sun that was already quite low. I needed to get down quickly or I would be alone on a dark mountain—alone with the bears.

I followed the paint marks on the rocks that indicated the trail direction. Hopping from rock to rock I suddenly realized that I had lost my way. There were no more paint marks. I looked and looked. They were gone. "What should I do?" I wondered as I tried not to panic. I sat down and closed my eyes. "God, if you're there, please help me." I opened my eyes and there it was—the paint mark! Whew! I flew down that mountain, arriving at my bus in the dark, exhausted and sore. I crawled into my sleeping bag and slept fitfully, nightmare after nightmare. The next morning, I headed for Cape Cod and spent the rest of the summer with my adopted family.

The Zieglers went to church regularly, and I was very impressed with the quality of their relationships. They had something special, and I wondered what the secret was. They knew I was interested in the Bible, and the following winter they sent me one. It came at a very low time for me. Why did life have to hurt so much? I was lonely, confused and probably a lesbian. "What could possibly be worse?" I thought. I started to read the Bible and the study guide they sent. For the first time, I understood that Jesus not only died, but he also rose from the dead and there was a reason for it all.

I didn't understand the stuff about being "saved," and "eternal life" did not have much meaning for me either; however, the idea that I could become a "new creation" appealed to me. I wanted a chance to start over again, especially knowing that God was on my side, helping me. The Bible said that the truth would set me free. Truth and freedom were both things I had been trying to find for so long. It also said that if I put God first in my life, everything else would fall into place and I would have what I really wanted—things that God actually knew better than I did myself.

I felt like I could not be a more total wreck. What did I have to lose by asking God to take over? So I sat alone on the floor of the little house that I rented in the woods and opened myself to God. I experienced peace and I knew God was really there. I sat alone in the dark for a very long time and God took care of me, giving me a kind of comfort I had never experienced before.

Things began to change after that. I read my Bible nonstop and thought I must be the only one to experience God in a personal way. I never understood any of this from the churches I had attended growing up. I decided I would wait a year, just to be absolutely sure it was real, before I told anyone. At the end of that year, I went out and bought Bibles for everyone I knew. I told them all about what I had done a year before and the new connection I felt with God as a result. It was obvious that something was changing in me.

I re-established good relations with both my parents and every other relative I could find. I went back to school and soon became involved in a campus Christian group, leading Bible studies and telling others what I had learned about how to experience God's love. At the time, I thought this was another way to bring justice and peace to the world. Looking back at that time, I now realize that I actually began to be more conformed to the images of others in that group than the unique individual I was created to be. It was great to be part of a group, but I wasn't really strong enough to trust God's unique work in my own life. Integrity was beyond my grasp.

I felt like I had to be like the other women in the group, even though it didn't feel like me. I thought it was what God wanted me to do. The Bible said that you had to "deny yourself," so that was what I thought I was doing. I went to classes, did homework, held a job, went to Christian meetings and Bible studies, read my Bible, and prayed. I had no time just to be myself, to use my own unique gifts and talents, to be the artist God created me to be, to meet my own needs. I was afraid to be me, yet as hard as I tried, I also sensed some rejection from the leaders of the group because they seemed to know that I was somehow different.

Graduation was drawing near, and I was offered a scholarship to a prestigious university to continue in my field, but I felt like God had other plans for me. The campus group I had been involved with practically begged students to join their staff after graduation. For some reason, however, they seemed to hesitate when I asked for an application. It didn't come as a surprise when I was rejected.

I began looking into other opportunities for service. Soon, I found myself traveling across the country to take graduate courses in preparation for service overseas. I applied to join a missionary organization and, to my surprise, I was accepted. I thought for sure when they read my answers to the questions on homosexuality they would reject me. I was intensely questioned by three older men in a tiny room. It was the most intimidating experience I've ever had. I answered their painful questions with painful honesty and that seemed to satisfy them.

I had been too preoccupied to develop any social attachments since becoming a Christian. Maybe *it* was gone? Maybe God had really changed me. No. That summer I had a great roommate and we were soon the best of friends. Once again, *it* was there. I was so disappointed. I pleaded with God to free me from same-gender attraction. I told my roommate about *it*, and I also told the young man who had become interested in me. Together the three of us prayed, and at the end of the summer we went our separate ways.

I went to seminary to continue my preparations, continuing my efforts to fit into the Christian subculture, at least in appearance. I never felt comfortable with Christian lingo. And I was beginning to learn that there was some diversity among Christians. Maybe I could begin to express myself again through my artwork? Whenever there was an opportunity to use my sketches in an assignment, I did and it felt great.

I developed a whole entourage of male friends. The Bible college/ seminary campus had very conservative rules to govern male/female relationships, and it was perfect for me. When some of the men expressed their serious intentions, I began to wonder about the possibility of marriage. Whatever God wanted me to do, I would obey.

I began a master's program at the suggestion of my organization. After two semesters, I found out the reason they were encouraging my studies was to give me more time to develop a relationship I had with a certain young man. I was furious. We were just friends. I decided that would be my last semester before leaving for my assignment overseas. However, during that semester, I met another young man who was so much like me! It seemed to me that most of the Christians I had met were alike—and I was different. But this guy and I had so much in common. It was so refreshing to me. We both liked the same kind of music, art, photography, the outdoors, bicycling—just about everything. And we only had about two weeks left before classes finished.

It was an exciting time, and we soon came to the same conclusion that God might want us to be partners. Within three weeks we were engaged. Before we made that decision, I told him of my homosexual tendency, and we figured God would make it go away. So, by faith, I accepted my role of wife four months later. I was determined to make it work, to trust God to work in me to be the perfect wife in every way. What I may have lacked in sexual enthusiasm, I tried to make up for in other ways.

We went overseas together in 1980 and soon became parents. My life was consumed with parenting and homemaking, as we developed relationships with the people in our isolated mountain village. Life was more about survival than anything else. The physical part of our relationship didn't seem to be getting any easier for me, as I had thought it would, but I didn't feel able to talk with my husband about it. I didn't want to hurt his feelings. Therefore, subconscious negative feelings built up in me that leaked into other areas of the relationship or occasionally just exploded.

On visits to town, we enjoyed friendships with other English-speaking expatriates. Occasionally I would feel twinges of attraction to other women, and it always disappointed me to think God still had not taken *it* away. We became friends with another married missionary who shared the same struggle, and gradually learned of a number of others as well, including one who chose to end his tormented life.

I sought counseling on several occasions with Christian counselors, and their responses varied from one extreme to the other. None was very helpful. Suicide entered my mind on a number of occasions and there was nowhere to turn. I felt God's presence always and asked for help constantly. I tried everything and nothing worked. Could it be that God didn't think there was anything wrong with me? Why did I think something was wrong, if God did not?

Some of the things I learned overseas have been very helpful in finding peace with life's mysteries. It is hard to live in a different culture without gaining a greater understanding of one's self and humankind— the unity and the diversity. There is value in both being the same and being unique at the same time. We become more flexible and able to live with ambiguity. We develop a wider perspective. Imagine how wide God's perspective must be—not seeing life through the narrow lens of just one culture or even a few but having an understanding of everything that transcends all cultures.

Because I lived in a different culture, I became aware of the way biblical concepts may have to be understood differently in different times and places. What is crucial in Scripture is the meaning that was intended, not just the words. How can someone in another culture understand the meaning behind "the bread of life" if they have no idea what bread is? How many other biblical concepts carry cultural information that we don't understand?

We had made our home in a far away culture for sixteen years, but our children were getting older, our work in the village seemed to be at a good stopping place, and my mother needed us back home. We packed up for the last time and moved back to the USA. The decision to return was harder than the decision to go.

One of the first things I did when we returned was to attend the annual conference of Exodus, a Christian organization that claims to help people change their sexual orientation. I attended worship services, prayer meetings, lectures, workshops, seminars, collected reading materials, and bought books. I talked with as many people as I could.

Most of the people I talked with who claimed to be "healed of their homosexuality" didn't seem to actually be homosexual in the first place. Some of them had suffered some kind of trauma, such as child abuse or rape, that set them on a path of distorted sexuality. When they began to heal from that experience, they gradually moved more toward their true sexuality. Others I met seemed to be bisexual, somewhere close to the middle of the gay and straight continuum. They were more fluid in their sexual orientation and could go either way, just as capable of feeling drawn to men as to women. The only people I met like me, people who had always felt far to the gay end of the continuum and did not recall ever having a traumatic experience, were wondering when they would be changed. When were we going to be "healed?"

I drove home from the conference with plenty of time to pray and think. God seemed to replace my turmoil with peace, and I was able to be thankful for being created the way I was. When my husband and I first considered marriage and a life in missions, we trusted God to take care of all our needs. At that time, the needs we thought of were financial support, good health, and safety. Those needs are still important, but we also need to trust for our deep personal needs. A mixed orientation marriage is complicated at every level, not just the physical. We need to learn how to be really honest with ourselves, and good, open, honest communication with each other is essential.

We visited a number of churches, trying to find a place where our family could feel at home, but none of them seemed to share the same values we had come to embrace. We were eventually invited to a Mennonite church and it was a perfect fit. We were pacifists and felt very comfortable with the entire ethos of simple living and service. In preparation for membership, we read the church's confession of faith and learned that Mennonites bravely held a number of beliefs that set them apart from other churches we had attended. They weren't afraid to be different. To "do justice, love mercy, and walk humbly with God" was actually a way of life. That was exciting to us.

Since moving back to the States, I have spent many hours reading and studying about homosexuality and what God wants. I have prayed and meditated about what I have studied in relation to my personal experience. I have spent productive time in both secular and pastoral counseling and worked through some serious depression as a result of my sexuality. It was never my choice, and I tried everything to make *it* go away. Now I feel content to be who I am. There are no easy answers. I now work at a Mennonite school where every day I face the conflict between mainstream Christianity and gay Christians—not just in my personal life. It seems as if even the Mennonite Church has gone to war. We travel the world over as peace builders, and yet I can't help feeling hypocritical, knowing we are helping in other conflicts while ignoring our own. Where is integrity?

What would happen if the Mennonite Church took up the challenge to transform the conflict with people like me? What would happen if homosexual young people could come to our churches and colleges and find love, acceptance, role models, and wise guidance? What would happen if the church blessed the love of same-gender couples who wanted to commit to each other? What is the alternative? Isn't it throwing lives away—pushing them into darkness, when it's light they seek; tossing them into promiscuity, when love and a stable home are what they want? To pose a serious question that has become a cliché: "What would Jesus do?" I pray and hope that we will all quiet our own inner voices and listen to God as we all seek to bring justice and peace to the world together.

We must be the change we wish to see in the world. ~ Gandhi

Pat Spaulding, who works at Eastern Mennonite University, is married with three children. Writing this piece for publication was very important to her because there are certainly others who share the same experience, and they need to know they are not alone. Also, the many people who have not had this experience need to realize that there are people they know personally who have secrets like this. It's more than an issue; it's people whom we know and for whom we care.

Pat would like to thank the many friends and family who helped her with editing. It was a very special project; however, it also worked together with increasing inner pressures that she has felt for a long time to accelerate some very hard talks with her husband and children. In an agonizing step toward personal integrity, Pat has made the difficult decision to leave her marriage.

* * *

Editor's note: *Sybil Heerdegen, Pat's mother, wrote the following reflections after her daughter revealed her lifelong secret and read the story written for this book.*

When my darling little daughter was born, I knew she was my angel and a miracle. The doctors had told me after an operation that it was possible, but not probable, that I would ever get pregnant. Therefore, you can imagine my joy and the joy of our family when she was born.

She was everything I dreamed of—almost. Instead of being a feminine little thing that I could dress in ruffles and lace, she wanted blue jeans and sneakers. Instead of dolls, she wanted trucks. I just had to realize I had a tomboy and let it go.

She excelled in everything and was musical and very artistic. She was an active participant in the Girl Scouts. Her teachers used to tell me how much they enjoyed having her in their classes. She skied all winter and spent the summers playing tennis, surfing, and riding her bike.

As she got older, she was very popular and immensely enjoyed group activities with her friends. When her girlfriends began to get boyfriends, however, she really wasn't that interested. She did have plenty of dates, but did not seem to enjoy herself. My husband and I just thought she was shy and laughed about it.

In college, she became very active with a Christian group and ended up going on to seminary. She always enjoyed travel and adventure and was interested in working outside the country. I didn't approve of this because I hated the thought of her being single in a far-away place. By that time, most of her friends were married, but she still was not interested.

Then one day a young man called to tell us that he would like to marry her. He will never know how pleased we were. They married soon and went overseas as missionaries together. I was heartbroken that they were so far away, but happy that she wasn't alone anymore. We corresponded and talked by phone for years. Every four years or so, they would come for a visit. Each time they would bring a new addition to the family. They made such a beautiful family. She and her husband seemed to be made for one another.

After they had been gone more than fifteen years, my husband died and I was all alone. I was not in good health and did not do well on my own, so I decided to move into an independent living retirement facility. My daughter and her family had been thinking about returning to the States anyway, so they came at that time to help me with the move and to be nearby in case I needed them.

It was the happiest time of my life. I was able to see my grandchildren grow up and enjoy my wonderful family. Their lives revolved around their church and church activities. The children seemed to be happy and didn't have any of the serious problems you hear about young people having today.

One day I asked my daughter what they were discussing in her Sunday school class. She told me they were talking about homosexuality. I was very surprised. I couldn't believe they would even talk about it in a Mennonite church. Then I saw my daughter reading books on this subject. It was difficult to believe she would be so interested in such a topic. She suggested that I read one of the books. I read through about a third of it and told her to take it back. I just didn't think it was a good thing at all.

Sometime later, as we were on our way home from the public library, my daughter mentioned that one of the people we had seen at the library had a gay son. I said that we were so fortunate not to have any problems like that in our family. She replied, "Guess what? We do." I thought she was just kidding, but asked what she meant. Much to my shock, she said, "I'm gay." I will never forget those words. Then she asked me if I would like to read the story that she had written for this book, and I agreed to read it.

I told myself I was too old to be hearing anything like this. My wonderful family, my wonderful son-in-law. I could not have a son I would love more than him. I guess I did not sleep much that night, but by morning I realized my daughter was still my angel, still my miracle, and someone of whom to be terribly proud.

Since she told me, I have read at least ten books on the subject and have changed my mind completely. I know she was born to be lesbian. She can no more help being what she is than I can help being who I am. All the prayers in the world won't change her orientation, and I am sure God would not want her to change. I don't know what lies ahead. I do know that God will be with us and guide us. I just want happiness for both of them and our wonderful family.

* * *

Editor's note: *Craig Spaulding, Pat's husband, has written the following postscript to her story.*

These last weeks and months have been extremely difficult and have challenged me emotionally, mentally, physically and spiritually. Three months ago, Pat decided she could no longer stay in our marriage. We have had a good marriage. It has had its ups and downs and challenges as any marriage does; however, ours has also had the additional challenge of being a mixed orientation marriage. I'm straight and Pat is gay.

As we have gone through an intense struggle discerning how to proceed, we have had the privilege of walking with twelve members of our congregation. They shared in our tears, anger, frustration, hurt, and pain, as they listened to our unanswerable questions and raised their own difficult questions. We have stumbled along in uncharted territory, trying to find the way forward that would be honoring to all involved.

However, there are no easy answers. My Christian upbringing and commitment tells me that marriage is a sacred covenant made before God, the church community, friends, and family, and that it is "till death do us part." Yet, even Jesus recognizes that it is an imperfect world we live in and makes provision for the ending of marriage.

When Pat and I first started getting to know each other, I did not understand that Pat's orientation was part of her core identity—who she is. I knew that she was attracted to women and had difficulty being around men who were romantically inclined. However, we both felt our relationship was special and that God had led us together in miraculous ways. She professed to love me and seemed to be attracted to me—at least enough to marry me, so I thought it was an issue that God would take care of. I admit that I was ignorant of how much this was an integral part of Pat. We were young—well, not too young—and naive. We were steeped in a conservative Christian worldview that believed God could and would "fix" Pat, if we only prayed and believed.

Twenty-five years of struggling later, this has not happened. It has been an extremely difficult road for her to travel. There have also been many frustrations on my part. It has taken me this long to understand how much pain and struggle it has been for her—so much so that she would even consider giving up our relationship and family as we know it. It's not only the constant longing to be herself and to be able to embrace all that it means to be a gay person, but it has also been a struggle for her to be with me as a male. Though she shared this struggle off and on with me and I observed it first hand, I still did not understand the depth of it and how much it is the core of her very being. I take full responsibility for not being more sympathetic and understanding of something over which she has no control and the torture it has caused her. This lack of understanding has also caused unfortunate patterns to develop in our relationship that have added to the stress. For this I'm truly sorry to both Pat and our children.

I know the last two years have been especially difficult for her. However, I will probably never totally understand what it's like to be trapped in a relationship, a church, and a society that doesn't understand or support gays and lesbians in their quest for living authentically as they were created to be. On the other hand, Pat will probably never be able to understand the depth of the hurt of having a partner and best friend for twenty-five years, thinking we would spend the rest of our lives together, and then facing the feelings of rejection that go along with her leaving. This rocks the very core of who I am as a person: my trust, my self-confidence, my judgment, and who I am in relationship to others and to God.

I feel like there is a tug of war going on inside me—like I am tied to a medieval torture rack that is gradually being tightened, tearing me apart, little by little. On the one hand, I have the pain of a twenty-five-year marriage that is now ending, a family that will no longer be together in the same way as it was before, and a "life companion" with whom I will no longer share the future. On the other hand, I see the person who has been in pain set free to be who she really is and to feel good about herself and rejoice in who she is.

This is tough for me and our three wonderful kids. Sharing so many wonderful experiences, common interests, values, and being great friends only makes this all the more painful and difficult. It has not been an easy journey to accept. There have been a lot of tears, anger, frustration, pain, sadness, and hurt expressed during this process. If I had my choice, we would still be together. However, it is not my choice. My choice now is how to proceed in light of the current reality.

So what is the way forward? We are both called to forgive each other. I need to try to hold in tension my pain and grief with Pat's joy and freedom to be who she is. She needs to try to understand that her choice of freedom to be herself is causing a fracture in our relationship, our family, and our church. I know that she doesn't take this decision lightly. I think for both of us it will always be a "catch twenty-two" situation—a mystery that has no answers, only the opportunity to embrace or reject this ambiguity, paradox, and mystery.

For me, the pain seems unbearable at times. Yet, it is something that I've chosen to embrace. It is something that I need to hold and be present with. The way forward is through the pain—to accept what is beyond my control, to be there for my children, and to choose to remain good friends with Pat, if that is possible. There is no other alternative, or at least no loving alternative that I can imagine. Forgiveness for both of us will take time—much time. It is not easy and it will not be a once-for-all process. It will have to be done over and over again as new situations arise. Pat and I both need to work hard at forgiving the church and society for their part in forcing people into relationships that are not consistent with who they are. Healing will come in baby steps.

This all has me asking the ultimate unanswerable question: "Why? . . . Why me? . . . Why us? . . . Why our family? . . . Why were we so confident that God was leading us together?" Yes, we each have responsibility for the way things started, developed, and ended, as does the church and society in general. But ultimately, there are no answers, only pain and silence. In some respects, it will always remain a mystery.

I am making the conscious decision to be open to and embrace this ambiguity and mystery. All these things need to be held in tension by both of us. We are called to live authentically, with integrity, compassion, perseverance, and yes—forgiveness. I hope that in time our experience will be transforming for each of us and will enable us to empathize, walk with, and help others who face life's ambiguities and mysteries.

* * *

Ambiguity implies a lack of closure, an inability or unwillingness to tie up all the loose ends, a recognition that all of the contradictions in life cannot be resolved. Ambiguity creates and reflects an element of uncertainty and mystery.[1] Howard Zehr

Our growth depends on openness to experiences of mystery . . . We are called to openness . . . Closing ourselves to mystery is closing ourselves to God.[2] Pat Koehler

---

[1] Howard Zehr. *The Little Book of Contemplative Photography.* Good Books, 2004.

[2] Ibid.

Craig Spaulding will be finishing his course work in the summer of 2004 at Eastern Mennonite University's Conflict Transformation Program, with a master's degree concentrating in restorative justice. He is working as the manager of Restorative Justice Initiatives at the Community Mediation Center in Harrisonburg, Virginia. Photography and rock climbing with his children and friends have been helpful ways for him to cope with some of the stress of these last months.

CHAPTER 21

Please Don't Be Afraid of My Happiness

Lin Garber

Most people whose stories are in this collection have felt a call to some kind of ministry throughout a good part of their lives as Christian believers. That is not the case with me. In the church of my childhood, ministers were nominated from within the congregation *by* the congregation, and if more than one was nominated, the choice between or among them was made by lot. When an (Old) Mennonite congregation needed to choose a new ordained man (they were all men in those days, of course), if anyone said that he felt called to the ministry and should therefore be placed in the lot, he would have become the object of much concerned expostulation about the dangers of pride.

My own experience of truth telling has cost me nothing, so I feel somewhat ill at ease in these pages. If anything, in recent years when I have become more vocal in the church setting on behalf of people whose longings and feelings of affection and expressions of gender identity don't quite match the expectations of the majority world, what truth telling I have done has rewarded me more than it has cost me anything. Having just turned sixty-nine, I have no aspirations to become anything beyond what God has already surprised me with; I merely remain open to any new ways of serving God, God's church, and God's precious gay and two-spirit people that God may place before me.

I can tell one story, however, to illustrate how hard it is for all the people in this book and the ones we represent to get a true hearing in the church at large.

"Being different is nothing new to me." That is how I began an autobiographical sketch several decades ago that was intended for a collection of true stories by people who lived "alternative life styles." It was to be published by Herald Press, the publishing house of what was then the Mennonite Church.*

The piece was accepted with thanks by the editor, but not long after that, it was returned to me with a sorrowful note. Herald Press had decided to cancel the publication. What they had been counting on was a series of stories about how miserable all these nonconforming people were, and instead they got stories of how *happy* they were! That would not do at all.

My story made one more journey before it reached its resting place here in my files. Faith and Life Press, the publishing house of what was then the General Conference Mennonite Church, was going to do a similar collection of stories, picking up some of the material from the wreck of the Herald Press project, and once again the editor was pleased with my offering.

Once again it came back to me, sent by the managing editor, with this explanation: the book as submitted to her included three stories relating to the gay experience. One was by the spouse of a gay person; another was by a gay person who had been mistreated by the church. The publication committee decided that there was too much gay-related material in the book. One of the three would have to go, and the reason for not using mine, the editor said, was that she thought it was so important for the church to be informed of the injustice of its treatment of gay people.

Here is the piece as originally planned, followed by part of my response to the managing editor's explanation.

1982 Autobiographical Sketch

Being "different" is nothing new to me. The condition was so familiar that when I learned in my midteens that I was gay it was only one more difference, and not a very important one.

My Depression-era infancy teemed with sisters, but I was a boy. I was definitely a boy—but all the boys I knew loved sports and hated books. I loved books and hated sports. I was a country-bred working-class Mennonite in a town where most of the working class were not Mennonite, and most Mennonites were academics and professionals. But I was also a city boy in a country church. I was "smart" in a "dumb" school. Being different, or at least in the wrong place, seemed inevitable.

My dream, my poignant longing, was to find a boy companion who was different like me. My family recognized this need and sympathized with it; it was not their fault if the potential friends they placed in my path never quite filled the bill. For always would come the physical test.

Throwing a ball, catching a ball, hitting a ball with one or another awkward implement—those skills defined American boyhood, and I was ludicrously inept at every one. Oh, I was always willing to try, but the Great American Ball, I soon learned, would always fall between me and my peers. Even the gym teacher gave up on me and sent me off to umpire the girls' games.

A few guys, however, were willing to give me another physical test: sex play. At least no particular skills seemed to be called for, but the point of such silliness eluded me. More than that it was nasty and distasteful (my parents and siblings left no doubt about that). So the kids who played those kinds of games were avoided by me, to the mystified disappointment of my sisters.

Puberty changed one thing. I found out what sex play was for. But even as I masturbated as frantically as any other kid; even as I grouped or coupled in adolescent experiment, I made no conscious connection between sexual activity and my misty hopeless dream of a boy companion. But one new factor was added to the dream: it would be nice if he had a body as achingly beautiful as those I was beginning to notice.

As my world expanded, I began to meet boys who came close to the dream image. In my fantasies I supplied their deficiencies, and in real life I tried to shape them into what I wanted them to be. Some responded with astonishing grace and patience, even affection; to this day I look back on friendships of this period with gratitude.

At sixteen, I learned what I was called. From first grade, to be sure, I had been called a sissy. I rejected the term, for I knew I was not (and never wanted to be) a girl. I had heard the word "queer" without knowing its specific application; it just meant disapproval. But I found a gay novel (God only knows how it penetrated the ghetto, and in fact I believe God must have put it there) and discovered myself on every page. To the world at large, it told me, I was a homosexual; to the knowing and sympathetic I was gay. And I was not alone!

What was I to do with this information? Above all I meant to follow Christ and be a good member of the fellowship of faith. But there were no rules covering my case. There were plenty of rules about girls: don't date before sixteen (a rule I broke, for which I was severely punished); don't hold hands on the first date; don't engage in petting, whatever that was. But, beyond a vague and to me nonsensical stricture against close friendships with boys, there were no rules about being gay.

So I made my own. I would never force my desires on another boy who did not share them, though the longing just to touch was sometimes past bearing, and though I was as much in the dark about what exactly we might do as any Victorian bride approaching her wedding night. But if God willed.....

It took six bittersweet years. In college I found a beautiful young man and fell in love (which was nothing new) and he was gay (and *that* was new!). First there was ecstasy. Then there was dissonance, and conflicting counsel from well-meaning but ill-equipped faculty and friends, with one glowing exception who may just have saved my life.

After graduation came a second gay encounter. I fled from looming promiscuity into an engagement (soon broken, providentially averting potential disaster). Finally I migrated to a metropolis, chiefly for professional reasons but also because I knew the Mennonite Church was not ready to accept that a person could be both gay and Christian.

*****

Now the church has asked for my story, and I look back on eighteen years of committed loving companionship. Because the rules covering a gay union are as scant as those on being gay and Christian, our commitment was marked by no ceremony, is recorded in no document, is enforced by no external human agency. Yet it grows stronger every day.

My dream has come true in all important respects. To judge by the delighted and astonished way many straight people respond to our relationship, its quality as well as its fact, that is yet another way I am different. Yet we know many gay couples, of both sexes, who have been together as long, as supportively and as happily as we have. Perhaps the single most important thing I can say to Mennonite young adults is this: anyone who tells you that gays are incapable of forming lasting relationships is simply not informed.

God gave me a joyful life and a companion to share it with me. Thanks be to God!

And there you have it: the story that was so menacing that the Mennonite publishing houses could not let it be told. Below is some of what I said to the Faith and Life editor after she had returned the piece to me (accompanied by praise for its literary quality, by the way):

As for your aim [making the church see its mistreatment of gay people], you have a good point. But what troubles me is a more subtle form of homophobia that thrives on "pity" or "compassion" or "redemptive love." Mennonites are especially good at this one. Tell them they are guilty of something and see them wallow. Tell them they are responding inappropriately to a case of human suffering and see how much they need human suffering to minister to in order to feel good. But tell them the object of their pity is actually in pretty good shape, then watch them flounder in frustration.

People have a variety of needs: they need to be accepted, respected, and to have their anguish recognized and alleviated. But they also need, fundamentally, to be able to share their joys. As a gay Mennonite, I seem to have been luckier than most. My family has long ago recognized my orientation and fully accepts my relationship as good for me. My home congregation and I have, by virtue of physical separation, been able to maintain correctly cordial relations, while that part of the New York Mennonite community that I am in touch with has been more than supportive and accepting. For my more persecuted brothers and sisters I welcome the steps, your publication included, that lead to recognition of their troubles. The church at long last is showing itself "willing to listen to gay people" recounting their woes. How soon can it listen to their happiness? *That* will be the sign of agape in bloom.

That was my own first exposure to the difficulty that gay, lesbian, and all sexual-minority people have in getting their truth told within the official fold of the Mennonite churches.

More than two decades later, nothing has changed in that regard. The book you are now reading had to be published outside of the official Mennonite press, and it is difficult to find its two predecessor books on the shelves of the Provident Bookstores, the official sales outlet for that press.

The history of another book reinforces the point: it is called *To Continue the Dialogue*, edited by C. Norman Kraus. It is an anthology of essays by Mennonites with a broad range of opinion on subjects related to its subtitle: "Biblical Interpretation and Homosexuality." A number of the essays give a positive picture of gay people. For whatever reason, the book, published by Pandora Press US (now Cascadia Publishing House), is one of only two Pandora US books not granted the co-publishing imprint of Herald Press, which means that it did not have the advantage of access to Herald Press's distribution system.

In 1998, a group of people formed the Welcome Committee, with its first goal the creation and placement of a full-page ad in *Mennonite Weekly Review*. It was called "A Welcoming Open Letter on 'Homosexuality'," and it appeared in the issue of 17 February 2000, with more than six hundred signatures obtained from all over the Mennonite world of Canada and the United States. Later additions have brought the number of signers to seven hundred or more.

That ad caused a storm of controversy in the letters columns of the paper and engendered two subsequent ads opposed to its encouragement of "covenant vows" between loving couples of the same sex. Two individuals placed those ads separately, and after their appearance the paper announced a policy of declining to accept further ads on either side of the subject. (The editors have continued to provide space on their letters pages for often lively discussion as well as to permit their columnists who are so inclined to speak up on behalf of gay and lesbian people.)

A further project of the Welcome Committee was to be a book. Discussions were held with Pandora Press US toward its publication, but when amicable differences made that collaboration impractical, four of the proposed contributions were accepted into the Kraus book named above (with some editorial alterations, as in the case of my own historical essay). The committee then changed its plan and began to issue a series of booklets. So far seven booklets have been published in the Welcome to Dialogue series—but they have never been made available through official church channels.

Mennonite officialdom has shown less reluctance when it comes to the production of books that are negative about the lives of GLBT people. In place of the project that was to have included, along with other testimonies of joy, my little story above, Herald Press chose to publish *Such Were Some of You: The Spiritual Odyssey of an Ex-Gay Christian*, by Kevin Linehan (Scottdale, 1979). Sad to say, the later life of this unhappy person provides a lesson quite the opposite of what its Herald Press promoters intended, and this title has long since mercifully disappeared from the active lists.

Two decades later, Herald Press encouraged Willard Swartley, a professor at Associated Mennonite Biblical Seminary, to collect into a book some occasional papers he had written over the years under the title: *Homosexuality: Biblical Interpretation and Moral Discernment* (Scottdale and Waterloo, 2003). There is not space here to do an indepth analysis of Swartley's volume. I can only say that even when Swartley quotes people who have a positive view of the sexual minorities (whom he persists, like too many authors on the subject over the years, in lumping together into the meaningless category "homosexuality"), he does so only to deny, without sound evidence, that their thinking has any legitimacy. On the other hand, when he quotes, as he frequently does, authors whose works reek of homophobia (most conspicuously, Robert A. J. Gagnon), he does so with approval. One might note that Swartley had already been given a voice for his views in Kraus's book, where he (with several other anti-gay spokespeople) was invited to write a response. What a contrast between approaches to dialogue!

At the Mennonite Assembly in Atlanta in 2003, I attended a moderator's forum, where God presented to me the awkward necessity of outing myself as a gay man. Atlanta 2003 was the first assembly in years—perhaps since 1979—that did not offer so much as a single workshop on the fear-inducing topic of "homosexuality." When someone in the forum pointed that out, it fell to me to announce that, hey, folks, here I am. One of *them*. Part of the moderator's response was to urge me to read Swartley's book, which was being heavily promoted at the convention. I did not tell him at the time that I was already quite familiar with some parts of it, and I can only say of that moderator: God forgive him, for he knew not what he did. It feels to me that what he did is analogous to recommending to a Jew that he read the *Protocols of the Elders of Zion*.

One small beam of light relieves this gloomy record. In 1999, Herald Press published *Sexuality: God's Gift*, edited by Anne Krabill Hershberger. Chapter 7 is by Dr. Willard Krabill, Anne's brother, with the title "The Gift and Same-Sex Orientation." But even this bright spot was tarnished when Choice Books, which distributes books on displays in high-traffic areas like supermarkets and transportation terminals, expressed interest in the title but asked for an edition from which Chapter 7 would be omitted. The editor declined permission, for which she will surely receive a beautiful gem in her heavenly crown!

There is so much joy in my own life, including the recent celebration of forty years with my life partner, that I wish could be understood and shared by people whose dread of me and people with lives like mine must be painful to carry around with them all the time. May the truth that is being told in this book, and so many others, finally shine a comforting light on those fear-shrouded souls.

---

* In 1999 the Canadian portions of the Mennonite Church and the General Conference Mennonite Church formed Mennonite Church Canada, and in 2001 their counterparts south of the national border merged to form Mennonite Church USA.

Lin was born **Verlin Garber** in 1935, the youngest of nine children, and grew up in Elkhart County, Indiana, living in the county seat of Goshen from second grade through college. He graduated with a degree in music and became a professional singer in New York, where he met Jay Schatt in 1963. Jay was born to a Jewish family in Brooklyn and lived in that borough all his life until he and Lin moved to Orange County, New York, in 1983. There Lin received wonderful spiritual sustenance from the Friends Meeting that he joined. In 1991, they moved to Boston and Lin became active in the Mennonite Congregation of Boston, which welcomed him by becoming an open and publicly affirming member of the Supportive Congregations Network. He is employed a few hours a week at Harvard, where the I.Q. score that stuck out so badly in grade school ("I was 'smart' in a 'dumb' school"—1982 Autobiographical Sketch above) now puts him into the category of "barely functional." Nevertheless, the Harvard folks are gentle and patient with him, and he is happy to be there.

CHAPTER 22

Born of Solidarity

Rachel Jackson

*Let us not be disheartened as though human realities
made impossible the accomplishments of God's plans.*
Oscar Romero

There is a joke among my co-workers in the sexual assault center where I am the community educator: "If you ever want to avoid small talk with someone, just tell them what you do for a living." Unfortunately it's true. When that information falls on most ears, I watch them choke back their surprise, and I have come to expect the subject change that follows. Once someone told me, after a pause, "....Oh, I'm sorry." The irony is that the silence that surrounds sexual assault is exactly the fuel it has always needed to exist.

I am sometimes asked by my students, "Are all the people who work at Rape Crisis Services sexual assault survivors?" The question is warranted. Most movements of peace and liberation are launched when those whom the violence and tyranny directly oppress cease to be silent. Indeed, the anti-rape movement began when survivors of sexual assault began talking to one another and speaking out. However, I know that there are others who work tirelessly alongside survivors to end the rape culture in which we live. Do they do it because it is a good deed? Or do they recognize something deeper that many people do not? Do they recognize that they too are victims? That we are all victims in a culture that permits and promotes violence?

We celebrated Thanksgiving of 2003 at the home I make with my partner Becky and daughter Havah. My parents and cousin spent the day with us. We went around the room, each saying what we felt thankful for this year, and my turn came last. I willed back tears as I explained that I am thankful for those who allow their hearts to be broken by the things that break God's heart. It is they who literally save lives, spiritually and physically. As I said that, I was thinking of those who, although they don't have to, hurt with those who are hurting. Who are these "God-sends" who have touched my heart and shown me Jesus? It is to them that I dedicate this chapter.

While my world formed around me as a little girl, I lived with a deep sense of God's love for me. I felt as though the Spirit of God had touched my spirit. I am thankful for the purity and warmth of that foundation. The simplicity of it has held me firm, despite the bewildering complexity of God's people in the world.

I was born and raised in Reba Place Fellowship, originally a Mennonite/Brethren intentional community in Evanston, Illinois. When I was sixteen, I was part of a small delegation to El Salvador. We arrived the day the cease-fire went into effect in El Salvador's decade-long civil war. While there, we listened to the people of Valle Nuevo with whom we hoped to establish a relationship. Their stories were of shattered lives ravaged by war. But they were also stories of strength and miracles. As the trip drew to a close, what I had witnessed and heard was more than I could contain or understand, so my heart broke. The experience was shell-breaking...and I was a mess. I realized that the point of hurting with those who hurt is not so that we're all in pain. Rather, peace and a new understanding (unattainable any other way) are born of solidarity.

Since college at Eastern Mennonite University (EMU), I have learned more about violence and pacifism. I now work with issues of violence every day. I have learned how violence is a continuum and is exhibited not just in the physical sense with strength and force, but also with antagonism, disunity, and domination.

While in college, I found a new joy in myself as a woman. It was real and raw and different from my earlier understandings. But the more I studied, the more I found myself perplexed by aspects of

Scripture that seemed abusive and devaluing of women. I grew up in an evangelical community and had been taught that the Bible is God's direct word. If it's in there, God said it, and it pertains to me. My feelings were deeply hurt. I began desperately to try to reconcile my foundational sense of being deeply loved by God with the Bible. It was then that I began one of the most meaningful spiritual experiences I've ever had.

One of my favorite books at EMU was *The Upside-Down Kingdom* by Donald B. Kraybill. The author describes how Jesus came into a culture (that is not too different from ours today) and was the counter to that culture, turning it upside down. He modeled justice, peace, compassion, grace, the seeking of light, communion, and love. In a world that held wide divisions and normalized violence, Jesus listened to those who were hurt and stood in solidarity with them. I fell in love with this radical. When I looked to Jesus, my hurt feelings were diminished. Regardless of anything or anyone else, I am his child, free and beloved.

This event laid another foundation within me. My guiding principle in the world is to let my heart be broken by those things that break God's heart. It is useful to me in my work as an anti-violence educator addressing issues of war, economics, and difficult controversial biblical questions, and in my role as a mother, partner, friend, and daughter. Not only did I discover a true relationship, I stumbled upon the model I want to use in everything.

It was also at Eastern Mennonite University that I first met Becky. After graduation, while living many states away from each other, we began to connect deeply through e-mail and letters. As time and our friendship continued, I realized that I had found the one whom my soul loves. Becky is my best friend and a major source of my smile and laughter. As my companion who makes me feel complete, she challenges me and is the inspiration behind profound spiritual and emotional growth for me. For everything she is to me, I hope I am at least that for her.

The home that Becky, Havah, and I have together is one of the happiest places on earth for me. We are a truly complementary family—from little things like the difference between cleaning "clutter" and cleaning "dirt" to larger things like how much Havah and I thrive on Becky's honesty and ability to see options. Havah, whose Hebrew name means "life," is our spirited event planner, always gearing up for the next holiday. She is cared for like a small child and respected like a big adult. Over the years, it has been beautiful to watch the relationship between Becky and Havah take on a life of its own. They are truly Family to each other.

We desire so much to share our family with our wider families of origin. Most people want and hope to be able to do that. However, too often sharing in family life for GLBT people is not possible or easy.

I remember when a childhood friend of mine came out to her family. Many months went by when they would not contact her. I could not imagine a more painful feeling when she told me she had resorted to trying to find a surrogate mom and dad to replace the parents she thought she had lost. Now I feel that pain in the losses Becky has experienced with her family. It's odd that when you love another so completely, their burden becomes so closely yours that your tears mix with theirs.

Becky is certainly human, but I realized two things as I was falling in love with her. One was that she is just about the most integrity-filled person I know. The other was her deep love for her family. She has eight precious nieces and nephews. Since Becky has been in my life, I have seen her love for them fill her so fully that it appears wet in her eyes.

At times, Christians' quest for righteousness ironically gets in the way of Jesus in the world. Becky received a letter from an in-law not long after coming out to her family. The in-law proclaimed firm disapproval of our relationship and warned that she would not be open to allowing her children to be around "that." The day was dark. The letter contained no "I want to hear about what's inside of you—I want to understand you. How are you doing, sister?" How quickly gay people sometimes are no longer brother, sister, aunt, or daughter when they come out. Instead, they represent something foreign—even an enemy. It's easier to blame the person and reinforce our understanding of our *own* righteousness than to learn how to love the way Jesus does.

Presently, Becky's parents both disapprove of our partnership, but Becky feels especially hurt and rejected by her mom. Her mother says she has lost a daughter. She does not realize that Becky is still the same caring daughter with a deep love and reverence for God that she was before she revealed to them that she is lesbian and that we have a relationship together.

My mother heart bleeds to see the gulf that exists between Becky and her mom. We believe in God's desire and ability to redeem this relationship. Becky longs to hear her mother's voice on the phone simply to encourage her in work and graduate school or to say happy birthday. Some family members have told Becky they don't pick up the phone to call her anymore because "it's just too hard." To be left out of her family's life is very painful for my soul mate. She loves them dearly. We often pray that her family will visit us and be blessed by the love in our home. Together we dream of compassionate interactions that involve our entire families.

Now we face what is becoming a familiar dilemma. Next summer, one of Becky's close cousins will be married. The whole clan will be there. If we go as a family, we risk a terrible situation. If Becky does not go at all, she misses her cousin's wedding, and it may appear that she has decided not to be a part of her family. But if Becky goes alone *our* family is split. What does that teach Havah? There are no easy answers.

Last summer my family had a large reunion of cousins, aunts, uncles, and parents. Becky and I were distraught with the decision of whether she should come or not. My mom and dad do not approve of my relationship with Becky. Initially they were kind, yet also not warm toward her. I am thankful they have never been hurtful. However, going to visit my parents has not been a relaxing time either.

Becky and I were at our wits' end over the decision when my brother's wife e-mailed me. She told me she sensed our bind. She suspected I had already dealt with the more "conservative" members of my family (i.e., my parents, herself, and my brother), and if I want my family to get to know Becky, she will need to be present at family gatherings. Decision made. In doing that, my sister-in-law did not insinuate approval, but made known her love for me, which also means loving

Becky. The reunion turned out to be an incredible blessing. The honesty with which we went and the right-ness of having Becky there made enjoying my entire family a renewed experience. I love them all very much.

My dear dad once challenged me to find even one homosexual leader doing the will of God. I thought about how the challenge, "Show me an African-American political leader in the late 1800s," would have been hard up for an answer. God may be calling all kinds of his children to spiritual leadership in the world. However, if the world does not receive them, it will be hard for them to be seen. My sister-in-law might not be exercising her gift and call of church leadership if her spiritual community remained fastened to a historical, traditional understanding of Scriptures that culturally bound women to be silent in church. I am glad that is not the case for her.

What happened next almost made it seem as if God heard my dad's challenge. I am not sure of what God has shown my father. But over the next few years, God brought some of the most Christ-like people into my life. Many of them are leaders. Many of them happen to be gay. And many of their stories are written on the pages of this book.

Our deep desire for good family relationships is similar to our search for a spiritual community. When I first moved to Illinois from Virginia, I attended New Covenant Fellowship in a withdrawn way. At the time, I needed the simplicity of anonymity to just worship God. Becky's congregation in Newton, Kansas, (New Creation) provided an amazing spiritual family for her. When she moved to Illinois, she was ready to seek that out since she missed her church in Kansas. I was inspired and realized I was ready for that also.

However, we did not seek out a small group. We spent time slowly getting to know people in the church. With the exception of a few people, we were not deliberate about making it known that we are a couple. I wondered (and truly couldn't tell) where the church rested its position on the honor of a same-sex couple. But I also didn't ask. I was afraid of the answer and was enjoying myself too much. When we did discover what the official position was, I ignored it. Maybe I thought subconsciously, "If we just lay low and try not to make waves, Becky and I can continue to worship with these people."

What transpired next resulted in us deciding to leave New Covenant. Our last official Sunday was a service of testimonies arranged by the senior pastor. We left early that day, but not before I stood at the back, crying and feeling like I was saying goodbye. One sister shared the horrible circumstances of how her husband cheated on her for twenty years and how God brought her through that. But, because it turned out that her husband also happened to be gay (previously unbeknown to her), she made statements in the sanctuary insinuating that homosexuality is poison and that the lifestyles of all same-sex oriented people are promiscuous and deceitful. Her pronouncements created the misnomer of "one homosexual lifestyle" and the implication that all people in same-sex relationships are not true Christians, even if they believe they are in a relationship with the Lord.

I felt as if my heart was breaking. I no longer wanted to keep silent about my permanent life-giving relationship with Becky. I believe Becky and I have much to offer together and as individuals. I am proud of the home we have created and the security we give to Havah. I'm happy to share our respectful, loving partnership with others. But I know I won't live fully facing the sun if we aren't functioning as a couple, as well as individuals, within our spiritual family. There comes a point at which we have to decide if we want to live with full integrity, available for God to use us to our full potential, or remain on the sidelines of true church involvement as if we're ashamed and secondary.

New Covenant had turned out to be the nearest thing to a true spiritual family I had ever had as an adult. The timing of this "orphaning" for us was especially grave because we already had so many issues within our families of origin. More than ever, we needed and wanted a spiritual family. Yet, we felt like the one we wanted to choose to worship with would not corporately choose us.

What happened next surprised us. Individuals came out of the woodwork at New Covenant and chose us. The co-pastor and his wife asked us to respond creatively and not leave altogether. They extended an invitation to join their small group, something for which we were so hungry and grateful. As we shared our spiritual journeys with that group, I described the day when we left the Sunday worship service. A woman in the group surprised me when she began crying over the pain she realized we had felt. I had never witnessed a heterosexual person who personally felt the pangs of GLBT people struggling to engage with their families and the larger body of Christ. Since then, these caring people have appeared everywhere—some at New Covenant and others from places like Eastern Mennonite University, Hesston College, and the Brethren/Mennonite Council for Gay, Lesbian, Bisexual, and Transgender Interests.

Our "creative response" has been to continue developing relationships with New Covenant. Our highest priority for a church is to find a place of spiritual resources for Havah. We still try to attend New Covenant on Sunday occasionally, often because it is depressing to send her without us. The people there are good servants who are truly seeking how to be a community where all of God's children can enter freely. However, we ultimately desire a home where we don't feel weighted down as our family walks in on Sunday morning.

When I think of the future, I look at my daughter, and I am not disheartened. It is with the heart of a child like Havah that God asks us into his kingdom. She is full of love, with a mind for justice. Through our actions, we desire to teach her integrity and real-ness. We want her to understand that when she so frequently puts herself in the shoes of another and stands with them, it is an act of solidarity. One evening last spring on a visit to Virginia, Becky and a friend were talking about the rare person Havah is. They spoke of challenges and how they seem to give her tenderness and make her stronger. After a pause, the friend looked at Becky and said, "Havah's going to save someone's life someday."

Maybe she already has.

Rachel Jackson grew up at Reba Place Fellowship near Chicago in Evanston, Illinois. "Home" to Rachel is anywhere with her partner Becky, a graduate student in education, and daughter Havah, an inventive second grader. A graduate of Eastern Mennonite University in Harrisonburg, Virginia, Rachel finds her deepest desire for work in anti-violence and justice issues. She is the sexual assault community educator in Champaign, Illinois, where she teaches junior and senior high school classes and adult groups in the surrounding four counties. She enjoys belly-aching laughter, cilantro, warm weather, salsa dancing, and has recently picked up scrap booking, which she loves, but it makes her feel old!

CHAPTER 23

A Life of Hope in the Margins

Lynn Dykeman

I did not expect to live my life in the margins of society. From the time of conception, I was slated for a life of middle class white privilege. Both of my parents grew up in poverty and struggled against remarkable odds to secure an education. My parents' goal was that my sisters and I would never experience the poverty that had underscored all aspects of their childhood. They were successful at ensuring we lived a life of middle class privilege.

Being a woman, however, I would soon learn of the structural inequality along gender lines in our society. This came as a shock to someone raised in a family where all offspring were female, and we were taught that we could be or do anything we wanted. The realities of being a woman were apparent throughout my life. As I entered the university community and the work force, I saw, and occasionally experienced, sexual harassment. I know what it is like to be unsafe walking alone at night. I work in a profession that is seventy percent female and, in twenty years, I have rarely worked for a female director. Social workers are generally women. Social work bosses are generally male.

I am marginalized, as all women are marginalized. I continued to live in white middle class privilege, nonetheless. For a woman, I had all the privilege that money and education could provide. There were few places where I was unwelcome. This all changed, however, when I finally recognized that I was lesbian. In this moment of knowing, I became "other"—unacceptable or unwanted in many parts of society. I can still pass as a straight woman if who I am remains unknown. If I allow myself and my life to be seen, I risk becoming unacceptable. Situations have become safe or unsafe, a kind of situational analysis unknown in my life prior to my coming out. I can choose to pass or I can risk rejection.

I believe there is a huge cost to "passing." To deny who we are—who God created us to be—generates an internal sense of wrongness, of shame, of unacceptability. When I hide who I am because I risk rejection, it is difficult not to internalize a sense of being unacceptable. It is a continual challenge to lesbian and gay persons to live proudly and not internalize the structural homophobia in our society. The importance of coming out, first to ourselves and then to others, in contexts of safety and sometimes in contexts that may or may not be safe, is part of the continual challenge of being gay. To choose to hide places limits on who we are to ourselves and who we can be in the world. This struggle has lived within me all my life.

People often ask me, "When did you know you were lesbian?" I wonder if people are ever asked when they knew they were straight? I never heard any discussion of homosexuality until I was well into my twenties. The unspoken knowing I learned through comment and innuendo in my childhood taught me that homosexuals were ill and evil people. Their inherent wickedness was unquestioned. In my teen years, I experienced a gradual awareness of same-sex orientation. At twenty-two, I finally said to my first counselor, "I think I am gay, and if I am, I am going to kill myself." For me this was the logical response to a life situation that could only be evil. Being gay meant that there was something very wrong with me that could only end with my death.

My therapist at the time assured me that she did not believe I was gay—something years later she said she never would say again to a client. Her comment, however, brought a huge sense of relief to me. Perhaps I could be cured; perhaps with therapy and counseling this situation could be resolved. For the duration of my twenties I struggled with this issue, convinced that if I worked hard enough to face my issues, my same-sex orientation would disappear. Maybe I was fixable.

I began seminary studies in 1986. My work as a social worker had always been rewarding, but I needed a context in which to explore my spirituality as I did my work. Seminary provided me with the context I needed to integrate my spirituality and my vocation. I routinely revisit the question: *"How does my faith, something central to my life, impact my work?"*

My spiritual journey happened outside of the context of my family of origin. I came from a family that attended church about once or twice a month. From the time I was about twelve, I usually went weekly. I remember desperately wanting to believe, but I experienced my faith as an intellectual knowing. When I was twenty-two, I had a profound conversion experience, and since that time I have never questioned the existence of God again, although my understanding of this Being has grown and changed with time.

I had my burning bush experience while I was at seminary. During a field trip with a religion and culture class, much to my horror, I was called forward from a congregation of several hundred and commissioned as a leader of the church—the only person who had that experience that day. My classmates enjoyed the teasing that came with this experience and asked me when I would be ordained. I had felt a call before this experience, but somewhere in my deepest knowing, I knew it was a call to which I would never respond.

As I entered my thirties, I was an extremely unhappy woman. I felt at war with myself. One of my close friends finally came out as lesbian, and through this friendship I began my entry into the lesbian community. At my first lesbian gathering I expected to meet some very odd, unbalanced people. I was shocked to learn that they were not unlike numerous people I had met before. Some I enjoyed, some I did not; some were conservative, some were not; some seemed at peace with themselves and some did not. The only difference between these individuals and the mainstream society that I experienced was their sexual orientation and their experience with living in the margins.

My coming out would be a process that I went through over and over again, as did many of my GLBT friends. One comes out to trusted friends, perhaps some family, some people at church, some people at work, and so the struggle goes on. Some stories are ones of great possibility. Others are stories of fracture and distance. My coming out has been a gradual process that spanned a decade. The walls of the closet lead to a profoundly limiting life, but coming out of this darkness involves many risks and much heartache along with the joy.

As I came out, I knew I would never be ordained. I went away on an individual retreat at a convent and mourned. I wrestled with the choices presented to me and knew I could not deny who I was and minister with integrity. For me there was no decision, only the appearance of one. I knew I had to acknowledge my sexual orientation and with that realization came the knowing that ordination would never happen. A chapter of my life had closed.

I sometimes wonder if I had been straight, would I have responded to my call? After a very public childhood, because of my father's job, would I have been willing to live such a public life again? Would I have been willing to make the many sacrifices necessary for ordination? These are questions that will never be answered.

Some of the losses I have experienced because of my sexual orientation have been quite overt. Others have been subtler. Although I rarely discuss my personal life in places of employment, some people realize I am lesbian. At one place of employment, an executive director told me that some students in her class had come out as homosexual, and she had cautioned them against doing so because it would have a lifelong impact on their careers. On another occasion, as I stood in a large walk-in closet, she made a joking comment about me remaining in the closet. She clearly told me that coming out would impact my career. I never had the courage to tell her that not coming out would impact my life even more.

The price of being lesbian includes some times of great pain in my relationships with my friends. My two best friends from my twenties and early thirties, both Christians, chose never to see me again after I went to their home to discuss my sexual orientation. Our friendship of fifteen years did not have room for an honesty I felt necessary to protect the integrity of the friendship. I have had no contact with them for ten years. I have not seen their beloved child in the last ten years. I sometimes wonder what she was told about my disappearance from their lives. She is grown now, but for me she will always remain the twelve-year-old I saw at the time of our last visit. Some wounds never really heal. You simply learn to focus your energy on other things.

The most painful place of marginalization in my life has been the marginalization I have experienced at the hands of the church. I have experienced the greatest condemnation in Christian contexts. In discussions of homosexuality within church settings, I have encountered remarkable rage and uninformed opinion. I have marched in parades and seen "Christians" waving signs saying, "Christ hates queers." I have been in church discussions where I have all but been equated with the devil. Then there are other church members who, while offering support, minimize our pain. They argue that things are really not that bad. Those who make these arguments are very likely not gay or lesbian.

Hiding who I am at church is one of the most painful experiences I have known. Church has always been a place of spiritual renewal, social justice, community, and connection. When I feel unsafe in church settings, the sense of separation from the community is particularly overpowering. For one who has known the feeling of a church home, the sense of isolation caused by passing at church is deeply overwhelming. I try to press for inclusion, for a broader understanding of Christ's message that included the marginalized.

One of the losses I have experienced with my coming out has been the ability to freely select a church community in which to worship. When I came to the Kitchener/Waterloo area in 1982 to study social work, I struggled to find a church home. I love much about the liturgy of the Anglican Church in which I was raised. My first real church home in Ontario, however, was a Mennonite congregation that I attended for ten years. When I came out, I felt less connected with this congregation. They went through great struggles with God-language which made me question any acceptance I could feel there as an out lesbian. For a while, I attended an Anglican church that was affirming of gay and lesbian inclusion. There were things I enjoyed there, but the early morning commute to another community made regular attendance difficult. I also did not feel as spiritually at home as I had in the Mennonite Church, because I am a pacifist and my spirituality has a strong social justice component. However, because of my sexual orientation, I do not always have the luxury of choosing where I will attend church.

In 1996, I began attending Olive Branch Mennonite, a place that has become a central part of my life, a place of healing and hope. I am "lucky" to have found an affirming congregation in my home community. Many of my lesbian sisters do not have this choice and have to commute long distances to attend affirming churches outside of their communities. If there is an affirming church, they often attend it regardless of its denominational affiliation. The church affiliation of gays and lesbians is often defined by who will accept us.

It is important to note that not all my experiences with the institutional church have been negative. I attend a church that embarked on a journey and became a congregation that welcomes gays and lesbians. It has become a safe church home. I have also been blessed with my involvement in the Brethren and Mennonite Council for Lesbian, Gay, Bisexual, and Transgender Interests (BMC). This is a place where we, the marginalized, join together for fellowship, spiritual enrichment and, from time to time, to knock on the doors of the institutional church.

Leaven, an American organization that works for social change in many areas, including sexual orientation, has always been a safe space, a place of regeneration and refreshment where I find the strength to continue my journey. My recent involvement in Christian Lesbians Out (CLOUT) has provided support and encouragement.

The parents' group of BMC is composed of people who will always have my respect. They support their children on their journey and continually challenge the church establishment to include gay and lesbian members. Sometimes when BMC members are too tired to write yet another letter, someone in the parents' group will write one. They have consistently been parents to those whose parents could not make the journey towards acceptance of their gay and lesbian children.

There have been life-giving moments in this journey. I sat with a friend when South Calgary Mennonite Church was given their plaque as they joined the Supportive Congregations Network. My friend questioned why we were crying. I suggested that it was because this was one group of people who said that we were not going to hell. I visited Germantown Mennonite Church in Philadelphia, the oldest Mennonite church in North America, shortly after they were kicked out of their conference in 1997 because of their support of gay and lesbian inclusion. It was a vibrant, spiritually-filled day. I attended WOW 2000 in Dekalb, Illinois, an interdenominational gathering of over a thousand gay and lesbian Christians from many denominations, listened to powerful speakers, and participated in life-giving dialogue. It is events like these that sustain me on my journey. My spiritual journey largely happens within supportive congregations and in gatherings of gays and lesbians. I am unable to actively pursue my spiritual journey in congregations where I must question my acceptance or where anger at my presence is evident.

One of the great challenges of being a lesbian Christian is to avoid beginning to see as "other"—as not part of the body of Christ—those who marginalize my community. It is a continual challenge to remind myself that they too are part of the body of Christ and that they are an important part of the Christian community. I continually remind myself that if I am insistent that I must not be seen as "other," I must not see them as "other."

I once had to leave a same-sex commitment service reception to get more film from my car. A sobbing woman was in the parking lot. Although I did not know her, I knew she came from a conservative Christian tradition and wondered if her tears were caused by the conflict between the values she had learned and the values she heard shared that day. I so wished to speak to her but as "one of the lesbians" in attendance, I felt that I must remain silent. I witnessed her pain and was deeply saddened by it. I so much wanted to say, "It is okay. Christ has room for all of us."

I see fear and terror mixed with rage when homosexuality is discussed. There is no question that "the other side" experiences pain. It seems that sometimes they are concerned that loving us compromises their faith. I do not believe that we will all ever agree on this topic. I do believe that Christ's real challenge was and is for people of different beliefs to work and live together. Christ brought together people of widely differing backgrounds and taught them to be community to each other. I believe he would say the same thing to the church today with regards to the issue of homosexuality—live together, work together, and know the Divine.

I often view the last six years of my life as something of a miracle. In my thirties, I came out to my sisters who worked hard to understand but both felt it highly unwise to tell my parents. In 1998, I went to a spiritual retreat in the Blue Ridge Mountains sponsored by Leaven Inc. There I met a woman who would become my life partner. I have never been one to keep things simple; Nora, of course, lived in Oklahoma. In 2004, after five years of a long-distance relationship, she is close to finalizing her immigration to Canada. In 2002, we had a commitment service at Olive Branch Mennonite Church that was attended by 130 of our colleagues from work, our families, and our friends. The BMC men provided an excellent catering service, and we felt unbelievably blessed. We were able to make our union legal in Ontario in 2003, something we chose to do with a much smaller celebration—five people in the library of our home. Nora always is clear that the real wedding was the church wedding. I can only agree.

That real wedding involved many miracles, which would take more time than I have to tell, and some are not mine to recount. I could tell stories of people who accepted their own orientation or the orientation of others. It was a day we will always treasure, as wedding days should be. One of the most powerful memories for me will always be the involvement of our families. Finally, in my forties, after much soul searching, I told my mother my secret and learned that she already knew of my sexual orientation. She, with my blessing, told my profoundly shocked father. Both chose to love what they could not fully understand and were present at our service. Nora's daughters, although somewhat hesitant, were also present as were all of our siblings. For me this will always be an unanticipated miracle. It pushes me to believe that there are other miracles of acceptance that can occur if only we can believe.

All three of our surviving parents and our siblings recognize that both Nora and I are the happiest we have ever been. I now have a playful and healthy relationship with Nora's daughters. I feel loved and accepted in two families. Coming out to my family transformed my relationships with them and tore down walls that had existed for years. Nora and I are indeed blessed.

While I will never be ordained, I have been given moments when I had the opportunity to voice concerns of the GLBT community to the larger church. I have spoken at Mennonite conventions and been a part of the Listening Committee of the Mennonite Church. I also had the privilege of interviewing seventeen lesbian women, many of whom were Mennonite, for my second seminary degree. In this research, I explored the experiences of lesbian women in the Christian church. I would say that perhaps some people at my seminary were not quite ready for that topic to be explored. I lead worship regularly at Olive Branch Mennonite Church, a community led by lay members, and recently I was privileged to co-officiate with an ordained person (non-Mennonite) at the marriage service of lesbian friends.

Despite the limitations imposed on my life by those who view me as deviant, I am happier than I have ever been. The relief of accepting who I really am far outweighs anything that society can dish out. My coming out story is not atypical and, in many ways, has been gentler than many. I consider myself to be a remarkably lucky person. I am out to and maintain loving connections with my family of origin, I know the joy of a loving partnership, I am known by many work colleagues as a lesbian woman, and I share in the life of a loving and welcoming church community. My journey has taken me a long way from the life of white, middle class privilege so desired for me by my parents, but it is the only life I could chose and live with integrity. It is a life where I have embraced my sexuality and my spirituality. I live a life where I know I am loved by God, by my family, and by my friends.

Lynn Dykeman, M.S.W., M.T.S., M.T.H., works as a clinical social worker and does some family medicine resident teaching at McMaster University in Hamilton, Ontario. She maintains a private clinical practice in Kitchener, where she lives with her partner Nora Clevenger and their two cats. She has studied social work and theology at Wilfrid Laurier University. Lynn and Nora attend Olive Branch Mennonite Church.

CHAPTER 24

Called to Serve the Lord:
Being a Good Boy for Jesus

Keith G. Schrag

All my life I have been aware of wanting to be and do what God wants me to be and do. From my youngest days, going to church and being part of God's people was central in my life. Because my father was our preacher, and because I was an oldest child, this awareness and involvement was reinforced regularly.

I don't ever recall that my parents indicated that they wanted me to be a preacher or pastor. I do know that I often heard them say and pray their desire that I grow up to serve the Lord. This was something that I just took for granted. I never questioned this desire—both theirs and mine. My prayer was, "Lord, how do you want me to serve you? What is your path for my life?"

Earnestly Seeking to Be a "Good Boy for Jesus"

I was the oldest brother, and my siblings knew I was far from perfect. I struggled for many years with a deep awareness that I was a sinner, that I "came short of the glory of God." I wanted assurance and a deep sense of peace. Most of the time that deep yearning went unful- filled. So I struggled. Although I read the Bible daily and prayed in my private devotions, and although our family had family worship at the breakfast table each day, and although I was baptized on confession of my faith at age twelve and became an active member of our congrega- tion, I continued to struggle with my sense of not being "in the center of God's will." How would I ever quench this tremendous longing? How could I ever find my way? Included in this dilemma was my attraction to other guys. These were my hidden tormentors daily.

My external life continued to progress, seemingly well. Although I grew up in rural northern New York, I found ways to connect with the wider Mennonite Church. As regularly as we could, our family attended church conferences. We traveled to Laurelville, Pennsylvania, and Little Eden, Michigan, to church camps and retreats and other meetings where I could meet others "like we were." As I matured, I became increasingly active in my local school and its activities.

I decided to spend my college savings to take my senior year of high school at Eastern Mennonite High School in Harrisonburg, Virginia. There I met many people, including youth and church leaders, who had a big influence on me. My college years at Goshen (IN) College expanded that aspect of my life even further. Those four years were pivotal in addressing issues of my love and respect for the Mennonite Church and my desire to be of service to God in a deeply meaningful way.

During my college years, I met my future wife and felt led by the Lord to pursue a long-term relationship, a lifetime companionship. It was my prayer that this would cure my attraction to males and give me victory over what I had not been able to curb heretofore. In those years my participation in church became even more significant to me. Many church leaders lived in our community and others visited and spoke. My enthusiasm and appetite for church service expanded. My reading led me further in that direction.

Therefore, I was not surprised that attending Mennonite World Conference at the end of our wedding trip (Kitchener, Ontario, 1962) was another pivotal experience. There I became even more committed to serving Christ and the church as a leader. Through many answers to prayer, I felt God leading me to seminary. My wife, family, and many friends affirmed me in this calling. Few of them knew of the inner struggle that I continued to wage with my thoughts and attractions. At that time I knew nothing about "orientation." I knew only of my "besetting sin" and my tremendous sense of shame about it.

Serving the Lord in Church Leadership as Self-awareness Expands

Following my graduation from Goshen Biblical Seminary in 1966, our family moved to Premont, Texas, where South Central Mennonite Conference and Mennonite Board of Missions were supporting an outreach among poor Latino families. That was followed by work in Wichita, Kansas, again with the support of South Central Conference.

As a young pastor and father of three young children, I often struggled to find a place in the denomination where my sense of peace and justice, my compassion for others, and my growing awareness of my orientation could be integrated. Increasingly, I was able to let my wife Rhoda be privy to the deepest secrets and fears with which I struggled. Gradually I was able to allow others into my circle of support and shared with them my yearning to be whole, as a man who was attracted to some other men, and also as a husband, a father, and a pastor.

It was during these years, from 1966-1987, that I became active in church leadership at many levels. I served on conference peace and justice committees, a conference executive committee, Mennonite Board of Publication, and on committees dealing with Student and Young Adult ministries. I wrote articles for our church publications and led workshops at church conferences. I was delighted that the gifts God had given me had been discovered by and were useful to the wider church.

Dis-ease and Controversy Grow

Living and working in Iowa (Des Moines and Ames) brought new challenges and opportunities. One of those was helping young adults and others in our congregation look at human sexuality. We used resources provided by our denomination as well as materials from other denominations and respected scientific perspectives. The search to be honest and to be faithful (a "good boy for Jesus") was taking me into areas that became increasingly controversial, locally and across the church. Our congregation in Ames continued to seek God's leading. One of the areas that we continued to address was sexuality (including homosexuality) and the church. My involvement with the Men's Movement and the regional American Friends Service Committee helped me to experience settings in which my gayness was openly affirmed and supported.

Eventually, the leadership of Iowa-Nebraska Mennonite Conference approached me about my position. Our area pastoral leaders met for a weekend of in-depth study, pursuing the awareness of conflicting viewpoints among us and our conference leaders. After much deliberation, our small Ames Mennonite Church was expelled from the conference. Since we were also members of the Central District Conference (General Conference Mennonite), we still had affiliation with another group of congregations. Yet we were now known across the broader church as radical, and I was deemed an unreliable pastor by many leaders.

As I worked with other people on issues of sexuality, I became aware that I could no longer continue believing that my gay orientation was a sin. I informed conference leadership (Central District) of that and was relieved of all pastoral duties, official and otherwise. No longer was I welcomed to write in church periodicals or lead workshops at denominational levels. No longer was I acceptable as a spiritual guide. Although I had finally found deep peace and integrity as a human being, the denomination would not acknowledge that as significant. However, God clearly affirmed to me that even if the Mennonite Church could no longer accept my leadership, I was still an ordained minister. My work for the Lord would now take on much broader and deeper significance.

By the end of 1987, I had officially been removed from all denominational responsibilities except my personal church membership. I had also decided that I could no longer live under the public definition of a married man, while secretly being gay. I broke up my marriage and family by declaring that I needed to be authentically me, to live publicly as a gay man. That caused deep pain and suffering for my wife and children and for numerous others. My family of origin supported me during my years of struggle and continue to do so. My former wife and my children, in spite of their pain and anguish, were also understanding and supportive to a large degree. I moved out of the family home and established my own residence where I could live as a man who is gay. That was both a great sense of freedom to me and a profound loss.

All my life I had sought and wanted the affirmation and acceptance of the church as "a good boy." All my life I had looked outside of myself for a sense of worth and meaning. All my life I had been seeking to live God's path for me, but without sensing a deep, inner peace. Now, in spite of my profound grief, I had that deep peace. I had the love and acceptance of many family members and friends but not of the church that I had so deeply loved and respected.

Grief and Adjustment

Increasingly I became aware that the community of faith that had formed me and had been my source of deepest identity and focus was no longer available to me. Although there were many friends within the church who were supportive, the institution—the organized denomination—abandoned me. As an alumnus of the seminary, I was invited to give money but not my concerns and suggestions. I was no longer welcome to write for our periodicals. I did attend a few denominational conferences but often felt marginalized. Even though many friends there welcomed me with open arms and ready ears, others kept a distance from me. I felt "on guard" and knew my presence was a source of dis-ease for others and myself. I soon quit attending such functions.

I began a deep journey into grief. I could no longer expect those of my faith family to understand me or seek out my gifts and services. I had to increasingly disengage myself from my lifelong hopes and dreams. I even encountered persons who went so far as to shun me, to behave as though I were not really standing in front of them and speaking to them. I began to encounter aspects of anger and hate that I had never expected to find from the people in my church and in its leadership. Articles, letters, and statements appeared in denominational periodicals that used hateful language and false statements against gay persons. I felt this hatred very personally.

This became a time for me to seek out sources of strength, peace, encouragement, and clarity that could help me find my way through the traumatic confusion. I found community in the Re-Evaluation Counseling community worldwide as I dealt with the issue of oppression, both external and internal. Gay spirituality resources became crucial venues for me as I continued to explore how God/de was leading me. (Throughout my life I have used various terms to refer to the Holy One. When I was young, I was comfortable using the terms "Jesus" and "the Lord." Later, it was comfortable to use "God" also. But in recent years, I tend to prefer "God/de." This is a much broader term for me since it reflects the awareness that the Divine is not restricted to the male gender, but incorporates both male and female.)

Increasingly I became conscious that the Anabaptist history that I have so much appreciated and respected was yet again coming to bless me. Just as those early folks had dealt with suspicion and rejection from their former communities of faith and love, so did I. Although I was not burned at the stake or cast into prison, my denomination made it very clear that my beliefs and practices were branding me as a heretic and therefore undesirable.

Serving the Lord in an Expanded Ministry

Through all this time I found that my inner life was becoming richer and deeper. My awareness of God/de and the ways in which the Divine is expressed expanded greatly. I became more and more authoritative as a human being with integrity (and one who is gay). My professional work as a Marriage and Family Therapist took on greater dimensions as I helped develop a Gay/Lesbian/Bisexual and Transgendered Caucus in my group, the American Association for Marriage and Family Therapy (AAMFT). I was asked to lead workshops and training sessions across Iowa and the nation.

My involvement in the Brethren/Mennonite Council for Gay, Lesbian, Bisexual, and Transgender Interests (BMC) increased and deepened, including service for several years on the board. We worked to develop the Supportive Congregations Network (SCN). We sponsored workshops at churchwide conferences in North America. I was also a co-leader of two workshops at Mennonite World Conference in 1990 in Winnipeg, Manitoba, along with Renze Yetsenga, my dear friend and fellow-pastor from Groningen, Netherlands. Later I was asked to be a resource to church leaders and seminary students in Germany and to speak at the annual Mennonite International Youth Congress (of European Mennonite young adults) in the Netherlands. These experiences were deeply gratifying and reassuring.

Ministry Outside the Institutional Church: An Ongoing Blessing

As time passed, I became increasingly aware that God/de had a much broader ministry for me than I had imagined or dreamed. Indeed, my ordination in Wichita in 1971 was the recognition of my call to serve in spiritual leadership. Since that time, persons of faith from many denominations and religious traditions have surrounded me. I have been amazingly supported and loved by my extended family. My local congregation has been a source of ongoing counsel, support, and nurturance to me. Many persons have appeared to be for me "The People of God/de."

My anguish at the reaction of my homophobic institutional church helped me to face my addiction—"church-aholism." I realized that my professional experience in dealing with addictions in others was a rich resource to me in facing my own. I have been in recovery for many years and still deal with the temptation to want the church to be my savior! This pain has moved me forward into an arena of blessing as I discover the wonders of the Almighty, the One who uses a Cyrus and a Tamar to accomplish Divine purpose. The wineskins are not adequate; the boundaries and boxes need to be redefined. Those places that had seemed "right" have now been exposed as mere places of comfort, areas where fear kept me restricted to what was familiar.

I have heard over and over again the Divine call to Abraham: "Go up from your familiar culture, people and patterns to a land which I will show you." It is an amazing call. I may no longer be considered "a good boy" by the institutional church but God/de seems not to be keeping score!

Sometimes the cries of my heart, like the Psalmist's, come in the form of a lament.

A Lament for my Denomination

O my people!
Why would you reject your sons and daughters,
Your brothers and sisters,
Your parents and your closest friends?
Why would you force your leaders to make decisions that please you,
rather than following my Spirit's call and leading?
Why would you choose to honor the voices of fear, condemnation, and
stereotypes—cruel untruths,
rather than searching your own hearts and my way of Love
and Justice?
Why would you choose to force ways of deception and double-speak on your
leaders,
rather than seek my Presence in the dark places,
the valleys of discomfort and terror,
the confusions of disagreement and diversity?

I have longed for you to grow in your discernment of my ways.
I have longed for you to learn that compassion, justice and peace
are my spiritual gifts, given for the good of the church as well
as the world.
I have longed for you to learn new ways to love and serve me.

But, you would not.
You insisted on cutting off what was giving you dis-ease
rather than seeking the deeper truths of my mysterious ways.
You insisted on making firmer and harsher rules and boundaries,
causing "the little ones," those on the edges, to be discredited
and dishonored.
You insisted on closing your ears to those you appointed to listen and study,
filing their reports and recommendations in "safely hidden places."
You would not listen to my voice, spoken by those who said the reports
on change and reparative therapies were unreliable, untrue,
and misguided.
Instead, you chose to abandon your confessions and commitments to those
you thus persecuted.
You were no longer willing to study and to be in loving dialogue with those
you distrusted.
You shut me out.
Oh my people.
How I long for you to grow in joy and peace!
How I long for you to move beyond fear and control!
How I long for you to live in Love and Joy and Hope!

And this is my vow to you, my people....all my relations...
I will NEVER abandon or forsake you.
I will NEVER cut you off or shut you out.
For The Eternal One has spoken, saying,
"I never fail. My mercy is forever."

Keith Schrag, M.Div., M.A., was born in Ontario, Canada, grew up in northern New York, and has lived in Iowa since 1975. His former wife Rhoda pastors and teaches in Elkhart County, Indiana. He has three adult children: Jonathan, living with his three children in Goshen, Indiana; Jerold, living with his wife Linda and their two daughters in Estes Park, Colorado; and Lisa, living in Chicago, Illinois.

After turning sixty-five in 2003, Keith retains his private practice as a Licensed Marital and Family Therapist in Ames, Iowa. He is also a holistic healer and teacher, leading workshops and rituals that assist inner growth and exploration. He is involved in many community organizations as a volunteer. His hobbies include traveling frequently, daily exercise and health care, attending world-famous music and dance venues at the near-by Iowa State University auditorium, and exploring internet friendships.

CHAPTER 25

Open to Strangers

Frank Ward

The 1996 Fourth of July weekend in Dallas was scorching. I can think of no other word to describe it more accurately. The Western District Conference (WDC) of the General Conference Mennonite Church and the South Central Mennonite Conference (SCMC) of the Mennonite Church were holding their annual meetings jointly in the same hotel. Business sessions were conducted separately. Since the Rainbow Mennonite Church I served was a dual conference church, several other members and I decided to attend the first business session of the SCMC. Attending business sessions has never been one of my favorite activities; I place it somewhere between bungee jumping and being a contestant on *Fear Factor*.

About an hour into the session, after taking care of the requisite items, the chairman called for new business. Immediately a pastor rose from his seat behind me and strode down the aisle to the lectern. As he passed me, I noticed that he held a copy of the *Mennonite Weekly Review* in one hand and a Bible in the other. *Uh oh, I thought, things are going to get hotter for the Rainbow Mennonite Church.*

* * *

By the time (1942) I entered high school in Philadelphia, my friends and I considered ourselves fully educated in the mysterious realm of sex. But our miniscule and faulty knowledge, certainly mine, was amassed from eavesdropped or whispered and giggled conversations with peers and culled from dictionaries where I was led on circuitous routes from one strange, unpronounceable word to another. It was also here that I developed what I thought—big mistake—was a clear understanding of homosexuality. That word and related ones were rarely used—there were others that were part of the high school vocabulary. Primarily they were used to ridicule and deride boys who were usually smaller and more timid. I sadly confess to my participation, even though I was sometimes the butt of the taunting myself.

It was about that time that I happened upon the First Mennonite Church in Philadelphia (which is another story). There I experienced a number of events that would eventually become life-changing for me. I found myself in a Sunday school class of boys taught by an untrained man from whom we learned *love*. Not the love we received from our parents—they *had* to love us. This was a man who *listened* to what we had to say, who paid attention to us for our own sakes. We delighted to express in class the most outrageous ideas, theological and secular, yet they never seemed to threaten him or his faith. It was years later that I learned what he knew then: that we were starting on the uncertain, fearful, and exciting path to adulthood. We were trying out our new-found powers on a man we knew—though wild horses could not have dragged the words from our lips—loved us, accepted us, and could be trusted.

The United States had recently entered World War II, the "popular" war, when another important event for me happened at the church. A group of young men, conscientious objectors, visited the church and spoke of their conviction that violence was not the way of Jesus. I had always carried a feeling, for as long as I could remember, that violence seemed a bad way to settle disagreements, no matter how serious. Now I heard young men speaking of following a different path. It resonated with me.

Several years later, there was a change in ministers at the church. I had a deep appreciation for the pastor who had baptized me and guided me into the church, but his successor was different in many ways. He was younger, related to some of my interests and, to the shock of some members of the congregation, he wore a sports coat on weekdays and even at the Sunday evening church services. I also discovered he went to movies on occasion! Films were then, and remain, a passion for me.

The new pastor quickly tore down my image of those who entered the ministry. It was built on the relatively few ministers I had met, seen, or heard, mostly in eastern Pennsylvania. In my undoubtedly biased view, I saw them as rather humorless, always dressed in white shirts, solid black ties, suits, and hats—Blues Brothers' garb without the shades.

But more important, he introduced me, with sermons and the loan of some books, to theology and biblical study. One evening as I passed him on the stairway to the second floor sanctuary, he suddenly reached out, grabbed me by the tie, and pushed me gently against the wall. *What sins of mine had he discovered?* He wagged a finger in my face and said, "Frank, you ought to be thinking about going to college and becoming a minister." He smiled and continued up the stairs while I stood there. As far as I knew, no one in my family had ever walked through a college door let alone attended one. If I remember correctly, in less than two years he was gone. I assume his theology was too liberal for the congregation or the congregation was too conservative for him; as a youth I was not privy to the details.

It was four more years before I made my decision to act on at least part of my pastor's shocking counsel. On the advice of the present pastor, I went off to a Bible college in 1950. I do not regret that three-year step in my journey. I learned much of the language and thought of conservative Christians. I still remember friends, both teachers and students, with great affection. It was there that, for the first time, I heard the word *homosexuality* used in a serious context. But what a context! I learned that the Apostle Paul was dead set against it, as were all the other biblical authors. Furthermore, because of his approval of marriage, Jesus was clearly opposed to it. The conclusion was short and not so sweet; homosexuality was sin and nothing less. That, it seemed, was enough for any Bible student—and any Christian—to know.

After three years, feeling that I wanted more than I was receiving at the Bible college, I transferred to a Mennonite college and seminary. That was an even more profitable experience, especially as I learned more about peace and nonresistance. But the biblical teaching regarding homosexuality was the same; it was sin. I cannot recall the topic being discussed in any of my college or seminary classes on psychology or counseling.

Toward the end of the fifties, I found myself pastoring a Mennonite church in a small town. The congregation was everything a new pastor could want: caring, forgiving, and willing to endure my fumbling attempts at preaching and teaching. But it was there that I ran headlong into "The Big Question." A young woman, recently out of high school, came to see me one day, distraught and inconsolable. Marie (fictional name) had been volunteering with a social service agency in a midwestern city and had been sent home when she broke down after having her first homosexual experience. It was with an older, more experienced woman. She had been forced to admit, she told me tearfully, what she had tried to deny to herself for some years—she was a lesbian.

In 1950, the Mattachine Society had been founded. In the early years of the decade, homosexuality began to receive a small amount of attention in some media. In 1953, it became sufficient reason to fire federal employees. There began to be reports of police brutality and harassment which could not be ignored. My straight world was gradually hearing about the suffering of gays and lesbians. I learned much about it one afternoon and in the months that followed. At our first meeting, Marie asked me a question—"The Big Question"—for both of us. With her voice full of anguish and despair, she stared at the floor and whispered, "Is God mad at me?"

As I write this the season is Epiphany, and I am reminded that a few days ago our pastor asked the adult education class if any of us had ever experienced an epiphany. The word is from the Greek and among its translations are "made evident" and "coming suddenly into view." I really don't know if I have ever had an epiphany, but I do know that the moment that distraught young woman asked that question, the answer was clear—as evident to me as anything I have ever known. I don't recall my exact words, but I told her that I was absolutely certain that God was not angry with her. Nor did she need to be angry at herself— God loved and accepted her as she was.

However, words are so often insufficient. "The best thinking," I had heard a psychiatrist say, not too long before I met Marie, "is that homosexuality is an illness, often caused by poor parenting." That idea held on even into the seventies. Marie consulted medical doctors, psychiatrists, counselors . . . the list grew. No one seemed able to help. I don't believe her family had any idea of the reason for her distress—she was terrified to tell them. She attempted suicide—a cry to the universe for help. She mentioned to me several times that she had heard that there was a community of homosexuals in San Francisco. Then one day, she was gone. Sometime later I accepted a position at the General Conference (GC) offices and moved to Kansas. I never heard from or about Marie again. I still pray for her.

I served at the GC offices from the middle sixties to 1975, a time of great upheaval in American society. It was an exciting time for me. By the time I left in 1975, Blacks (the politically correct term at the time) had made some significant progress in the society. Homosexuals and women were becoming more vocal about their needs. But bringing about change and acceptance in the Christian church was as difficult for those groups as it was for the Blacks. When I left my position in the office there was, in my mind, little to cheer about.

Wanting to return to the pastorate, I accepted a call to Rainbow Mennonite Church in Kansas City, Kansas. I could not have asked for a better group of people with whom to work. Together we asked questions, struggled for answers, and asked more questions. What did it mean to have faith in our society? What was God's intent for the Rainbow congregation? What was our role in our community? There were more. We neither received nor expected complete, final answers to our questions; we knew that we were on a journey.

After my unforgettable experience with Marie, I began to pay more attention to the question of homosexuals and the church. I discovered D.S. Bailey's book, *Homosexuality and the Western Christian Tradition,* some years after it was published. However, I could find little after that until the eighties when publishers began to sense a market as the topic gained some prominence. In 1978, I had a number of helpful conversations with a member of Rainbow who was a teacher at a university and a counseling psychologist. As a result, it was decided that we should offer a three-day workshop in our church building to

Western District (WDC) and South Central Mennonite Conference (SCMC) leaders and other interested people. The purpose was to present an alternative view to the prevailing one in Christian churches that homosexuality was a sin.

Among the speakers we invited were the pastor and several members of a local Metropolitan Community Church. We wanted the participants to have a chance to meet and converse with real human beings who happened to be homosexual. A reporter from *The Mennonite* attended the workshop, and for the first time, I believe, a Mennonite paper carried a substantial article dealing with the situation of gays and the church. My mail was interesting for a few weeks. Some messages offered support; a few spoke of judgment to come.

In 1979, the Rainbow Mennonite Church Council agreed that the congregation would accept as members all persons professing faith in Jesus Christ "regardless of sexual orientation." In 1989, our congregation was invited to join the Supportive Congregations Network (SNC). By joining, we would support the Brethren/Mennonite Council for Lesbian and Gay Concerns (BMC), an organization of gays and lesbians who wished to become members of Church of the Brethren and Mennonite congregations without hiding their sexual orientation.

After a special meeting in 1990 to discuss the implications of such a move, the congregation passed a motion to join SCN by a large majority. The problem was, however, that we had joined at a level that kept our name from being publicized by either the SCN or BMC. No one except our own members knew that we welcomed gays and lesbians (today I would use the acronym, GLBT) as members!

Finally in 1996, the Church Council, with the approval of the congregation, decided that we would move to the "Publicly Affirming" level. This meant that now the SCN and BMC could make our name known to other similar organizations and use it in their publications. On June 27 of that year, ten days before the annual sessions of SCMC and WDC were scheduled to meet in Dallas, Texas, the *Mennonite Weekly Review* carried a front page article in which it reported that our congregation, along with others, had publicly joined the SCN. The result was a call at that first business session of the SCMC for the disciplining of congregations—ours—who would open their doors and offer member-ship to gay people on the same basis as it was offered to everyone else. The heat was on; we had crossed the line. Shortly thereafter, we were informed that we must recant and remove our membership from the SCN or face discipline from the SCMC. The irony was that during all this time we had no openly gay members.

In September, the congregation met to discuss our response. There was a strong consensus that while we wanted to remain an SCMC con-gregation, we also wanted to continue our membership in the SCN. This was not acceptable to the conference. A small task force was ap-pointed at Rainbow, and we discussed with the congregation how best to deal with the situation. For the next year, meetings were held, telephone calls made, and letters sent between the congregation and the SCMC. The relationships were always cordial, but there was little progress.

Our task force met twice with a small group appointed by the SCMC Executive Committee. We shared biblical interpretations but found nothing to agree on. Finally it was agreed that, rather than deal-ing with the issue again on the conference floor at the annual sessions in 1997, the question would be put to the conference delegates by a mail-in ballot vote. Later we changed our minds and suggested that a special meeting of delegates be held at which time we could thoroughly discuss both homosexuality itself and the matter of the relationship between the conference and congregations who were willing to accept homosexuals as members. We were not surprised to learn our sugges-tion was rejected and early in 1998, a ballot was mailed to all SCMC delegates.

On March 9, I received a conference phone call from the confer-ence moderator and the conference minister. We had been prevented from meeting in person because of a snowstorm. They read to me the decision the executive committee made after tallying the votes:

Moved that we inform Rainbow Mennonite Church of the majority decision of the delegates, that we loose them from membership in the South Central Conference, and that this become effective March 1, 1999. Between now and March 1, 1999, their status will be restricted, to be interpreted to mean without vote.

After almost forty years of membership in the SCMC, we would be completely cut off in a year unless we would remove our membership from the SCN and refuse membership to human beings born with a sexual orientation different from "straight" people. In 1999, the action was made complete. As I write this in 2004, the Rainbow congregation remains "loosed" from the SCMC.

In the fall of 1998, just before I turned seventy, I retired from the church and moved away from Kansas City. This was an arrangement the congregation and I had made together more than a year before. It was not, as some supposed, over the disciplining procedure. But it was unpleasant, to say the least, to realize that after twenty-three years, I was leaving the congregation during the process of being disciplined.

I have passed over many of the details, the twists and turns of that procedure, but I am convinced that sometime in the future, church historians and theologians, if they care enough to study it, will see it as flawed—another of the many blunders that Christians make because we are human. However, in my estimation, it is a blunder with appalling consequences for the many fine and wonderful people who long to belong to an Anabaptist congregation but are prevented because of the prejudice, fear, and legalism that bar the church doors. They continue to press against those doors. Some call it antagonism and dissension-sowing, but I see it as a yearning for justice, acceptance, and peace—entities for which Mennonites have long claimed they stood. And I am convinced that someday they will prevail and all the doors of all the churches will swing open.

Throughout the entire discipline process I found myself not so much angry as sad. Nevertheless that sadness was balanced by my joy at the amazing strength and commitment of the Rainbow congregation each time they made decisions in the matter. More than eighty-five percent of the congregation was supportive, and the church was never in danger of dividing. At the time we made the first decision to accept people with homosexual orientations and at each further step, I could not help but remember Marie and wonder what changes it might have made in her life if she could have been part of a faith community where she could have felt accepted by the people, by God, and by herself. I pray that she has found a full and free life—and the answer to The Big Question.

After my retirement in 1998, my wife and I moved to Hawaii, her home state—still a territory when we married. Here we found what we consider a gracious gift from God—a church that like Rainbow and others contains a statement of welcome in its bulletin every Sunday. Part of it reads, " . . . we celebrate our diversity in religious, racial and ethnic backgrounds, in abilities and sexual orientations, and in age and gender." A significant portion of the membership is made up of GLBT people. I can't say how many...I don't know. It is a question we do not ask, not out of embarrassment or caution—it just doesn't matter. There are many more important things to discover about each other. But we do not hide from our differences; during worship someone may request prayer for a husband or wife, another for a partner. We pray for each one. Every Sunday morning after a prayer of confession, we "pass the peace" with handshakes, hugs, and even kisses (remember that old Mennonite custom?). Sometimes we sing Brian Wren's wonderful hymn, "We are your people." I especially like the third verse:

> Rich in diversity, help us to live
> closer than neighbors, open to strangers,
> able to clash and forgive.

What a wonderful gift from God!

Frank Ward was born and raised in Philadelphia. He received his B.A. from Goshen College and his B.D. from Goshen Biblical Seminary. He studied at Eastern Baptist Theological Seminary in the post-graduate program. He has served as pastor in two Mennonite congregations. Between the two pastorates, Frank served on the General Conference Mennonite Church's Commission on Education. In 1998, he retired after pastoring the Rainbow Mennonite Church for twenty-three years.

He lives in Mililani, Hawaii, where he and his wife Margaret Makino celebrated their fiftieth wedding anniversary last year. They have a son, daughter, son-in-law, grandson, and granddaughter. Frank and Margaret are active in the Church of the Crossroads, United Church of Christ, in Honolulu..

CHAPTER 26

Two Faithful Congregations

John Linscheid

I am not a pastor. Denominational leaders put an end to that in 1984. Their action, designed to deflect controversy and protect the *status quo,* released me to participate in a collective ministry. The witness of that ministry may one day encourage healthy responses to conflict and replace the worn out *status quo* with a truly energizing Mennonite reality in Christ.

The revocation of my pastoral credentials was a small (though heart-felt) loss. The real loss has been the wider Mennonite church's failure to avail itself of the gifts of uniquely faithful congregations. These congregations, expelled or simply marginalized for welcoming a fuller complement of God's children, often have provided models of Christian discernment. They have much to teach. As spiritual descendants of the Anabaptists, they have seriously applied New Testament principles of prayer, discernment, scriptural inspiration, and accountability to making decisions about challenging social issues.

True ministry demands *honest* grappling with life's realities. Embracing messy human processes and risking uncomfortable conflict can yield growth under the tutelage of the Holy Spirit. The Mennonite Church USA and its predecessor denominations could have learned from these congregations to trust God enough to enter the uncertain realm of profound spiritual engagement. Instead, they sought the comfort of authoritarian solutions. Fearing attacks from factions that demand simplistic answers above faithfulness, Mennonite leaders have, except for brief moments, reiterated old prejudices and shut down honest, though uncomfortable, discernment.

* * *

I came out of the closet to the Lawrence Mennonite Fellowship—now Peace Mennonite Church—in 1983. This gathering of Mennonites in Lawrence, Kansas, had been given funds by the Western District Conference Home Missions Committee to aid its church-planting effort. In 1980, the fellowship had called me, fresh from Associated Mennonite Biblical Seminaries, to be its first pastor.

Idealistically, we sought to apply Anabaptist/Mennonite perspectives to Christian faith in everyday life. As a peace church, we were among the spiritual leaders of the local peace-and-justice movement. We worked at making our worship and congregational life express our discipleship in how we cared for each other and made decisions. So, when I told the congregation I was gay, it naturally sought the Holy Spirit's leading through mutual discernment, Bible study, and prayer as a gathered community. Some members ardently opposed the idea of retaining me as pastor. Others argued that our commitment to God's justice and equality demanded nondiscrimination with regard to sexual orientation.

This was before the Mennonite denominations adopted litmus tests on homosexuality and while the General Conference Mennonite Church still existed. The General Conference, to which Lawrence Mennonite Fellowship and the Western District Conference belonged, placed a high value on local congregational discernment. Lawrence's approach to the issue at hand conformed not only to its Anabaptist/Mennonite faith but also to our denominational polity and process.

Our engagement of the issue got messy at times. We got angry with each other. We engaged in fierce biblical and theological debate. We wrote and exchanged papers. But we did it all face-to-face, attempting to remain fully accountable to one another in love. Those who disagreed with or got angry with me came directly to me. People even asked permission before discussing each other's viewpoints when they could not be present. All this took place in the context of our life before God, as we continued to meet for common prayer and worship. I felt love and unity with those who disagreed with me just as I did with those who agreed with me.

After two meetings, we reached a consensus to put the unity and life of the congregation foremost, even though we remained divided on the issue. We agreed that none would threaten to leave in order to pressure others. We would remain fully open to the Spirit in our deliberations and transparent with each other. We had already invited a representative of our partner, the Western District Conference, to the second meeting.

What we perceived as a healthy, caring, and thoroughly Anabaptist approach to conflict confused district leaders. Focused on the potential fallout in wider church politics, they could only perceive our careful deliberation as a failure to dispose efficiently of a threat. They moved to "fix" the situation by revoking my pastoral credentials and threatening to cut off church-planting funds unless I was fired. There was no prior dialogue or attempt to clarify things with the congregation or with me.

In response, the congregation called a meeting to mutually discern how to proceed. Even those who felt I should leave the pastorate had not wanted the decision made this way. We considered our options. Could we continue without district support? How would conflict with our district detract from our church-planting mission? We came to a consensus, and I resigned.

However, the Lawrence congregation confronted district leaders about their impersonal process. It made two requests. First, it asked that the Ministerial Committee meet with me face-to-face to discuss our views. The meeting was not comfortable, but it did provide the opportunity to confront one another and see each other as people.

Second, the Lawrence Fellowship pointed out that no discernment had taken place regarding the issue of homosexuality. It suggested that a district forum should be organized for such a discussion.

A little over a year later, the district organized a workshop for congregations to study the issue of homosexuality. It invited a woman from the Brethren/Mennonite Council for Lesbian and Gay Concerns to tell her story and a man who identified as ex-gay at the time to present his. It invited me to present my views on interpretation of the relevant Scriptures and another man to present the opposing views. District leaders had taken Lawrence's concerns seriously. In a respectful atmosphere allowing for balanced points of view, participants engaged in honest discussion while acknowledging important disagreements.

Several years after that, a member of a subsequent Western District Ministerial Committee talked with me. She suggested she might approach the committee about reconsidering its earlier decision. However, I had moved out of the Western District, and the process did not seem practical to me. I also ran into the man who had chaired the Ministerial Committee when it revoked my credentials, and we shared some grief over the pain of the former events, achieving a better mutual understanding.

I cannot help but believe that Lawrence's Anabaptist/Mennonite model of discernment and the integrity of its approach had opened hearts over time. For at least one brief period, the congregation had achieved a level of healthy dialogue seldom seen in church conflict. The district could have used Lawrence as a resource to shepherd other congregations through similar discord. Although the opportunity was lost, Lawrence's ministry had some wider effect. Unfortunately, the door that started opening would be slammed shut later when a denominational merger would make condemning gay and lesbian people a litmus test for good standing in the new organization.

* * *

In 1985, soon after I left Lawrence, my partner Ken White and I moved to Philadelphia, Pennsylvania. Here we became involved in the continent's oldest Mennonite congregation, Germantown Mennonite Church. This congregation, too, had seriously engaged the issues of sexuality. In response to a request for membership by Don Winters, who was gay, the congregation embarked on a process of biblical and theological study and discernment. It also chose an Anabaptist/Mennonite approach and sought consensus despite serious conflict. Shortly before Ken and I arrived in Philadelphia, it had reached a decision to hold same-sex and heterosexual couples to the same ethical standards of faithfulness and covenant.

Germantown's process was also messy sometimes. At Germantown, a number of people left before the decision was finalized. Some disagreed with but came to respect the sincerity of the majority view. They chose to stay and not to block consensus.

Although Germantown had long been affiliated with the General Conference (and its Eastern District), during the late 1970s and early 1980s, the congregation's strongest ties were to the Franconia Mennonite Conference of the Mennonite Church denomination. About the same time that Germantown's study resulted in more openness, Franconia Conference adopted a contrary view. The conference declared heterosexuality God's ideal, implicitly viewed gay and lesbian people as inferior, and advocated conversion to heterosexuality. Every gay or lesbian person I knew who saw the statement found it degrading and offensive. Noting the discrepancy between the congregational and conference positions, Germantown informed Franconia leadership of the congregation's position and conversation ensued.

After several meetings, representatives from Franconia and Germantown came to an agreement. Germantown would rescind its explicit decision to hold church members in same-sex and heterosexual couples to the same moral standards. It would not officially oppose but also would not adopt Franconia's position. It would take *no* position on homosexuality. Franconia would respect Germantown's decisions regarding church membership as a "pastoral" matter. This would permit Germantown to receive gay and lesbian people into membership— including some who were in covenant relationships. Many found it painful for Germantown to step back from its earlier decision. Still, the agreement presented an opportunity to base decisions about membership on faith journeys rather than sexual orientation. Moreover, it preserved the congregation's unity with the conference.

The conference moderator of the time later noted that all Franconia's representatives to the talks had explicitly acknowledged that they had opened a door at Germantown. Now people in gay and lesbian relationships could become members. (But the agreement was not publicly announced.) One representative, a pastor, even recommended Germantown to a gay member of his congregation.

Germantown had met a controversial challenge with much integrity. It had not been a perfect process. There had been some casualties.

Disagreements over homosexuality continued and arguments took place. People's feelings got hurt. But members sought forgiveness from one another and endeavored to respect each other in the love of Christ. At Germantown, as at Lawrence, I found a congregation that trusted the Holy Spirit to lead it through a complex situation. It achieved an unusual measure of Christian maturity that was reflected in relationships within the congregation.

In the larger North American context, more and more evangelical leaders sought to increase their influence by playing on society's prejudices against gay and lesbian people. Some of their Mennonite adherents began to leverage the issue to gain power in Mennonite circles. They discarded Anabaptist/Mennonite principles of mutual Christian discernment in favor of doctrinal absolutes. They denounced all who disagreed with them as "against the Bible," "soft on sin," and "unfaithful." Noting the inclusion of gay and lesbian people at Germantown, detractors who were part of Franconia Mennonite Conference demanded that conference leaders "do something about Germantown."

Protecting the anonymity of Germantown's detractors, conference officials passed along their complaints. We took a cue from Matthew 18:15 and offered to meet with those who felt offended by our openness (we did not know who our detractors were). When our invitation was relayed, it was not accepted.

When an article in *Dialogue,* (a publication of the Brethren/ Mennonite Council for Lesbian and Gay Concerns—now Lesbian, Gay, Bisexual, and Transgender Interests) reported Franconia's accommodation with Germantown, the controversy exploded. Some leaders from other conferences who were leading crusades to cleanse the church of gay and lesbian people feared that Franconia's accommodation would undermine their efforts. They joined in pressuring their Franconia counterparts to adopt a similar intolerance.

In response, Franconia's leadership abandoned its prior agreement with Germantown. They requested an investigation of Germantown's ministry. That fostered the appearance that they had been unaware of Germantown's openness. When the "investigation" revealed what had never been hidden, the conference demanded that the congregation comply with its official position.

Now Germantown faced an impossible choice. The heterosexual members of the congregation could say to their gay and lesbian brothers and sisters, "Get out! We have no need of you." This would violate Christ's demand that the church be one and Paul's injunction not to divide the body of Christ (John 17:20-21; First Corinthians 1:10-13; 12:12-27). But standing firm also threatened the body of Christ—the implied threat from Franconia leadership was to divide the body of Christ by excommunicating Germantown.

A few hopeful souls from the conference met with representatives of Germantown to attempt to find a "third way." A truly middle ground could not be found. However, Germantown agreed to consider a form of non-voting associate membership to preserve our connection with the larger church. Conference leaders refused to bring the proposal to delegates for a vote, favoring excommunication.

When delegates heard testimony of Germantown's faith and process, however, they hesitated. A few supported us. Some wanted more time to decide. Many considered excommunication too extreme. The vote fell short. At the next assembly, the pattern was repeated. Finally, conference leaders resorted to an impersonal, mail-in ballot to finalize the expulsion. Soon after the ballot deadline passed in October 1997, conference leaders brought word of Germantown's excommunication to our congregation. To make conference leaders take responsibility for what they were doing, my partner Ken demanded that the conference moderator walk him to the door to symbolically cast him out and she did so.

Again, a congregation witnessed to the larger Mennonite church about working for unity in conflict. It could have provided a model of Anabaptist/Mennonite approaches to Christian discernment. Again, its gift was repudiated.

*   *   *

Germantown remained a member of Eastern District Conference and the General Conference Mennonite Church. However, a few years after Germantown was excommunicated from Franconia, the parts of the General Conference Mennonite Church and the Mennonite Church in the United States merged to form the Mennonite Church USA. To achieve the merger, the General Conference surrendered its tradition of congregational discernment in favor of the Mennonite Church denomination's authoritarian conference structure. In addition, the new denomination made condemning gay and lesbian people the single litmus test for faithfulness in the organization. This left Germantown vulnerable to having its last official tie to the larger denomination severed.

In September 2001, Germantown's positive response to a gay member's request to be considered for ordination provided the needed excuse to sever that tie. (See chapter two by David Weaver in this book.) After a short series of dialogues between Germantown representatives and Eastern District Conference leaders, the outcome was clear. District leaders would entertain no viewpoint that did not affirm the new denomination's official prejudices against sexual-minority people.

Germantown again appealed to the New Testament command not to divide the body of Christ, but our differences with the district could not be bridged. So, Germantown delegates invited Eastern District to join us in adopting a confession of our shared sin of dividing the body of Christ. District leaders did so, recognizing our mutual failure, but they were unable to see another solution. Germantown was excommunicated. In May 2002, the oldest Mennonite congregation in North America lost its denominational affiliation.

* * *

At Germantown and at Lawrence, small congregations eagerly sought to follow Christ seriously. Each embraced the challenge of applying Anabaptist/Mennonite principles to complex real-life conflicts. Each took mutual discernment seriously and were led to open their hearts to teachings from the Holy Spirit that did not conform to popular opinions. Despite foibles and faults, both achieved an unusual degree of success in maintaining the unity of the body of Christ within the congregation.

Unlike traditional Mennonite communities where church participation is the social norm, the Mennonite communities of Lawrence and Germantown exist by choice. Even members from "ethnic Mennonite" background tend to participate because of their specific commitment to Mennonite faith. Because "Mennonite" has to do with their faith identity, they value connections to the larger Mennonite world. When their discernment puts them at odds with comfortable traditional views, they do not threaten to leave if they don't get their way. Instead, they seek to maintain a unity in Christ that will transcend disagreement.

Congregations such as Lawrence and Germantown live the essence of Anabaptism and Mennonite faith. They should be guiding the Mennonite church. Instead, they are driven to the margins. Yet they are the North American Mennonite church's brightest hope for its future.

* * *

I have not been a professional pastor for over twenty years now. My training has faded. My skills have atrophied. I doubt I could successfully exercise pastoral responsibilities should the opportunity present itself. But God has given me much more than I have lost.

I know authentically what it means to be a member of the body of Christ. I know the visionary reality of ministry practiced together by disciples in congregations thrown into the crucible of moral challenges. I know what it means to be Mennonite. I have seen the promise of unity transcending diversity in the church.

I am no longer a pastor, but I am part of Christ's ministry. That ministry still has the potential to teach the larger Mennonite church the life-giving, unifying power of Christ, our Savior.

John Linscheid earns a living as Office Manager and Assistant to the Chair for the Department of Chemical and Biomolecular Engineering at the University of Pennsylvania. Together with his partner Ken White he has led workshops on and authored an article about gay spiritual identity development. He and Ken are members of Germantown Mennonite Church. John knows that others will remember the details differently. He acknowledges that conference and denominational leaders and other members of the congregations would tell these stories in other ways and invites them to do so. Other articles by John are available at www.seas.upenn.edu/~linsch/JLpage.htm

CHAPTER 27

"Small Deaths and Little Resurrections"

Anneli Braul

Recently, I completed a Master's thesis, "'Making Room' The Praxis of Hospitality and Journey to Inclusion: An Inclusive Model of the Church for North American Anabaptist-Mennonites." I argued, based on a reading of liberation theologies (including Latin American and North American feminists) and Anabaptism, that the time is right for the church to proclaim the good news of inclusivity and to "make room" for all people regardless of race, gender, and sexual orientation. I learned that the radical reformation of the sixteenth century with its emphasis on the spirit is highly regarded by both Latin American and North American liberation theologians. In fact, they point to the contributions of the sixteenth century radical reformation as an important frame of reference and as a catalyst for reform and change in today's church.

As a proclaimed and baptized Anabaptist-Mennonite, I feel strongly connected to a long history of persons, stretching as far back as the sixteenth century (and perhaps even beyond that), who risked speaking out about the social, economic, spiritual, and political abuses of the church and the state. They were prepared to say that membership in the church was voluntary, based on a commitment to follow Jesus; that all individuals were equal before God; that all persons were "priests" and had opportunity to "offer a psalm, a text, a prayer, or an interpretation." Two other principles were important: freedom of conscience and listening to the spirit (discernment) within community. I am also aware that Anabaptism as a movement down to the present is flawed, not pure, with abuses and faults of its own. Still, I affirm many of its tenets, though with a critical eye to ways the church has excluded, shunned, or discriminated against persons it does not agree with.

For the purposes of this reflection I want to use an idea that I found while researching my thesis. In her book on the practice of Christian hospitality and its biblical roots (*Making Room: Recovering Hospitality as a Christian Tradition*, 1999), Christine Pohl suggests that the practice of hospitality—welcome and inclusion of all in the church—is both costly and rewarding. She describes the consequences of hospitality as "small deaths and little resurrections" (187). The work of hospitality is costly because it is exhausting, full of ambivalence, uncertainty, the unknown, and irony. It is also rewarding, Pohl says, because "as we make room for hospitality more room becomes available to us for life, hope, and grace."

My personal journey of faith and my work as a co-pastor within a publicly affirming congregation have been radically impacted and enriched. I have experienced both losses and rewards. There is a cost for speaking the truth; there are also immeasurable benefits. This is the irony of inclusivity. Rather than attempt to outline a history of Calgary Inter-Mennonite's journey toward inclusivity, I will be speaking in my own voice and experience about what it means to be a member and co-pastor in a publicly affirming congregation.

Let me share a little piece about myself first. I was born in 1955 in Ascuncion, Paraguay, to parents who were at that time General Conference mission workers from Canada. I cannot remember a time in my life when I did not feel a love for the church and a strong connection to it. I grew up, quite literally, in the shadows of a church steeple (First Mennonite on George Street in Waterloo, Ontario). My modest childhood playground extended to the churchyard just across the street from our home. From our front stone porch, we could see the comings and goings of the congregation, and the "path" between our front door and the doors of the church was well worn.

I loved the singing of hymns, the organ music, the warm woodwork, and the stained glass windows enlivened by the sun's light streaming through. I loved hearing my father's sermons in which he often "painted" descriptive and moving word pictures. From early on, my consciousness and imagination have been permeated with ideas, questions, wondering, and talk of God, Jesus, and being a faithful disciple in the world. I have, from my earliest recollections, carried a sense of God around in my heart/soul.

I was a shy child, often within my own thoughts, comfortable in quiet reflection, sitting and watching and listening to what was happening around me. I can remember feeling a gentle protective attachment to a young boy in my Sunday school class who was different. Though I was still very young, the one way that I knew how to show him he was not alone was to sit beside him, sharing a songbook. I believe the seeds of dismay towards injustice and discrimination were sown in my heart long before I gave voice to them. (I also sometimes muse that my inclination and attraction to the theologies of liberation arise from my birth on Latin American soil.)

Following graduation from a private Mennonite high school, I studied theology and philosophy at Canadian Mennonite Bible College and the University of Manitoba. I married, had three children, and supported my husband's upwardly mobile career path. Throughout this time, I did not stop reading, thinking, reflecting, and questioning.

In the spring of 1987, when our youngest daughter was barely four weeks old, we moved to Calgary, Alberta. On our first Sunday, even before we began to unpack, we attended Calgary Inter-Mennonite Church (then known as South Calgary Mennonite Brethren Church). This church was recommended to us by a friend. Being an active participant and member of this congregation over the past seventeen years has changed my life. I was encouraged to express my ideas and thoughts within a congregation that was open to theological inquiry, exploring other faith traditions, social justice, and simply asking questions or wondering. The congregation was founded on principles of welcome, openness, and respecting individual faith and personal journeys. Our young family was warmly welcomed.

The community respected my contributions in worship, education, music, and service, and I nurtured and sustained many friendships and relationships. In the fall of 1995, CIM affirmed and commissioned me as part of a co-pastor team. Though I have resisted spiritualizing this affirmation to be a minister in a congregation, I recognize this part of my journey as a significant opportunity—a place to learn and grow, an incredibly wonderful place to stretch my perhaps latent gifts, and a rich context in which to contribute to the church I love. It has been a distinct privilege to be part of a team in leadership at CIM. It has been an amazing experience to be part of a congregation living, worshipping, and working its way to public affirmation and inclusivity. It has been an equally amazing experience, though eye opening and sobering, to be part of the wider church conferences struggling with their response to one congregation's decision to follow its conscience.

This brings me to the questions I have set out for myself. What have been some of the "small deaths" for me as co-pastor of a publicly inclusive congregation? What have been some of the "little resurrections"?

The many hours of meetings with conference representatives and constituency (within three denominations regionally and nationally) took their toll. The nature of the "dialogue" or conversations was in many instances emotionally, psychologically, and spiritually draining. It was difficult to hear painful comments. Many times I wished I could have been spared the anger and attributive language, not only towards homosexuals but also towards their families and allies. I was told by leaders in the conference that "now is not a good time" to be public about your welcome. They reminded me that there were Mennonite congregations and leaders who were practicing their welcoming, quietly, without disturbing the whole group. I experienced persons who were privately supportive and said so, but in public they said something else or nothing at all. Perhaps the most painful moments of all have been discriminatory conference actions towards the youth and young adults of Calgary Inter-Mennonite.

I have come to realize that the sentiments expressed by well-meaning leaders within conferences and congregations are duplicitous. It is acceptable and even preferable to be privately inclusive. It is okay to chastise and frown on those who are inclusive and say so aloud in the public arena of church and conference life. This raises interesting questions about a church that stands in a long faith tradition that was born out of freedom of conscience, public voluntary confession of faith, and taking risks to do so—a faith tradition that values congruence of "word and deed."

Another loss relates to association or connection with peers, colleagues of the Mennonite collective in Alberta, and the wider regional and national Mennonite church family. It is sometimes difficult to be seen as variant or an aberration. One of the consequences of CIM's public inclusivity was the loss of my credentials with Mennonite Church Alberta. Conference leadership could no longer endorse me as a minister under their auspices. As co-pastors, we have been told that we are not welcome at certain provincial/regional pastors' gatherings. It was also stated that if I stood in front of an inter-Mennonite gathering as worship leader, I would be like a lightening rod, hindering the ability of some persons to worship. It is a curious experience to be seen as a threat and someone to be feared.

In the bigger picture, the loss to the broader church when it is not inclusive and welcoming to all is considerable. There is the loss of valuable life experience, giftedness, and the souls and bodies of persons loved by God—made in the image of God. This is what I grieve.

These examples of various isolated incidents from my experience are not life-threatening by any stretch of the imagination, though they are hurtful. Nevertheless, they do communicate something about the larger spirit, beyond the mere actions or words themselves. They communicate something about collective fear, anxiety, and the need to silence others. By being known as someone who would advocate publicly on behalf of marginalized persons, I have also experienced marginalization, albeit in a small way. However, this leads into the notion of "little resurrections"; for me, this whole experience as a leader within a publicly inclusive congregation and everything that this entails has brought "death" to a faith and practice based on fear, held captive by an unknown and uncertain future.

It is an amazing freedom to be released from censorship to follow one's own spirit. I feel gratitude that I am part of a congregation that tries to the best of its ability to speak about and live a theology of grace. This means to abandon a theology of fear and judgment and to accept individuals as loved by God—equal, gifted, and responsible. I am glad that I can speak freely, honestly, and responsibly in both private and public places without a veil or from behind a constricting policy or confession. This is a powerful benefit. Though there have been significant costs, there are also innumerable rewards of positive and life-giving consequences in this experience.

I credit the nurturing, open, and hospitable spirit of CIM for much of my own ability to embrace an inclusive posture. I have learned a lot over the years from the perseverance, fortitude, resolve, and honesty of the members of our congregation and from their capacity for ongoing learning, diligent work (study, worship, reflection), and emphasis on relationships. I have seen the integrity, respect, and value that is placed on each person. I have seen compassion towards those who are vulnerable, even in the face of an uncertain future for the collective.

It is no small thing for a group of people to bring word and deed together (a core Anabaptist concept) so that they are integral parts of a larger whole. The congregation chose deliberately to care about the lives of human beings over institutional conformity to documents or statements. The religious experience of each individual within the community receives high priority. One of the ironies is that while it has been an exhausting journey, it has also most notably been an energizing one. It has been my distinct privilege to stand in public solidarity with a congregation, with marginalized and isolated persons, their parents, family members, and allies across the continent as one "prophetic voice."

I have also found life-giving connections in the work of the Brethren/Mennonite Council and Supportive Communities Network. I had wonderful experiences helping to plan two BMC/SCN sponsored retreats, held in Canmore, Alberta, in recent years. I had an opportunity (thanks to CIM's generosity) to attend a SCN sponsored Pastors' Retreat in the spring of 2002. I also find connection in an ecumenical ministerial body in Calgary. It is important to be networked and supported in friendly places.

I have gained relationships with many people across Canada and beyond who relate to CIM because they want to be connected to a congregation that is publicly affirming and where they can choose freely whether they want to belong or not. It has been humbling for me to hear many stories shared by individuals and parents—stories of loss, pain, suffering, and isolation experienced through church/conference policies of exclusion (membership requirements, statements about family, human sexuality, marriage, confessions, etc.). It is particularly painful for parents to know that their gay son or lesbian daughter is not welcome as a fully participating member in the life and leadership of the church. Knowing that I am part of this group of "diaspora," though not always visible or identifiable to the institutional church, grounds me and infuses me with hope to keep going. I carry their faces, their stories, their encouragement, and their hopes within me. They offer a rich and profound source of courage.

Feeling somewhat isolated and perhaps frustrated by a disappointing church experience, one person wrote to me, "I do not have a pastor who understands," and in the next sentence this friend continued, "What am I thinking—I actually have two pastors!" I have heard Calgary Inter-Mennonite described as a beacon of light and hope. CIM has been affirmed for its courage to publicly affirm that which is unspeakable and feared. People have said, "Even though we cannot attend regularly because of distance or other commitments, we know you are out there. Thank you for your support, for caring, and for listening." I have discovered that it is not possible to determine, gauge, or quantify the effect that a public affirmation of inclusivity has. The effects, I believe, ripple out as a series of "little resurrections" beyond what we can even imagine, many of which we may never see or hear about.

Inspired by the congregation and its many friends and supporters, I have also gained personal confidence in articulating what I believe and why it is important to say so out loud. I have gained personal resolve and courage to speak and write. Resurrection is about new life. New life and possibility are what Jesus lived and taught. To move towards what is life-giving in faith and discipleship is the key. This means that it is sometimes necessary to move out from behind a "dead letter" position—a policy, confession, or belief that does not foster or promote a fullness of life (spiritual and physical) for all who wish to be a part of the church.

Although I belong to an "excommunicated" congregation, I am still an Anabaptist-Mennonite. My identity as a child of God within a particular faith tradition is not taken away. I am not excommunicated from the roots of my faith nor dismembered from the wider global church. Therefore, I will continue to search diligently after the spirit of love and compassion that was demonstrated and made visible in Jesus. I will continue to speak for justice and equality in the church. As a person of faith, I am not relegated to silence or to invisibility unless I choose to be so. Though walls or barriers may be raised, I am still responsible to participate in all the ways I can to dismantle prejudice, fear, and discrimination in the face of institutional intransigence.

The spirit of life and love—the spiritual dimension of the radical reformation (Anabaptist movement) is not confined to the sixteenth century record or history books. The spirit of God (elusive perhaps, definitely mysterious) is not limited to our own perceptions or understandings, but moves where it will. This is where life is found, where hope and joy find expression—newness of life—where glimpses of "little resurrections" are shared. The reward for speaking truth is personal and corporate integrity.

In my belonging to CIM and as a co-pastor of a publicly inclusive congregation, I have felt keenly the "deaths" and losses (some small and some not so small) that are consequences of this decision. I have experienced many "resurrections"—little glimmers of newness and significant life changing events. In reality, we are constantly moving between losses and gains, costs and rewards, pain and hope, death and resurrection.

History has shown that individuals or movements within the church that challenge the status quo are often seen as heretical, subversive, threatening, disruptive, and troublesome. The Mennonite Church is obviously not immune from this, given its own history of first being shunned and sanctioned and then sanctioning, shunning, disciplining, and excommunicating those it fears as a threat. The stuff of resurrection is not easy; it is an outrageous claim. Resurrection definitely disrupts the ordinary flow of life. It is a call to transformation and the hard work of living life. It means turning away from everything that leads to death of possibility and to death of the soul of individuals and collective church communities. This is some of what I have learned through my experience as an active participant and co-pastor of a small urban congregation that went public with a compelling private conviction born out of an earlier congregational principle: "We will welcome whomever God sends through our doors."

It is the right time to speak out. It is the right time to say what is true from within our souls and our life experience. It is time to "make room" and to say that discrimination against certain groups of people within the church is not right. It is time to dismantle duplicity, to uncover fear, to shatter covert silencing, and to step out from behind institutional barriers (arbitrary and finite). It is time to embrace our freedom as responsible people of God—a people of the resurrection—whatever the cost. It is time to grasp life in all its dimensions and diversity, creativity, and richness. The highest principle of which Jesus spoke was love. It is love that keeps us human, seeking a way toward peace and justice.

Anneli Braul has lived in Calgary for seventeen years. She has a deep interest in geography and landscape and a passion for photography and travel. In 2003, she joined the BMC Canada Board for a three-year term, representing a Canadian perspective on the Justice and Community Committee (JAC).

CHAPTER 28

Gifts on the Journey

Brenda Manthorne Dyck

(* names changed to respect privacy)

The scene is indelibly etched on my brain—the first floor of the library of Acadia University that I attended as a young woman. I can see the checkout desk, the tables for reading and research; I can smell that distinctly papery, musty odor of books. My friend Charles* from drama class approaches. I smile, give him a hug and ask, "Have you seen John* today?" A look that I cannot read crosses his face. He hesitates, then taking a deep breath, says, "Brenda, when John isn't with you, he's with me." I say, "Yes, I know. You're good friends."

He repeats it more slowly this time, as if hoping his meaning will sink in. I respond, slightly annoyed, as it seems he thinks I am dense, "I know, you're good friends......." My voice trails off as awareness washes over me. I don't remember how the conversation ends; I only know that I walk through the next several days in a fog, trying to take it all in. Slowly the pieces begin to fall into place. My journey toward an understanding of the range and complexity of sexual orientation has begun. It is a journey that I could never have charted for myself.

About a year following this event, in the summer of 1973, I was feeling restless and ready for an adventure. By this time, I had completed two years of a Master of Divinity degree. Deciding to explore another part of Canada, I moved from Nova Scotia to Calgary. While still new to the city, I attended a workshop where I met a charming young man with dancing eyes and a great sense of humor. From early on we knew that we were kindred spirits. We shared a similar faith perspective, frequently arguing with God, questioning tradition, and grappling with Scripture texts. Some months later, out of his own sense of integrity and his friendship with me, he told me of his feelings for another man. With his disclosure, I began a long, painful process of letting go of the hopes and dreams that I had for our relationship.

In 1979, I married Art, a friend whom I had met seven years earlier. We lived in Ottawa for nine months until a job opportunity for him brought us back to Calgary in 1980. One of the commitments that we had made to each other was to find a church community where we both felt at home. While visiting a retreat center, we met a mutual acquaintance who told us of a little Mennonite church in South Calgary. The first Sunday that we attempted to visit South Calgary Mennonite Brethren Church, we were greeted by a sign on the door that read, "Gone camping." That seemed a very hopeful omen to us; a church that could camp together had something going for them. Our next attempt at visiting this church worked and we were greeted warmly.

What I noticed from the beginning was the freshness of the worship. One of our early experiences was a wedding held within the context of the worship service. The simplicity, beauty, and reverent nature of that morning I hold in memory to this day.

We soon learned that this church had monthly congregational meetings and, as new adherents, we were welcome to attend. I was intrigued by the honesty and openness of these meetings with their animated discussions. Everyone was encouraged to speak, no topic was taboo, and folks freely expressed a whole range of views on a topic, seemingly without animosity. This was a group who worked and played hard at being church.

Both Art and I settled into this community quite quickly, attending worship, participating in choir, and serving on committees. For Art, in some ways, it was returning to his faith roots, that of the Mennonite Brethren Church; for me, it was relinquishing my United Baptist roots and history and embracing a new tradition. I've learned since that time that I cannot, nor do I choose to renounce my tradition; it is simply a part of me and my story. What was compelling for me was that although my birth name was not Mennonite, the church welcomed me with my gifts and limits that I brought into its life. My seeking after God and my commitment to this group were enough.

From its beginning, the church attracted Mennonites with other conference affiliations. In the mid to late eighties, the congregation initiated a process to explore the possibility of becoming affiliated with two other Mennonite conferences. After a comparative study of the theological beliefs of the Mennonite Brethren Conference, the General Conference (now Mennonite Church of Canada), and the Northwest Conference (formerly Old Order Mennonite), we concluded that the greatest difference among them was around praxis in such areas as baptism. The tenets of peace, social justice, and service—core values for our group—were found in all these traditions. We affirmed that we would proceed toward affiliation with these two other groups, while at the same time we informed the Mennonite Brethren Conference of our decision. In 1990, when the process of tri-affiliation was complete, we initiated an annual Celebration of Community worship service to replace the former concept of membership lists.

On a Sunday morning in May of 1991, a pivotal event happened in our congregation. The worship service was proceeding as usual until meditation time. That morning, the speaker came out to us as a gay man, poignantly recounting the struggle, the sleepless nights of tossing and turning, the fervent prayers that it would not be true. He spoke about his call to ministry and his plans to attend seminary in the fall. I was touched by his courage, by his wonderful sense of humor in the midst of all the pain and uncertainty, and by the immense trust he had placed in his community. This young man had been a member of the congregation for twelve years, sang in the choir, taught Sunday school, gave meditations occasionally, led worship, performed dramatic pieces, and played piano. He was known and loved. At the end of the service, folks gathered around him, hugging him, and expressing words of appreciation and affirmation.

In the next congregational meeting, our pastor very wisely said that we needed to talk about homosexuality. In that meeting a committee was mandated to design a study. The result was an eleven-week exploration of the biblical, theological, sociological, and psychological dimensions of homosexuality. It was led by resource persons from within and beyond our church.

I was one of fifteen members in that group. The study had a clear liberation theology perspective. In a safe setting, we owned our understandings and feelings about homosexuality, we heard and told stories, we studied relevant Scripture texts, and we accessed information from disciplines such as family therapy, medicine, and psychology. I came to that study with my heart already converted. I knew and cared about a number of gay and lesbian persons, including a colleague who had died of AIDS. I left with my mind changed, having had the opportunity to grapple with the "clobber texts," those familiar Scriptures that have been used against gay and lesbian persons. As we looked at these texts in their cultural contexts, I discovered that things were not as clear as they appeared to be and that one could interpret the texts in various ways.

In the study, I remember particularly an article by Walter Wink, a theologian whom I respected, that began by saying that the Bible did not have a sexual ethic; it had only a love ethic. The other challenge that this piece articulated for me was that it wasn't gay and lesbian people who needed to change, but it was I who needed to change my attitude. In fact, looking at homosexual orientation and behavior as sin was a prejudice in Wink's assessment, a view that I now shared. A new milestone appeared on my journey, a place where I could identify my movement from viewing homosexuality as a morality issue to seeing the welcome of gay and lesbian persons in the church without condition as a justice issue.

At the end of the study, we as a group assessed our learning and then created a statement that benchmarked the range of understandings that existed in our group. I was one of several group members who agreed to speak in a worship service about what we had learned. In my talk, I stated among other things that, as a result of this study, I believed that the church needed to offer covenanting services for same-sex couples who wished to declare their love in a public way. I said that I wanted to be a part of such an initiative. Throughout this period of time, the church, through our pastor, continued in dialogue both with the faculty of the seminary and with the young man who was studying there.

In April 1995, the current pastor resigned from Calgary Inter-Mennonite Church. After due process, the congregation then hired Anneli Braul and me for the positions of co-pastors, initially on an interim basis. Shortly after we were employed, I received a phone call. "My partner is dying with AIDS. Would you be willing to journey with us through this time?" I said yes, albeit with fear and trembling. That sojourn from April to July was a bittersweet time, filled in Annie Dillard's words with "both beauty and terror." I witnessed the fierce tenderness between two dear men, the candor, the warmth, the intimacy, the care and devotion, the small kindnesses. My heart asked, "How could anyone think that this love is wrong? There is such beauty and compassion in this relationship."

I had been invited into a holy place. It was a time of stretching for me, of learning how to respect the boundaries around what they wanted and needed, of learning not to make assumptions, of learning to ask when I didn't know, and of learning to trust my instincts. At the memorial service, almost every household in our church was represented. The deceased man's partner said that they experienced the presence and overwhelming support of our church at this time of loss and grief as a blessing on their relationship.

One of our early experiences as pastors was at a North American Mennonite General Conference gathering in Wichita, Kansas, in July of 1995. Because our church was grappling with gay and lesbian concerns, we went to sessions focused on this topic. We heard stories from parents telling of the pain of having their children rejected by the church—of the terrible dilemma of feeling they had to choose between the church and their children. We heard stories of persons who claimed to have changed their orientation from gay to straight. We heard other stories about churches working creatively at ways of being in solidarity with gay and lesbian members and their families. From gay and lesbian individuals and their families, we heard a challenge. How liberating and meaningful it would be to know that there was a church where they didn't have to hide their identities, where they could worship freely, where they could attend with their partners, where they could bring their gifts and participate fully in the life and ministry of the church. It seemed that it was time to come out as a publicly welcoming church— to "talk our walk."

Coincidentally perhaps, early in 1996, as I was working with the church's twentieth anniversary committee, I looked back at the May 1976 minutes of the first meeting. One of the founding principles stated, "We will welcome whomever God sends through our doors." This principle articulated an ethic of hospitality that had undergirded the life of this church from its inception, a principle that would challenge and guide the church into the future.

After a number of congregational meetings in 1996, our church made the decision to join the Supportive Congregations Network (SCN) of publicly welcoming churches, a program of the Brethren/ Mennonite Council for Gay and Lesbian Concerns (BMC). There was some discussion in the congregational meetings about whether to discuss our decision with the conferences with whom we were affiliated, but no consensus was reached. In retrospect, this was probably another critical turning point in our journey.

In October of 1997, Calgary Inter-Mennonite Church played a strongly supportive role in the first Alberta BMC/SCN retreat held in Canmore, Alberta. Fifty-five persons from Canada and the USA attended. There were worship services, workshops, coming-out stories, feasting, and visiting. There was communion as ritual and as reality. One woman remarked, "I was reading this queer magazine and there it was—an ad for a Mennonite gathering for gays. I thought—Mennonite and gay in the same sentence in Alberta, no way—this has to be a typo!" This same young woman, after the Sunday worship that concluded with communion, came with tears streaming down her face and expressed her gratitude. She added, "I haven't received communion for eleven years. I didn't feel welcome in my church." In her situation, God's table of hospitality had become a place of exclusion.

At this event, the executive director of BMC presented a plaque to us as a community that declared our church "a publicly affirming member of the Supportive Congregations Network," an affiliation of Mennonite and Church of the Brethren congregations that welcome gay, lesbian, and bisexual members." (This statement has been updated to include persons who are transgender, thus the acronym GLBT. The broadened scope of ministry of these organizations is reflected in their new names: Brethren/Mennonite Council for Lesbian, Gay, Bisexual, and Transgender Interests and Supportive Communities Network.)

A reporter from a denominational paper, who was present, asked to do a story about our church and the retreat. In its final form, this story emphasized our church's status as a member of SCN with little detail of the experience of the retreat. When the story broke, the phone calls began to come from persons in denominational leadership. They wanted to meet with the pastors of our church to discuss issues of accountability and interpretation of Scripture. Anneli and I brought this request to the Calgary Inter-Mennonite Church Council who in turn took it to a congregational meeting. In response, the congregation agreed that we should tell the story of our journey to becoming a welcoming church. They mandated seven people as a committee to represent the church. Thus began a long series of meetings.

The dialogues with each of the conferences with whom we were affiliated were, on the one hand, extremely painful, exhausting, and energy-sapping; on the other, they were joyful, energizing, and exhilarating. Invariably, individuals would come to talk with us, tell us their stories, affirm us, and share how our church was a pocket of hope for them. Others felt free to question our faith, our integrity, and our ability to interpret Scripture. Our experience in some ways mirrored the "coming out" process of GLBT people.

In the space of three years, our church was "dismembered" from two conferences and chose to take a five-year leave of absence from the third. I found it unconscionable that churches and conferences would take away from their sons and daughters their rights of belonging and the rites associated with them, uprooting them from their faith communities and their histories.

During this process, there were other experiences—times of joy and hope. In 1999, I was invited to be a co-celebrant with a United

Church minister at a covenanting ceremony between two women, one Mennonite and one from the United Church. Although our church had declared itself a publicly welcoming church, it had not looked specifically at ceremonies of commitment. When I raised the issue of officiating at this service, the congregation gave me permission to follow my conscience. In my view, this was a very Anabaptist decision. With delight, I met with the couple along with the United Church clergy to plan their service. On the day of the ceremony, the joy and celebration that filled that gathering place was palpable as eighty people gathered to publicly celebrate the love these women shared. As part of the ceremony, the couple had asked both ministers to reflect on the meaning of covenant. In my reflections, I said:

> Today as women of faith who love each other, you are claiming your birthrights to the rites of the church, God's blessing on your union mediated through God's people. To the wider community, this ceremony today is a proclamation of hope that one day, lesbian and gay unions will be celebrated freely everywhere as authentic relationships of love and commitment without remark.

> In the time that I have known you, I have experienced you as women of faith, of courage, of integrity, who in the face of a world that is often hostile to your love, have remained steadfast, passionate, and compassionate. In extending blessing on your union, my hope is that the church that has sometimes been a source of pain and wounding to you, may now be a place of solace and healing.

In a statement written to BMC in the summer of 2001, I described another experience of healing.

> The incarnational nature of BMC was best expressed for me in January 2000 when the BMC board arrived in Calgary on the coldest day of the year. You came, twenty-three of you, all bundled up against the elements, to work together. Most importantly for us, you came to be in solidarity. We were recovering from the painful encounters in our "dialogues" with three conferences of which we were members. Your presence with us was a soothing balm, a healing oil. You worked long hours, but you still had time to play with us. You ate and slept in our homes, met and enjoyed our families.

Our Sunday morning worship service rocked as you added your voices and gifts to ours! Your energy and commitment to justice, peace, and compassion were contagious. Weeks later, as I walked through our little church basement, I maintained that I could hear echoes of laughter, of singing, of prayer, of animated discussion. Your energy had permeated our walls and our spirits. It remains with us as a joyous, hopeful, and healing memory.

In September of 2002, I had the honor of leading a ceremony of commitment for a gay couple. The ceremony began with a gathering in the garden by a pond with a flowing fountain. The couple welcomed those attending, introduced each person and shared their connection to them. We then moved inside for the homily and the vows. In the homily I said:

Your community and your world need to witness with our own eyes the sanctity of your relationship. It encourages and inspires us in our own loving. Where love is, God is present and that is a holy place. Love is not something to be hidden, but to be shared. The world that is often hostile to your love needs to see it celebrated and honored in an open, holy way. You have dared to speak love's name, and I, for one, am grateful.

As part of their ceremony, they chose to use a lovely Quaker tradition where the gathered community was invited to sign their vows as an act of witness and solidarity. Then we feasted! Following the meal, a time of welcome from the families was given to the respective partners. The gathered community had opportunity to tell stories about the two men and to share "words of wisdom." From my perspective, it was a joyous, blessed event celebrating the love between two good men of faith.

As I reflect back on our church's journey, I must acknowledge that certainly there has been some painful fallout from our decision to become a publicly welcoming church. I will cite a few examples. Some of our youth have experienced discrimination around leadership positions in denominational youth and camp programs. Members of our congregation have felt ostracized in some Mennonite gatherings. Because our licenses to perform marriages were revoked, the church had to seek credentials from the provincial government for Anneli and me. This was a process that took much time and energy. In addition, Anneli and I have experienced isolation from our colleagues in other Mennonite churches. We are unable to pursue ordination as Mennonite clergy at this time, should we choose to do so.

On the other hand, GLBT folk see our church as a "beacon of hope" where they can receive all the rights and rites of the church. Families who are feeling disenfranchised by their own churches have a place to visit and feel safe. We are able to connect GLBT individuals and families to a community to help overcome their sense of isolation. Finally, we have immense freedom to welcome anyone who walks through our doors and to respond to their needs and gifts as they present them.

I have immense respect and gratitude for Calgary Inter-Mennonite Church. Throughout a difficult time, this congregation has persisted with compassion, wisdom, and integrity in seeking to be followers of God's way. I am also deeply grateful for those GLBT individuals and their families who extended grace to me by inviting me into their stories and their lives. I am grateful too to Art, my beloved, and to our sons who do not always understand or agree with me but love me anyway! For all this, thanks be to God, Companion on the Journey!

Brenda Manthorne Dyck, M.T.S., was born and raised in a fishing hamlet in Nova Scotia, Canada. Her faith tradition was United Baptist until she met and married her partner Art. They have lived in Calgary, Alberta, for twenty-four years and are the proud parents of three sons: Benjamin (Ben), Bernard (Bernie), and Andrew.

Brenda is currently a co-pastor of Calgary Inter-Mennonite Church in Calgary, Alberta. Her pastoral passions include work with rituals, pastoral counseling, spiritual direction, and social justice. She has worked in the fields of rehabilitation, social service, and teaching. Her hobbies include attending movies, live theatre, and concerts, entertaining at home, singing, and throwing pottery. Relationships, beauty, and humor are priorities in her life.

CHAPTER 29

My Journey Toward the Light

Vida S. Huber

From an early age, I understood that the life and work of the church are of ultimate importance. This understanding has been an important motivator for most of my life decisions. I was born in 1937 in Ohio where my parents served as superintendent and matron of an orphanage for fifteen years. When I was two we moved to Kansas, and my father served as business manager at Hesston College for four years. After being involved with church agencies in several settings for more than twenty years, my parents decided to return to Delaware where their parents had moved after leaving the Amish Church to begin what became the Greenwood Mennonite Church, a part of the Conservative Mennonite Conference. I was six years old at the time of our return and instinctively sensed as we settled into the Greenwood community that our family life experiences differed from those of my many cousins who were a part of that church community.

Our family had been influenced by the diverse experiences of a less conservative part of the Mennonite Church during our formative years. This resulted in both theological and lifestyle differences. Nevertheless, my parents were committed to living according to the expectations of the church, so the piano that had been part of our life in Kansas was left behind because it was not acceptable in Delaware. What I recall most from those years was my desire to belong and be like my cousins, many of whom were near my age. My parents gave my sisters the option of wearing coverings* without strings and light colored hose as they had done in Kansas, even though this differed from the common practice in Delaware. Wanting to belong, I requested adding covering strings when I "joined church" and for a time asked to wear dark stockings.

My childhood life centered around the church. In addition to attending the same church, my friends were my cousins and classmates at our church school. In spite of the conservative style of clothing required by the Greenwood Church and a fairly limited exposure to the world outside the church community, as a young child I had a strong sense of being cared for and belonging. The adults, many of whom were my aunts and uncles, made me feel important, listened to and valued. This was a critical factor in my strong identity with that community. During that period, there was an open spirit, and we had visiting speakers from across the church on a regular basis. These early formative experiences were significant in shaping my allegiance to and active participation in the church.

Things began to change, however, as I moved into my mid-teens. There was a narrowing of perspective within the church and concerns about "change" were expressed. During my late teens, I became aware of the limited role I could take within the church as a female. I was disappointed to discover that my involvement with InterVarsity Christian Fellowship was suspect because it was not Mennonite and that my attempt to help create a Greenwood Mennonite Youth Fellowship as part of the wider Mennonite denomination's program was not acceptable. I felt a tension about how to fulfill my desire to serve the church when the gifts that I had to offer were not utilized because I was born female.

Fortunately, the development of my inner voice was sufficient to continue my personal search for a spirituality that had meaning for me rather than silencing it to meet the expectations of church leadership. I recall that it was painful, while knowing it was necessary to follow my own inner voice.

I share these glimpses into my early spiritual development because I believe it to be foundational to experiences that have occurred in the intervening years. While I remained open to new understandings and trying to be attentive to the God within, for many years my basic behaviors and my theological understandings remained consistent with the early teachings I received at home and within the church. I taught Sunday school and summer Bible school, sang in the church chorus, dressed according to regulations, and gave evidence of being a compliant church member. During my two years at the public high school after completing ten grades at our church school, I raised questions about why my male peers from church could participate behind the scenes in class plays, and it was not acceptable for me to be one of the cast. I was troubled by the fact that the dress code with which I needed to comply caused me to stand apart from my peers in high school, while my male church peers could easily fit in with the crowd. Even though I questioned this and other practices, I complied with the directives of church leadership.

Throughout this period, my spirituality included the belief that God noticed and kept score of all of my behaviors, and it was very important to me to have a good score. Compared with some of my friends, I was eager for new experiences and knew that higher education was in my future. While at times I wondered why my life path was on a different trajectory, I had an inner knowing that it was important to follow where it led. Always there was a deep longing to experience God within my understanding of what that meant.

During nursing school, college at Eastern Mennonite College, and even in my graduate study in New York City, I changed very little externally in terms of dress and basic practices. As my spiritual journey continued, I was at peace with being different from my peers. It had become a way of life with which I was comfortable and of which, to some degree, I was proud. It provided safety; certain "temptations" did not enter my radar screen.

Because of my capacity to excel academically, I found affirmation and recognition in this arena rather than in other more socially based relationships. Exposure to diverse religious expressions through friends from many denominations, both in nursing school and in New York City, was enriching and stretching. I began to question certainties I had accepted about who God is and how the Christian faith was to be expressed.

Early in my days in NYC, I met Harold Huber, now my husband, and recall the unsettledness I experienced when he raised questions about things I thought were unchangeable. Deep in my soul, I understood that if I acknowledged that perhaps there was a different answer about things like wearing a covering, a chink would be created in my wall of certainty and other understandings would need to be examined as well. While this created deep fear within me, the drive for honesty kept me on a continuing journey around a variety of issues.

Upon returning to EMC in Harrisonburg, Virginia, in 1967 to lead the development of the baccalaureate nursing program, I was questioned by the Religious Welfare Committee of the Board about how I had gone through graduate school and retained traditional values, remaining in their words "unchanged." They were of course referring to externals and my traditional responses to their theological questions. They seemed amazed. I began to realize that I had made only minor changes in my thinking and yet sensed that change was happening. Interestingly, that seemed easier to do within the "safety" of the church institution, though maybe it was just an issue of timing. I discovered that on many fronts I began to question, to change perspective, to challenge traditional thought, and to gain new understandings. I am grateful that throughout the years, even though questioned and challenged from within and without, I was given the inner strength to follow the light as it led me.

I pay tribute to my mother for the model she provided of a woman who was able to be who she was in a society where limits were imposed on women. I learned that being true to oneself was of great importance even though my parents made accommodations to fit within their church. In their later years, some of my choices went beyond their comfort zone, yet I was not ostracized by them.

During my early life, I was minimally aware of homosexuality even though upon reflection I am aware that I had friends who were gay and lesbian. I did not confront this issue early, and my views were very traditional. I was in my thirties and a teacher at EMC when I first had the opportunity to walk with a good friend as she came to acknowledge to herself that she was a lesbian. The depth of our friendship, the high regard with which I held her as a spiritual friend, and the integrity of her struggle in coming to terms with her identity made it impossible for me to leave my own assumptions and beliefs unchallenged. This began a twenty-five-year evolution that started with knowing that I could not judge my friend and call her sexual orientation wrong.

I moved through a time of uncertainty about how to integrate my intuitive sense with my theological understanding. That evolution continues with my current stance of openly affirming persons regardless of their sexual orientation and preference. I must confess that it still remains difficult to comfortably counter family and friends who hold a strong opposing view. I have a deeply held knowing within, yet it is not easy to articulate my position without getting defensive. Most often, I don't engage in conversation beyond the surface unless I sense a desire to understand and a readiness to seriously engage on the part of another. I simply indicate it is not my desire to argue.

Harold and I have been a part of Broad Street Mennonite Church in Harrisonburg for thirty-five years. We began attending there before our marriage because it was small, open, and reminiscent of our years in New York City at Seventh Avenue Mennonite Church in Harlem. Last year, our small congregation was expelled from Virginia Mennonite Conference because we made our building available for a same-sex commitment ceremony, would not comply with the request to "dis-invite" the couple, and affirmed that we would welcome them as members of our congregation.

To understand this recent action and the stance of the congregation, it is important to put it in context. Broad Street Mennonite Church was started in 1935 as a "mission" to the blacks of Harrisonburg, and throughout its nearly seventy-year history it has been a fringe congregation on a variety of issues. As a "mission to the colored," the Virginia Mission Board insisted that the congregation abide by the mores of then-segregated Harrisonburg. When the superintendent of the mission was uncomfortable with the mandate to avoid cross-race expression of the "holy kiss" and to use individual communion cups, rather than a common cup, his leadership assignment was not renewed.

In later periods, the church was on the fringes in pushing for racial equality and justice and was one of the more active within the district in providing local leadership around human rights. As a result, on several occasions it was looked at askance by the more traditional churches within the district.

During the years Harold and I have been at Broad Street, we have participated in congregational actions in a number of arenas that placed us clearly outside the mainstream of local district and conference positions. It was not our intent to be on the fringes or to push the edges. It was a result of our internal desire to live in ways that would be true to our understanding of the call of Christ on our lives, as well as ways that would be relevant in our current setting.

Throughout the congregation's history, there has been a passion for justice and a desire to live out the hard sayings of Jesus. Arenas in which the clash with the local conference became apparent included the early stance around issues of racism, the charismatic movement, women in leadership, ordination as a system of power and control, methods of mutual decision making within the local congregation, inclusion, and other areas of congregational life. Thus, the more recent affirmation by the congregation of persons with varying sexual orientation is consistent with the stance of the congregation throughout its history.

Our recent experience around homosexuality has evolved over time. Several in the congregation had family members who were gay or lesbian, and they had grappled with this situation in the family context. While we had no gay or lesbian members at the time of the conference action, there have been times in our history when persons involved with the congregation were known by some of us, though not publicly, to be practicing gays and lesbians.

At that point it was not raised directly as an issue, although in one situation we learned after the fact that an individual left the congregation because the leadership questioned his suitability to teach a children's Sunday school class. This was not dealt with or acknowledged at the congregational level but happened behind the scenes. I was uncomfortable and sad, yet my journey was still in process, and I did not view the situation as an issue to be resolved. My subsequent friendship with the individual mentioned earlier, who was also attending Broad Street, was the instrument that brought the issue of homosexuality directly to the forefront of my thinking and gave me a reason to examine my personal position.

In 1991, a sizable group of individuals, including a leadership couple who had been called to the congregation almost a year earlier, left the congregation over disagreement about a number of issues, including forms of leadership and decision making (consensus had been our pattern for many years), openness to individuals not holding orthodox positions, and the understanding of Jesus as the exclusive way to knowing God. This was a very crucial time in the life of the congregation. It became even more painful because the district censured us, our participation in the district was curtailed, and we underwent a time of examination and interrogation.

After about a four-year period, we were "reinstated" after providing assurances that satisfied the allegations. As I remember that time, it was with the sense that we worked hard to meet their requirements and that belonging became the top priority. While not dishonest in what we said, it was not a complete statement of our position. Understandably, the experience left a deep scar. I believe this experience, along with the earlier marginality of the congregation, is important as a backdrop for understanding our more recent interchange with the leadership of the district and of the conference.

Several years ago, during a retreat, the congregation discussed the option of becoming an openly welcoming congregation. We shared our experiences and understandings, and while there seemed to be common agreement, a compelling reason to move and officially become a welcoming congregation did not emerge at that time. Whether we were not ready, I can't be sure. I recall it was said that it felt like we would be operating in a vacuum and no action was taken. I view this hesitancy to move ahead with an official position as a formative stage of our church life. I believe our hesitance was in part due to the still-remembered and painful experience of discipline by the district some ten years earlier. Intuitively we knew that taking such action would have repercussions.

The painfulness of the earlier time of discipline by the district and the later hesitance to become an officially welcoming congregation stand in stark contrast with our recent experience. This experience has been beautiful because of the unity within the congregation about our decision and the inner peace we feel in knowing that we acted in keeping with our values in the face of opposition by the district and conference. This is not to say it was not a difficult time. However, the choice was clear, and the sense of integrity that we felt was powerful and sustaining. We feel freedom and new life as a result.

We were strengthened by the many expressions of support from individuals and groups across the church. Frequently we have friendly visitors joining us during our Sunday morning worship. A banner hangs in the front of our sanctuary; a dove hangs at the window, and a trumpet hangs from the limb of a large plant. We are grateful for all these expressions of support from the broader church. Our official installation as a member of the Supportive Communities Network occurred the day following our expulsion from the conference, and we felt welcomed and blessed.

The chain of events that resulted in our expulsion was rather simple. When a couple asked if our church building could be used for their same-sex commitment ceremony, our answer was positive. When someone questioned whether we were prepared for the reaction that might follow, some of us—including me—naively said that there would be no repercussions. Several in the congregation were friends of the two women who wanted to be married in our church, but many of us did not know them at the time. Regardless, we agreed to make the building available and were surprised to learn later that the reverberations of our position were so widespread. Our overseer reported that he received around fifty phone calls and e-mails a week regarding Broad Street. It was almost amusing that such a small group could create such a stir.

It wasn't long until individuals within the broader church raised questions, and we were approached by district officials to verify whether we had in fact agreed to the use of our building in this way. Our affirmation that it was true resulted in a series of conversations between members of the district council and individuals in the congregation. When asked to rescind our invitation during the meeting with the District Executive Council, those of us present indicated that such an action would need to be a congregational one, but we felt certain there would not be agreement to rescind our decision. During the same meeting, we volunteered the information that while we currently had no gay or lesbian members, they would be welcome to become a part of our congregation. This resulted in what was referred to as the "Broad Street issue" and became a major focus of conversation within the district and conference for some time.

At one district meeting, six of us were invited to attend and engage in conversation. On other occasions, we were largely excluded from the conversation. After the initial processing at the conference level, a small group with representatives from Virginia Mennonite Conference, Harrisonburg District, and Broad Street was created for discernment and to bring recommendations. I was part of that group. There appeared to be little or no interest on the part of most members to engage in serious dialogue, so only one meeting was held. Further processing without our participation within the district and conference resulted in our expulsion, effective immediately, during a delegate assembly on February 1, 2003. It was heartening that a sizable number of individual delegates spoke against our expulsion and that the vote passed with only seventy-one percent in favor.

On February 1, as our Broad Street group sat in the delegate assembly listening to the comments supportive of and opposing our action, I was overwhelmed at moments with what felt like totally false accusations, misinterpretation of intentions, and harsh, judgmental attacks on our character. It felt bizarre that after the vote was reported, and without any further comment, the business meeting immediately moved forward to other items on the agenda. We had anticipated the action, yet I felt numbness and deep sadness. However, there was also a sense of freedom and relief that has continued throughout the year that followed. I would not for a moment have done anything differently than what we did. I value highly the personal sense of integrity that I feel. I became aware that I could let go of my fear of the reactions of church authorities as a motivator for my behavior. That was an important outcome for me.

Although as a congregation we were unanimous in our action, I know that the experience was also individual for each of us because of factors that we had previously encountered around this issue and the difficulties we have experienced with church institutions in other settings. Personally, I have grown increasingly disenchanted with the organized church over the past twenty-five years because of instances where I have experienced the "dark side" of church organizations and institutions. However, though I totally disagree with the position taken by the leadership of the district and conference and have felt angry because of their actions, it is not my desire to vilify them.

Gradually my anger is being replaced with a desire to help create a positive future. As one steeped in love for the church and having given significant parts of my life to its work and institutions, I recognize that perhaps the greatest gift we at Broad Street have to offer at this point is to continue to be who we are and to welcome all who would like to join us as we journey onward. There is much healing needed in the world, in our churches, and in individual lives. I long for the day when the Mennonite Church can exhibit comfort and readiness to engage in open dialogue around this and other areas of disagreement. I dream of a time when all will find welcome and inclusion, and I am committed to do what I can in the remainder of my life to assist in bringing that dream to reality.

---

*A covering is a small net cap that represented the Mennonite interpretation of First Corinthians 11:1-16 for many years. The covering is no longer a membership requirement for female members of the church.

Vida S. Huber, R.N., B.S.N., M.A., Ed.D., was born in West Liberty, Ohio, lived four years in Kansas, grew to adulthood in Delaware, and has lived in Virginia since 1967. She is married to Harold E. Huber, a historian, who formerly taught sociology at Eastern Mennonite University and currently works in the Historical Library there. They have one daughter, Heidi, who is a clinical social worker living in Baltimore.

After a short career as a practicing nurse, Vida spent most of her professional life in nursing education. Beginning in 1967, she led the development of EMU's nursing program and served as department chair. She began working at James Madison University in 1988 as nursing department head. Since 1999, she has served as Associate Dean of the College of Integrated Science and Technology, and now also serves as Director of the University's Institute for Innovation in Health and Human Services. Active on the boards of several community voluntary agencies, she has a passion for helping make dreams become reality. Since graduating from Shalem Institute in 1988, she provides spiritual direction to individuals from diverse backgrounds. She has been involved for many years in leadership roles at Broad Street Mennonite Church, Harrisonburg, Virginia.

CHAPTER 30

Lament of an Outlier*

Glenn M. Kauffman

An outlier is a member of a set of entities or measurements that does not conform to the mean, the norm, or the central tendency of the group. For example, in a set of experimental measurements of some quantity a distribution of values is always obtained. The result is expressed as a mean or average value of some sort, but the quantity is not completely expressed as the mean unless the standard deviation is specified which indicates the spread or diversity of the actual measurements. An outlier is a value that does not appear to conform to the mean.

The empirical question is whether or not such a value should be included in the determination of the mean. The significance here is that the outliers are real measurements with no known errors. The mean, on the other hand, is an abstracted value that has no empirical basis itself, i.e., it is not itself a measurement. In social groupings where each individual is different, is a "particular," the means or norms of the group are much less real or significant, because no two individuals actually conform to the norm. Frequently, we use these means or norms to represent ideal traits to which we are to aspire, with no expression or measure of the actual variation of the trait that exists in reality.

My Manifesto

I believe it is the task of the church to minister to human needs, both inside and outside our church walls, in all of their variation and diversity. The subject of sexual orientation is an extremely complex one at the biological and socio-developmental levels. I am not a biologist, but I can appreciate the complexity of this issue. The theories of causation of minority sexual orientation used by some of our church leaders are inadequate to account for the complex etiology of this aspect of our lives.

To base church doctrine and policy on the assumed universality of deficient theories is morally reprehensible and is abusive to many of those who, in their created nature, do not conform to the official norms of our church. It seems to me that the only valid ethical position one can take at this stage of history is to withhold judgment on the issue, accept the variety of persons as they are, and allow their experiences to play out in the life of the church.

This book, of course, is about the church leaders and potential leaders who have lost their positions or had their work compromised because they tried to be inclusive of this diversity.

Several of the poems in this collection are directed toward our church leadership. These leaders, in my mind, have largely failed to lead for the last twenty-five years. Many deny the reality of the natural variability of sexual orientation itself, believing that minority sexual orientation can be "corrected" or "overcome." They have failed to educate themselves or the church membership, many of whom have no knowledge of or direct experience with GLBT persons. Furthermore, they refuse to accept or work with those leaders who do have different understandings and beliefs from the official position.

Until this situation is changed, we will continue to lose valuable experience and potential leaders in the church. We will continue to be divided, just as our secular society (which we strongly resemble) is divided. One must ask whether the majority votes at our assemblies are not simply a reflection of the social and political biases that are extant in our secular society. Unfortunately, too many pastors and church leaders reinforce these biases.

Preface

Do not expect
pretty poems
from me.
Not while queer folk
are quarantined

and defenseless teens
are pressured into being
what they cannot be
'til some even opt
to not be.

Is not their blood on our hands?
On the hands of the church?
Is there not blood on the hands
of the bishops?

Entropic Topics
[The H-word]

Entropic Topics
which disorder our settled minds,
and upset our comfortable pews,
which wreak havoc with our frames of reference,

produce apparent chaos,
a word most feared
by bureaucrats,
accountants,
and bishops,

but make possible the emergence
of new ideas,
new creation,
new love,
and
new truth.

Taize [1]

I lit a candle for Tom
who is losing his job
for errors of being
and loving incorrectly.

Expendable
in a community built on love,
but operating in fear
for political rectitude

as if the world were so awash with love
that deity would choose to discriminate,
as if amid the myriad variety of beings
and the limitless types of hate and fear
God could accept one kind of love alone,
as if we can presume to judge
between a rare and rarer commodity.

One might think that in our world
God would welcome anything that
even resembles love
as we build our
Babel castles and protective moats
ignoring what is fine and good around us.

I lit a candle for Tom
who is losing his job
a prayer that he continues loving
even though we fail.

I should have lit a candle for us all,
for we are the losers;
a prayer to clear our vision,
to strengthen our courage,
to release us from fear
so we can love, however weakly,
well.

Broad Street 2002 [2]

Who are these people?
What is this place?
The significance of this time?

A collection of outliers?
A gathering of castaways?
The collateral damage of
church merger and self-preservation?
Detritus of dysfunctional truth?

Through a glass darkly we seek light
perhaps to find mirrored there
the glimmer of a new and different truth.

Through chinks in crackling, crumbling wine skins,
we see vistas
unencumbered by preordained conclusions
and traditional exclusions,
unbound by extrapolated laws
which emasculate the souls of those who beg to differ,
freed at last to love.

What is this place?
A place of celebration
of particularity,
of gifts of grace from marginalia,
no genitalia left at the door
in denial of who we are.

We celebrate love,
the resonance of souls
that binds us together,
disparate though we are,
that gives us hope to continue
the quest for love and justice,
the promise of Shalom.

I Do Not Cede You My Church

To the amorphous powers
who speak for the church,
who pen edicts and interpret scriptures
and tell us what our confessions mean:
I do not cede you my church.

You say the church's position is this
or the church believes that,
you collect the majority votes to prove it,
but you do not speak for all, not for me,
and I do not cede you my church!

My church has diversity of thought;
my church believes more than one thing.
It is not confined by your tradition;
its truth does not lie only
with those who set boundaries
which enclose the timid ones
with carefully constructed norms
fearful of new truth.

Fences that also protect the powerful
in their castle pulpits,
in their fortified committees and boards,
sanitized from dissent and diversity,
content with the hubris of their Truth
and fearful of new ideas.
I do not cede you my church!

Truth is living and emerges
in the powerless,
in the hearts of the poor, the meek,
the young, the gay, the disenfranchised,
who love without precondition
and hope against hope for Shalom.

I fellowship with the outliers
with odd frames of reference;
there I find truth and love.
There is my church.
I will not cede you our church!

[1] Written after a Taize service at Park View Mennonite Church, Harrisonburg, Virginia, September 3, 2003, after learning of Tom Arbaugh's dismissal from his position at the local Mennonite university.

[2] Reflections after a weekend meeting of MennoNeighbors, a group of supportive congregations and individuals who met in Harrisonburg, Virginia, at Broad Street Mennonite Church, shortly after the Broad Street group was expelled from Virginia Conference for their support of GLBT issues.

Glenn M. Kauffman was born near Goshen, Indiana, in 1938. The third of seven children, he moved at the age of eleven with his family to Harrisonburg, Virginia, where he still resides with his wife Mary (Schrag). They have two adult daughters. Glenn attended Eastern Mennonite College and Goshen College and obtained a Ph.D. in Physical Organic Chemistry from the University of Pennsylvania. He taught in the Chemistry Department at Eastern Mennonite University for thirty-eight years, retiring at the end of 2003 as Emeritus Professor of Chemistry.

His interests include the philosophy of science and religion, and gardening, with a special emphasis on rhododendrons and the native East Coast azaleas. His musical interests are exercised in the choir at Park View Mennonite Church, where he and Mary attend. He has been active in various GLBT support groups in and around EMU and Harrisonburg for the past several years. As left-handed, Mennonite, and chemist, he surely knows what it is like to be in a minority. He has been well-tutored on gay issues by his brother-in-law and very dear friend, Keith Schrag. He occasionally writes poems on various topics of interest.

CHAPTER 31

God's Table and Churchland Security:
Creating Welcome Within a Culture of Fear

Anne Breckbill

Preamble:

The following speech, entitled "God's Table: Y'all Come," was delivered at the 2003 Mennonite Church USA convention held at Atlanta, Georgia. It was the keynote address at the Brethren/Mennonite Council for Lesbian, Gay, Bisexual, and Transgender Interests (BMC) luncheon. It provides commentary on the political climate in society and in the Mennonite denomination during the summer of 2003.

In the United States, we were at war with Iraq though we had found neither weapons of mass destruction nor Saddam Hussein. The Department of Homeland Security suggested we stock up on plastic sheeting and duct tape in case of chemical warfare. Countless innocent individuals had been detained during the time since September 11, 2001, with no explanation or legal representation. Those who questioned governmental decisions were chastised and labeled "unpatriotic." We were told to trust that the Bush Administration had our best interests in mind.

In our denomination, Mennonite Church USA had been formed as a result of the Mennonite Church and General Conference Mennonite Church (MC/GC) merger, but integrating individual conferences had been less successful. Questions of membership and polity—specifically as related to the inclusion of GLBT-welcoming congregations and individuals—proved to be the sticking point for some local conferences.

Regional conferences had used a variety of disciplinary means to gain the compliance of welcoming congregations to the parts of the Mennonite Confession of Faith that addressed marriage and sexuality. Some congregations had already been expelled from their conferences, including the oldest Mennonite Church in North America (Germantown). Over fifteen years had passed since the Purdue and Saskatoon statements that called for dialogue, but BMC had never yet been granted booth space at a national convention where dialogue might have started or continued. We were also encouraged to trust that the church leadership had our best interests in mind.

It is an honor for me to address you today. Thank you for joining me in my musings regarding our beloved denomination and its reluctance to offer an unbridled "Y'all Come" invitation to all who wish to eat at God's table. I offer the following by means of introduction. I am a forty-one year old born and bred Mennonite. I am the vice-president of BMC, having been on the BMC Board for six years. My partner Jane Ramseyer Miller and I are longtime members of St. Paul Mennonite Fellowship. My political bias is left of the Democratic party. I spend my workday supporting internet banking applications for credit unions. And, yes, Bill and Ina Ruth are my parents.

I don't address you as a representative of any of these groups or people today. I address you as a sister Mennonite seeking God's will for my life and the life of our denomination. In the interest of clarity, the Mennonite Church that I refer to today is the Mennonite Church USA, as that is the context in which I have lived and experienced the church. For both its social and political significance, I have intentionally chosen to use the word "queer" when identifying gay, lesbian, bisexual, and transgender individuals. This term, adopted and reclaimed by the GLBT community, aptly describes both the playful and profound difference of GLBT peoples' experience in a heterosexist society.

The worldwide Mennonite Church is less well-known to me and may or may not fit the generalizations I will make about Mennonite Church USA. Mennonite Church Canada shares many of the same traits as Mennonite Church USA, yet it too functions in a different political environment. The critique I offer of our church is grounded in the love I have for this church. If I did not love the church and believe that it has a theology that can bring me closer to God and to who God wants me to be, I would have left many, many years ago. But I am here still, issuing this challenge in the hope of calling out the very best in all of us.

I live in Minnesota, which until recently was a comfortable political fit for me. However, like most states last November, we took a wild swing to the right by electing an extremely conservative governor. This governor is so conservative that Garrison Keillor actually pines for Jesse Ventura! Thanks to this new governor and the conservative backlash that elected him, the following situation is typical:

> You go to a concert. You sit down and wait for the lights to dim. Just as a hushed anticipation comes over the crowd, a voice says, "Please respect the performers by turning off all cell phones and beepers. Firearms are not permitted on the premises. Thank you."

> You enter a restaurant. As you enter the front door you see a sign: "No weapons." The maitre d' greets you by saying "Firearms are not permitted in this restaurant. Table for two? Smoking or non-smoking?"

The little piece of legislation that has store clerks, wait staff, and ministers alike talking about weapons with everyone they greet is called the "Personal Protection Act." Under this legislation, any adult without a criminal record can get a gun license with no waiting period. Also under this act, *concealed* handguns are allowed in every public indoor and outdoor space except for schools unless a sign prohibiting them is posted and every person who enters that space is verbally informed that firearms are not permitted.

What is the need for the Personal Protection Act? Why are we arming ourselves? What is the fear that made all these nice Minnesotans feel like they would be personally less vulnerable by packing heat to the grocery store, the park, the theatre, and church? Has there been a glut of murders and violent deaths in Minnesota in the last year or two? There have been too many murders to be sure, but the recent murder rates are well below the peak of crime we had back in 1996. I hope some of you have been able to see Michael Moore's movie "Bowling for Columbine." If you have not, I highly recommend it. It is at times comical, terrifying, tragic, surreal, and sad. In it, he explores the US's fascination with guns, killing, war, and the right to bear arms. Though many factors play into the US's unrivaled murder rate, Moore's ultimate conclusion is that what makes us different is fear.

We live in a country right now whose greatest commodities are its people's fear and its antidote, security. Much of the fear currently being sold does not represent genuine danger and much of the security promised does not represent true safety. Seemingly, our national appetite for this vague fear coupled with illusive security has no end. It is this appetite that is being taken advantage of by our warmongering leadership. Our fears are played against us. They are used as the foundation for war, imperialism, obscene excesses, and abuses. Our fears are used to silence those who question the course of action our government chooses and those who articulate dissenting opinions to those in power. These fears are paving the way toward fascism.

We know from the lessons of history that the Nazi regime wielded its power through three major tactics—building the fear of "others," promising security in exchange for blind faith, and promoting nationalism. The horrific deaths and abuses of the holocaust began by generating fear of others—Jews, homosexuals, physically disabled people, gypsies. Without fear, security would not be relevant and nationalism would seem narrow. Adding the fear of an outside threat makes a decision to trade blind allegiance for security and mind-numbing national pride appear a sensible and reasonable conclusion. Without the commodity of fear, fascist leaders and dictatorial regimes would be impossible.

As our nation allows its fear to balloon out of control, what is the witness of the Mennonite Church? Are we actively teaching openness and inclusion? Are we modeling honesty in relationships, respect for one another and openness to the "other"? Are we teaching compassion? Are we living "a true faith that casts out all fear" . . . or perhaps a true fear that casts out all variance?

I do not belittle the peace witness of the Mennonite Church, the efforts that have been and are being made to stop our government's violence and arrogance, and all of the many, many things Mennonites around the world do out of love for the "other." However, given the dire state of affairs in this world, does it not seem that the Mennonite Church has spent an obscenely inordinate amount of time in church basements and fellowship halls talking about sex? As our world, country, and communities are embroiled in hate, we Mennonites spend our precious energy trying to legislate and regulate love! Where is the soul of this dear Church?

Our denomination is caught up in the torrent of fear that surrounds it—

- our people have adopted the fear for survival and suspicion of the "other" that dominates our culture;
- our leadership has, perhaps unknowingly, assumed some of the same characteristics that mark our government's reign through fear;
- we all have been co-opted by an ideology built on the polarization of threat and security, an ideology that is inconsistent with the good news of Jesus Christ.

As a longtime member of a congregation identified as being "at variance" with Mennonite Church statements, I have had many opportunities to listen to and experience the processes, language, paradigms, and relationships that are crafted as our denomination tries to deal with difference. Too much of what I have seen smacks of the culture of fear in which we live.

Variance is difference. Variance is the "other" embodied. When I worked in the non-profit social service world, difference was called diversity and was highly desirable. In the Mennonite Church, difference is called variance and is highly undesirable. In the social service world, there is a value placed on being accessible, meeting people where they are, and developing an understanding and respect for cultural identity. Extending invitation and open-mindedness is the key to building respectful diversity.

In the Mennonite Church, unfortunately, ultimate value is placed on being in agreement. Certainly, there are cultural aspects to being

Mennonite. Those cultural pieces, though clearly still present, have become a bit more inclusive over time. We no longer impose the same inflexibility and impermeability in our Mennonite culture as we once did. But what about in our theology?

Shared theological beliefs are less frequently derived from our shared experience or mined from the spiritual lives and communities of our membership. Rather, they are regulated and enforced as the documented position of the Mennonite Church. Variance is not pursued and understood. Variance is rooted out, managed, subverted, contained, and hidden. And, if we are to be honest, the current variance is nothing more than a euphemism for a queer-welcoming congregation. When we consider our theology and the spectrum of belief reflected in this denomination, it is stunning to realize that the only variance worthy of response is whether we believe that same-sex sexual activity is a sin. That alone defines our threat to the denomination.

As a result, the words "at variance" have begun to sound like "code orange." Oh no! We have to do something! We need to protect ourselves—to root out evil—to manage the threat—and, as always, report anything that appears to be strange or out-of-the-ordinary. Just as Tom Ridge at the Department of Homeland Security (dubbed, incidentally, by Garrison Keillor as the "Department of Scaring People") would have American citizens wrapping themselves in plastic sheeting and duct tape to protect ourselves from the imminent yet nonexistent threat of chemical warfare, the Mennonite Church has donned its own metaphorical duct tape and plastic wrap as it approaches its own diversity.

I believe the people of this denomination are good people who mean well, yet the fear and distaste of true difference and dissent is palpable among us. Five years ago, the Twin Cities queer advocacy organization, OutFront Minnesota, held a conference at a hotel in northern Minnesota. When the attendees sat down for the banquet, the hotel wait-staff served them wearing latex gloves. That situation has become a metaphor for me. I know when someone "handles" me with latex gloves, whether I can actually see the gloves or not. "At variance" churches have learned through painful experience to expect duct tape and plastic wrap as a denominational response to the diversity of thought and practice they represent.

The fear that George Bush, Donald Rumsfeld, and John Ashcroft wield over the American populace is completely stripped of complexity and ambiguity. Complexity and ambiguity lessen the fear. They make one think. The last thing this administration wants the American people to do is to think. So, we have clear, unambiguous rhetoric. Our administration arrogantly decrees three countries to be the "axis of evil." The world is put on alert that "you are either for us or against us." Our aggression is redefined as an act of compassion. We are told that the "evildoers" have no soul. This administration has successfully compelled us to circle our wagons and clearly delineate who is in and who is out. Dissenting views are not just discouraged; they are punished. We rename French fries "freedom fries" to punish the French for their dissenting views regarding Iraq. We parrot freedom rhetoric as we strip our neighbors of free speech, free expression, and the right to dissent.

Rightly or wrongly, I see malevolent intent behind our current administration. I see greed and a lust for power. I see ego and control. I don't see that same malevolence behind our church leadership in regards to issues of variance. What I see is the culture of fear that feeds the need to secure and contain, the wish to placate and avoid, the impulse to silence dissent and a longing for less ambiguity. In reaction to this fear, we have begun to use the Confession of Faith as the Pledge of Allegiance and the Membership Guidelines as the Patriot Act.

The identity of a congregation who could pose a "potential terrorist threat" is a congregation that has joined the Supportive Congregations Network. Such congregations may be detained for further investigation. Another potential terrorist threat is an employee of our denominational schools who may not agree with every point of the Confession of Faith. He or she may also be detained (and may also be unemployed). Variance is to be reported to leadership and leadership is to manage that variance and, hopefully, make it vanish. We are encouraged to stay alert and report anything unusual. Again, I am reminded of the rise of Nazi Germany. Fear was so encouraged and nurtured that people became vigilantes, reporting friends and family alike in an effort to secure their place inside the political circle of safety.

But safety is elusive. When security becomes the ultimate goal, the need to protect is unending. The more we have, the more security we need and the less secure we feel. When we feel insecure, we must become more vigilant, which will only lead to feeling less secure. When fear reigns supreme, goodness loses. Ideals, values, integrity, relationships—all are up for negotiation when fear reigns.

I see members of the Democratic Party selling their integrity and acting against their ideals in order to maintain the broadest, wealthiest constituency possible. Where acting out their beliefs could serve as a powerful role in creating peace and modeling tolerance, they choose to violate those principles in an effort to hold together the biggest voting bloc they can. I see the moderate middle and moderate leadership of our denomination in a similar position. In an effort to maintain the unity of the body, moderate Mennonites are violating their own beliefs and values about inclusion, diversity, and the ongoing revelation of God. These are good people with good intentions and good ideals. But while personally supportive, they are reticent to take a public position that would in any way threaten their own position in the church and the acceptance they enjoy. They too often violate their own consciences. And when they do, they pay dearly and those who are the "other" experience the rejection of their friends.

Two weeks ago, I attended the Central Plains Mennonite Conference as a delegate from St. Paul Mennonite Fellowship. On the docket was a Conference Council proposal that our congregation be moved from full membership to provisional membership. In an effort to be clear that we wished to continue as full members, our congregation wrote an honest, personal letter to all of the conference churches describing our beliefs and urging them to vote against the proposal. After the proposal was presented, an opportunity was given for discussion. There was silence. Not one delegate of this conference, of which we have been members for nearly twenty years, spoke in support of our congregation. The vote passed by 83%. I had expected argument—I was not prepared for the silence. As we left the session, I was reminded of the Martin Luther King, Jr. quote: "In the end, it is not the words of our enemies that we will remember, but the silence of our friends." Indeed!

But we are a people who know the Good News—that love conquers fear—that Jesus taught a new way to respond to fear! We are a people called to be in the world but not of the world! We are a peculiar people! How did we come to adopt this mainstream culture of fear? How did we come to attempt to manage it by using the same constructs as our government? Early Anabaptism's ultimate goal was certainly not security. It was fraught with risk as believers stood firm on their dissenting beliefs. Despite the life-threatening dangers, these believers remained true to their convictions. Authority in their lives was no longer placed on government or religion or creed or a person. Authority was placed on their individual and communal understanding of God and God's word. Authority was placed on the communal experience of seeking God.

The early Anabaptist experience was about freedom, empowerment, and the calling forth of passion. It was a social, religious, and sexual liberation. These brothers and sisters moved from the celibacy and austerity of cloistered life into vibrancy, exuberance, hope, passion, and spiritual connection with God. They explored the difference between a religion of power and greed and a religion of the Spirit. They lived their faith, grappled together with their doubts and questions, and strove to live God's will as they understood it. They made mistakes, they lost their lives, but they lived their lives fully spiritually engaged. In fact, this vitality—the very essence of Anabaptism—is precisely what was threatening to the powers of church and state. If congregants were going to start thinking for themselves, having individual and communal relationships with God, what would happen to the established church? Who would be in control? Would everything have to be re-thought? Would everything be changed?

Anabaptism was a terrifying threat to the powers of the day. The Anabaptists, of course, were far from perfect. They, too, eventually adopted a pursuit of communal conformity designed to strengthen their influence even as it compromised a key tenant of their movement. Despite this, they remained true to their voice of collective dissent. When legislation failed to control the Anabaptist movement, violence was instituted and rogue Anabaptists who refused to recant their beliefs, who refused to give power back to the church as it was, were burned at the stake, drawn and quartered, drowned, buried alive, hanged, and stoned. And yet the movement grew.

Where is this Anabaptist spirit—that fully-engaged, fervent seeking of God—in the Mennonite Church today? Have you felt it here in Atlanta? Did you feel it at your regional conference? Do you see it working in your congregation? Is that spirit and tradition reflected in the way we name and address variance? Does it inform our approach to new people and new ideas? Does it inspire us as individuals and congregations to experience God in new ways?

One cannot be open to experiencing God in new ways and not be open to experiencing new people, new information, new feelings, new ideas. Openness is, by nature, a vulnerability to change. Openness does not exist where fear and security are in control. In addition to risk, openness brings with it vibrant life. I have seen this life at work in the church. In my work with BMC, I have the pleasure of visiting with many variant congregations and variant individuals, and I see them offering an invitation to return to our Anabaptist audacity. They are bringing a passionate, sensual openness back to worship. They are claiming their relationship with God as the cornerstone of their faith and are unwilling to recant in order to be in compliance with statements that do not ring true. They are inviting the church to change—to step outside of fear and embrace dissent.

The Mennonite Church rejects these congregations and individuals at its own peril. When those who make room for passion and risk and vitality in their spiritual lives are censured, silenced, or removed from this denomination, we suffer a collective loss of life. Our joy is silenced, our work for justice is compromised, and our purpose obscured. To exchange a passionate life for one of policing and patrolling for the sake of Churchland security is to trade away the essence of the Spirit we mean to nurture. We have already made this error too many times. We need to stop.

So how, practically, do we begin to be open to the Spirit of God in the "other"? How do we end the reign of fear and offer exuberant welcome to new people, new ideas, and a new church? How do we return to the passion and conviction of a people rooted in their personal relationships with God and community? How do we create welcome within a culture of fear?

First, we must release ourselves from the obsession with fear and security. We need to remember that faith conquers fear and that Jesus gave us a new way to approach danger. Next, we must embrace ambiguity as a virtue. God's world is complex. It is messy. It does not lend itself to neat categories of good and evil, right or wrong. If it were that simple, leading a Christian life would not involve faith at all. It would merely be following a recipe for doing all the right things at the right time and choosing good over evil. Instead, the Christian life is one of seeking to understand, learning to discern, grappling with one another in the search for truth, and experiencing grace when we falter. Being able to be honest about the ambiguities and incongruities of our faith and life is an invitation of welcome to all who seek the Divine.

It is imperative that we be a body of dissent. I don't mean that we need to be open to having dissenting views, but that we *must* have dissenting views. Without them our spirits, convictions and passions wither and die. Those least empowered to defend themselves lose when a society eliminates dissent. A healthy community must be able to disagree. Dissent is not to be merely tolerated; it is to be encouraged. If we are to be open to the promptings of the Spirit, we need to be open to those with whom we do not fully agree. It is in articulating our own faith in response to another's that we are changed and our faith is deepened.

We must also reject the uncritical use of power in the church. We owe it to our leaders and to ourselves to question decisions and demand accountability. When we put our faith struggles and discomforts into the hands of our leadership with the expectation that they will handle and fix these issues, we resign our Anabaptist legacy. We must own our own spiritual journey and struggles. In the end, doing our own spiritual seeking and practicing dissent will sharpen our witness as a denomination.

I truly believed that Amy Short (then the Executive Director of BMC) was joking when she told me the theme of this convention was "God's Table: Y'all Come." In addition to finding it patronizing of a culture we do not largely represent, I was unbelievably offended by the image. BMC has been trying to come to this table for over twenty-five years and has never yet been afforded an invitation. My home congregation has been attempting to hold on to a few meager place settings at the Central Plains table for its fifteen or so members. Two weeks ago, when we were voted from full membership to provisional membership in our conference, the message did not sound like, "Y'all come," but more like, "Well, you can't sit at the main table, but we will put up a little card table in the kitchen where you may sit if you like." There was no joyful welcome there. The Germantown and Broad Street congregations are not even sitting at a card table. Their invitation has been an invitation out. And then, there are the equivocating invitations for so many other churches: Maple Avenue, Southside, Assembly, Atlanta, Ames, Oak Park, Calgary, etc.

Perhaps I'm not asking the right questions. Perhaps the irony of this convention's title is not about the invitation at all. Perhaps it is about the table. Is this table really God's table? Does it have the look and feel of the tables where Jesus chose to sit? Is Zaccheus at this table? Mary Magdalene? Peter? John? The Samaritan woman? Thomas? Judas? Is the risk and diversity of Jesus' church represented at this table? Perhaps we are looking for an invitation at the wrong table.

Christ's cavorting with passionate, sometimes unsavory characters created problems. His openness to all and the change that openness wrought on his world eventually got him killed. Yet his lasting legacy is about true love, compassion, and welcome. Ultimate welcome occurs when the one who welcomes is prepared to risk as deeply as the ones seeking welcome. Christ is the embodiment of perfect welcome and an unbridled invitation to the passionate life.

May God forgive our imperfect welcome, our fear of the "other," and our obsession with securing the church. May we open ourselves to encountering God's spirit embodied by the stranger and to the ensuing transformations of our faith.

Printed in Booklet # 7 of the *Welcome to Dialogue Series*, titled "*These, too, are Voices from God's Table.*" Published here by permission of Ruth Conrad Liechty, series editor.

This booklet and the six preceding ones are available for $2.25 each, postpaid, and can be ordered from Ruth Conrad Liechty, 1568 Redbud Court, Goshen, IN 46526. E-mail inquiries may be sent to rliechty@juno.com

Anne Breckbill and her partner Jane Ramseyer Miller live in St. Paul, Minnesota. She attended Rockway Mennonite School (Kitchener, Ontario) and graduated from Goshen College (Goshen, IN) with a major in English Education. She taught high school English at Iowa Mennonite School (Kalona, IA) and Bethany Christian High School (Goshen, IN). During the 1990s, she worked at a non-profit women's center where she developed an outpatient chemical dependency treatment program and served as Associate Executive Director. She currently works with credit unions as they implement internet applications. She has served on the BMC Board for over six years.

Anne deeply cherishes her biological and church families as well as her friendship with ten-year-old Charlotte and twenty-year-old Dan—young people to whom she has been a mentor over the past thirteen years. She and Jane are long-time members of the St. Paul Mennonite Fellowship where they, along with all other members of the community, serve on the pastoral team. In addition to writing and speaking, Anne enjoys phone calls with her parents, coffee with friends, satire, cooking, watching Minnesota Gopher women's basketball games with Charlotte and, above all else, reasons to laugh.

CHAPTER 32

Why I Believe That
Gay, Lesbian, Bisexual, and Transgender People
Should Be Included in the Church on an Equal
Basis with Everyone Else

Eighty-Four Response Statements
with One Hundred and Eleven Signatures

My understanding of God is not one who condemns but one who loves, nurtures, and affirms; therefore, the church as the body of Christ has a responsibility to do the same. We are all stewards of God's creation and share the duty to love, nurture, and affirm each other. Who among us has the wisdom and power to decide who has access to God's love and guidance and who does not? GLBT folks need and deserve love and compassion as all God's people do, perhaps even more because of the unique challenges they face daily. Doesn't Christ welcome everyone with open arms?

Adam J. Barkafski ~ Lancaster, PA

God loves all creation. Passing judgment on what we do as individuals, churches, and nations is God's job. Jesus taught us to love God first and then to love our neighbors as ourselves. That's my job. I intend to do that to the best of my ability. I will love all my neighbors, including the GLBT community, as I love myself. I can do no less. That includes welcoming the GLBT community into my home, my circle of friends, my church, and every other association I am part of. Welcome friends, into all my world.

Al Holsopple ~ Baltimore, MD

I do not accept the belief that GLBT people are abnormal, mentally sick, or morally depraved. My search for understanding has brought me into dialogue with my lesbian sisters and gay brothers. I have come to the conclusion that sexuality itself, including all sexual orientation, is not evil and can be lived out either positively or negatively. I cannot put myself in a situation where I would be a part of a church that discriminates against GLBT people because of who they are. **Anna Kreider Zook ~ Boise ID**

I thank God each time I see another lingering obstacle to full inclusion and acceptance of GLBT people crumbling! Our society and churches are in dire need of the gifts of GLBT individuals. It's high time that we follow Jesus' teachings of welcome and nurture and end all silencing. He has cleared the way and provided direction for revisiting the texts that were once used to humiliate our GLBT brothers and sisters. As a mother, I want my children to enjoy the full privileges of membership and leadership, no matter what their orientation. Surely God wants nothing less and offers everlasting arms to each beloved child.　　**Anna Lisa Yoder~ Quakertown, PA**

I first became aware of the normalcy of diverse sexual orientation when I was a student nurse, and in all my sixty years, I have never had a moment's doubt that GLBT individuals are acceptable to our Creator God. I know them as "people" and experience them as having common ground with me. I cannot accept the biblical interpretation that these dear people are not acceptable to God. Whatever happened to Jesus' model of church? "For where two or three are gathered in my name, I am there among them" (Matthew 18:20). God, help us to love each other!

Anne Kratz ~ Telford, PA

"Now we see dimly. I know only in part; then I will know fully, as I will be fully known. Faith, hope and love abide with the greatest of these being love" (First Corinthians 13:12-13 – author's paraphrase). I believe that GLBT people should be invited and welcomed with love into the fellowship of the church on an equal basis with everyone else. These people are unaccepted by society and, unfortunately, by the church. My frustration is that these talented children of God are not accepted in leadership positions. We are the losers and they are judged unfairly.

Ardis L. Zerger ~ Dearborn, MI

I believe that GLBT people should be allowed to be members of our churches on an equal basis because they are just as acceptable in God's loving eyes as any heterosexual. God's boundless creativity has obviously been at work in the variety of sexual orientations that exist. Let's celebrate our diversity, not only in skin colors, body sizes, accents, talents, opinions, and personalities, but also in our various sexual orientations.

Becky Beachy Felton ~ Quakertown, PA.

The United Church of Christ is currently running a wonderful, thought-provoking TV commercial. It opens with several people "guarding the gates" of a church, while a line of diverse people wait to get in, among them a lesbian couple. Some are told, "You can go in," but others hear the words, "You can't go in." Then a voice-over assures us that this is not the way the UCC church operates. My prayer is that someday soon our Mennonite churches will accept everyone, including our openly GLBT children, with open arms as I believe Jesus did.

Becky Brubacher ~ Millersburg, OH

We are not whole and fully god/de's children when any part of the family is not truly welcomed at the table. When women's voices were missing from biblical scholarship and the pulpit, we were impoverished. We are impoverished now because of the gaping hole of rejected GLBT folks. In part because of the Mennonite Church's entrenched homophobia, we now attend a church where GLBTs are fully present as singles, committed couples, couples with children, and formerly on the pastoral team. There we are learning from each other about "suffering well," standing against all kinds of injustice, and celebrating with abandon and great joy.

Bob and Carole Hull ~ Newton, KS

When our daughter told us she was a lesbian, we read, talked, and searched for support. BMC conventions, Connecting Families retreats, and the shared stories in Roberta Kreider's books were a catalyst to help understand, even in a small way, who GLBT persons are. I've found that they can be very talented, caring, thoughtful, humorous, and God-loving. Unfortunately, they are also hurting because much of society and most of our churches make it difficult or impossible to share their gifts openly. This is unfathomable! They must be allowed the same privileges the rest of us take for granted.

Bob Brubacher ~ Millersburg, OH

For many years, having GLBT people as part of the Mennonite Church was a non-issue for me. That changed when a mother flew into town for the purpose of outing her son and his partner in my church. She felt God wanted her to warn us of the sinners in our midst. My God would not have given the blessing to any mother to humiliate and hurt a son in this way. If the church would spend half the amount of energy on feeding the poor, housing the homeless, and caring for the mentally ill as it spends trying to oust GLBT persons from their churches, the work of Jesus would truly be done.

Bonita Kreider Nussbaum ~ Eugene, OR

We believe that no matter if one is born in or out of season, or whatever one's biological makeup, or what sins we may have committed, all of us are equal when kneeling at the foot of the cross in need of God's grace—grace freely given to all of us. Therefore, we willingly bear witness of this grace to others, including our GLBT sisters and brothers. We can do no less if we claim to follow Jesus who himself walked with all sorts of people, many of whom were rejected by those claiming to uphold the moral codes of that day.

Carl and Gladys Keener ~ State College, PA

Christian growth and maturity come with much time, along with a true desire to become more like Christ. I often wonder how Jesus would feel and how He would reach out to various situations. I know God dearly loves every person He created, and that includes all races, cultures, and genders. Our hearts should be *full* of deep love, compassion, kindness, and understanding towards everyone—not just those we feel fit our lifestyle. Jesus said, "Whosoever will may come and drink freely of the water of life." That leaves no one out. God welcomes all who love Him into His family with open, arms! **Carol Kreider Kearbey ~ Parker, CO**

God is a God of inclusion, love, compassion, and relationship. We need only to look at how Jesus treated people to be convinced of that. Whether or not we believe certain sexual/gender orientations are sin, we are called to love one another fully. To me, that looks like being open and invitational. It's saying: "Hey, I want to get to know you as a fellow child of God. Come on in. Let's talk. I want to listen to you." After we gain a glimpse of who each of us is in God's eyes, we can decide if the stone-throwing needs to happen.
Catherine Bargen ~ Vancouver, B.C., Canada

Jesus said, "Whoever comes to me I will never drive away" (John 6:37). Peter learned that God's acceptance of people was based on their faith, not on ethnicity or human labels. Ought we not follow God's way?
Charles Longenecker ~ New Holland, PA

GLBT children of God are needed in the Christian church, because many of them bear witness to a loving (agape) God who needs to be more widely heard in the world. Many of them have developed skills in witness, service, and administration that are desperately needed in all levels of ministry. No denomination has enough good workers. Yet many churches refuse to affirm this category of God's children. The change toward accepting the God that Jesus worshiped is slow. We are making slow progress toward accepting females and blacks. Let's continue to move forward with the GLBT community. **Clyde Carter ~ Daleville, VA**

God in our own image is a human constant. We assume God confirms us in our deeply-held beliefs. This is good and probably inevitable. But it can easily become complacency if we assume that God thinks as we do. God then becomes little more than the boundary enforcer of our culturally established comfort zone. The Holy Spirit is always engaged in breaking down such boundaries, showing God in new ways. We need GLBT fellows beside us with full integrity to help us see where we have created God in our own heterosexual image (the essence of idolatry) and become morally complacent. Marantha! **Daniel Liechty ~ Normal, IL**

Five years ago, I helped to begin a new Christian Church, Disciples United Community Church. One of our key principles was welcoming all people, regardless of sexual orientation. This philosophy attracted to our community many GLBT folks who used their talents and creativity to help us grow and flourish, including serving in leadership positions. Our congregation consists of families with children, college students, adult singles, couples, and senior citizens. We value our diversity and the richness it brings to our religious experience. We welcome GLBT folks because we feel it is what Jesus would do. **Darlene Zerbe ~ Lancaster, PA**

Membership in the body of Christ is not based on human measurements and barriers, but is for all who have received the gift of the Spirit and evidence this by bearing the fruits. In God's new creation, we are all one in Christ, including GLBT people, and are joyously welcomed by God. In this new creation, the words of Isaiah 56:3-5 with regard to those formerly shut out by human barriers, can be fulfilled: "Do not let the eunuch (read glbt) say, 'I am just a dry tree.' For thus says the Lord: 'To the eunuchs...who...hold fast my covenant...I will give a name better than sons and daughters...'"
Don and Marilyn Brenneman ~ Greensboro, NC

For two decades now, and counting, we have been attempting to stand with gay and lesbian church members against a false reading of the Scriptures and an ignorance of the etiology of homosexuality. We have opposed creedal statements that condemn and exclude, and counselors who deny that etiology. We wish that the church would confront the issues Jesus spoke of—housing, clothing, and feeding the poor and hungry—instead of reflecting our present homophobic culture and would move on to understand how much we all have in common with the persecuted among us.
Donald and Elsie Steelberg ~ Wichita, KS

There is something of God in everyone. I believe that people are like the seeds that become pearls in oysters. Looking at the outside, you can't tell the size of or value of the pearl inside until the oyster is opened. It takes hard work for the oyster to make that seed grow into something valuable. Everyone has gifts to be used for God's work. Everyone is on the journey. God does not make mistakes. Can we risk throwing out the most valuable pearl in God's collection because we don't like how the oyster "looks"?
Doris Hopwood Dunhan ~ Bakersfield, CA

Since *all* people are made in God/de's image, on what basis can any group of individuals categorically be excluded? The notion of those in power excluding any category of persons as unworthy of participation—particularly in the setting of organized religion—reeks of judgmentalism, hierarchy, and "we/they" mentality. The basis for determining what is "okay" today is subjective—depending on leadership, changing times, and new understandings—and therefore prone to error. To deprive the church of the many gifts GLBT people have to share and to deprive those who want to give them is, I suggest, sinful.   **Dottie Wine ~ Lomita, CA**

I don't understand why we use a few negative passages to say that GLBT people can't be Christian. Why not use the positive criteria? Are you a follower of God? Do you confess Jesus as your Lord? In John 13:35, Jesus said that people will recognize us as his disciples by our love for one another. First John 4:7 tells us that God is love and that anyone who loves "is born of God and knows God." Add to this the signs of God's spirit listed in Galatians 5:22-23, and it is easy to tell where God is dwelling.

Doug Jantzi ~Schwenksville, PA

The American Anthropological Association recently concluded that a century of research on kinship shows that many family types, including those with same-sex parents, can contribute to stable and humane societies. It is time that we include GLBT people as honored members in our churches and communities. I have enjoyed getting to know many of them who are making wonderful contributions through teaching, public service, and raising children. Some Bible verses seem to justify male domination, slavery, and violence, but the human prejudices of the writers do not drown out the biblical message of God's love, faithfulness, and care in all relationships.

Douglas Hertzler ~ Mount Rainier, MD

I still remember that wooden sign prominently displayed in our United Methodist Youth Fellowship room. It read, "I know God loves me. God does not make junk!" Years later, that sign was put to the test. The church didn't love me, and I was junk. Today, love abounds with conservative compassionism. Now we "love the homosexual while hating the sin." God loves me again...but I'm still junk. However, love means accepting a person completely. It does not judge and compartmentalize. Real love creates a relationship of equality and respect. Isn't that what Jesus taught?

Duane Romberger ~ Elizabethtown, PA

Jesus was open to everyone He met. No one was turned away. Jesus met the needs of everyone who asked help from Him. No one was excluded. I think the church needs to model Christ's life. Jesus promised that anyone who comes to Him will not be turned away (John 6:37). The exclusion of GLBT people from churches is a matter of justice. If Jesus did not turn anyone away, why should we? We need to open our doors to welcome each one who desires our fellowship, regardless of how they are viewed by society.

Ed Meyers ~ Perkasie, PA

Christians are well acquainted with John 3:16, "the golden text of the Bible." "For God so loved the world that he gave his only begotten son, that whosoever believeth in him should not perish, but have everlasting life" (KJV). I see Christian GLBT individuals as part of that great *whosoever*—brothers and sisters possessing eternal life, who should be totally accepted in the Christian community. If the Lord gave them the same gift that he gave me when I believed in the Lord Jesus Christ, who am I that I should hinder God?   **Elaine Sommers Rich ~ Bluffton, Ohio**

God created all of us—we are all different, but God accepts us if we sincerely believe in him. The church needs to be a place where people are accepted for who they are and all who believe in God are welcomed.
Ella Bohrer ~ Sellersville, PA

God has given our GLBT friends many gifts that can bless the ministry of the church. Why would God have done so if it was wrong to have them used in this capacity? It is clear to me that God, who loves diversity and created so much of it, would have us benefit from what *all* of us have to offer. We have rejected GLBT people for too long; let's follow the example of Paul's lesson on Cornelius's rooftop and include all who sincerely wish to serve God.
Esther Becker ~ Gordonville, PA

A loved relative in the Groves family, another on the Bohn side, and lesbian and gay friends taught me that Christians have more commonalities than differences, no matter what their sexual orientation. We hurt and deprive ourselves and our GLBT friends if we do not accept them as equals in the church. National pediatric, psychological, psychiatric, and medical associations now acknowledge that sexual orientation cannot be changed, though some people repress it. We should give thanks for sound, stable families, whatever the sexual orientation. Sacred vows, faithful marriages, and loving Christian families are good for the community and the nation.
Esther Bohn Groves ~ North Newton, KS

All GLBT people should feel welcome in our churches. I believe that their sexual orientation is part of their development before birth. Jesus says that the greatest commandments are about loving God with all our hearts and loving our neighbors as we love ourselves. Therefore, we must care about everyone as Jesus did. To judge others is wrong. We often burden the GLBT children of our churches by our prejudice and drive them away instead of being as Christ to them and welcoming all seekers with love. Jesus still invites, "Come unto me all you who have heavy burdens" (Matthew 11:28).
Evelyn Krehbiel ~ Bluffton, Ohio

At no place in my Bible does it say that some people should be favored over others. Even the sons of Levi were superceded by unrelated people. I personally know GLBT people who have contributed to the church's life and others who have been broken-hearted and their talents were lost to the church because of prejudice or hate-filled attitudes. As one young, straight Brethren man said, "It's a matter of justice."

Grace A. Black ~ Baltimore, MD

Sexual orientation is not a choice. Our Creator God is a lover of variety. If this were not so, why is not every flower a sunflower or every snowflake of one design? Why is it that every human being has a different DNA? The church calls GLBT individuals unclean. In the vision recorded in Acts 10, Peter was instructed: "What God has made clean, you must not call profane." Jesus said, "Anyone who comes to me, I will never drive away" (John 6:37). Why should the church insist that GLBT believers must change their orientation in order to be accepted by God?

Harold Kreider ~ Sellersville, PA

Based upon the often painful testimonies of Christian brothers and sisters, I've come to understand that a homosexual orientation is not something sought or chosen; it's given. It's kind of like being bald; I didn't ask to be bald and do not prefer being bald, but it was given to me. I don't know why in God's providence I have been given a heterosexual orientation and others have been given a homosexual orientation. But I believe we are *all* created in God's image. As followers of Jesus, we are called to invite everyone, regardless of sexual orientation, into Kingdom communities of grace, nurture, and accountability.   ### Henry D. Landes ~ Sellersville, PA

In my professional, academic work, some of my employers, mentors, and important colleagues have been gay. I have enjoyed singing in choirs with GLBT choristers. A few older members in the small congregation my wife and I attend are openly unwelcoming to such people. I feel uneasy, knowing that there is an imposed gulf between my exclusively heterosexual Sunday morning faith life and my workday world at the university with individuals of a variety of orientations. If conferences or individuals in our congregation force me to take sides, I will need to leave the Mennonite world.

J. Evan Kreider ~ Vancouver, B.C., Canada

The God whom I know and worship offers unconditional love to all who respond to the Gospel call of Jesus Christ. But for too many centuries, the established church has discriminated against disciples of Jesus with a gender orientation other than heterosexual. The handful of biblical texts that have been used to support such censure must be understood in their original context of warning against idolatry and acts of sexual exploitation and abuse. The Gospel message calls everyone to a high standard of honesty, loyalty, and fidelity in personal relations, including sexual relations. Those same standards should apply regardless of orientation.

J.R. Burkholder ~ Goshen, IN

Our conceptualization of church is of a group that comes together to seek greater understanding of life's meaning, of universal mysteries, of our roles in building a whole and healed world: i.e., a greater understanding of God. How could that search for understanding be complete with ten percent of our sisters and brothers excluded from the process? We cannot accept the policies that have these precious people in a permanent quandary regarding the requirements of the church they are drawn to and what their souls are telling them. To us, a church without GLBT persons is not a whole church.

Janelle and Jason Myers-Benner ~ Harrisonburg, VA

On my Christian journey, and when I worship, I need all my brothers and sisters to walk with me on this road of life, to help me learn, to help me grow, to help me love more dearly. To accept all of God's children into the fold is simply the Jesus thing to do; it is the just thing to do; it is the merciful thing to do; it is the humbling thing to do. This is what God requires of me; this is what God requires of us all. It is simply........the right and compassionate thing to do.

Janet K. Hartzell ~ Souderton, PA

For most of my life, my church community was my entire community. Now I am a believer living in self-imposed exile from the church. As a heterosexual, I was never rejected by the church for my sexual orientation, but until GLBT believers are welcome in the church on earth, I am not welcome either. I sometimes miss a sense of "belonging," but if the price of "belonging" is the willingness to exclude others, I cannot pay. God does not ask my help in determining who will enter His kingdom. He asks, instead, that I love others as He loves me—responsibility enough for one flawed human being.

Janet Lipsi ~ Telford, PA

I have many GLBT friends who are demeaned because of their orientation. They believe in and serve the same Lord that I do. They are gifted and intent on bringing God's love and justice to all. Yet in most churches they are denied the right to serve.

Jean Lersch ~ St. Petersburg, FL

LGBT individuals are made in the image of God, who is beyond gender, and are God's beloved children, as we all are. These members of diverse sexual orientation in God's family bring unique gifts of ministry and grace of which the church has great need. When we open ourselves to God's word in its fullness, we see how tragically misguided the condemnation of our LGBT sisters and brothers has been. When we open ourselves to share in their lives, we know we can no longer afford to ostracize and marginalize them, and we can no longer deprive ourselves of their faithfulness, their insight, and their love.   **Jean E. Snyder ~ Edinboro, PA**

When I was young, I was always the last one picked for "choose-up" soft-ball. I wasn't a good athlete. The rejection I felt then is still a vivid memory. It is clear to me that Christ, who rejects no one, would want me to welcome our GLBT Christian friends, not reject them. We may interpret Scripture differently, but one thing is certain: Christ admonishes us to love the Lord our God with all our heart, soul, and mind, and our brothers and sisters as ourselves. I welcome my friends with the arms of Jesus.

Jep Hostetler ~ Columbus, OH

"LGBT" suggests a prayer to me: "Lord, grant us blessings and tender mercies." We live in an age where many find faith irrelevant. Yet I find among my LGBT sisters and brothers faith that moves mountains. Unfortunately, many Christians remain unwilling to accept them into communion. Even the Law of Moses commanded God's people to accept the stranger in their midst as their equal (Leviticus 19:33). Jesus broadened that law into the law of love that includes all people. With faith and love, may we fervently pray, "Lord, Grant us Blessings and Tender mercies."

John Burt ~ Pittsburgh, PA

God's Spirit within me bears witness to the fruit of the Spirit abundantly manifested in the lives of my GLBT brothers and sisters. The church is the loser when GLBT folks are not welcome to share their many gifts. I have walked with some of them through the despair of believing that they cannot be both Mennonite and gay. The cruel words and disrespect they experience from "Christians" is heart breaking. As I seek to follow Christ's example, I choose to respond to all of God's children with respect, compassion, and love.

Joyce Hostetler ~ Columbus, OH

"Everyone Welcome" declares the sign in front of many Mennonite churches that now include handicap ramps, elevators, childcare facilities, and Christian education for all ages. But not *everyone* is included in this welcome! Because our Mennonite Church was not willing to listen to the personal faith stories of GLBT people, we left the church and joined the Disciples United Community Church, an open and affirming outgrowth of Lancaster Theological Seminary (UCC). We pray that someday every church will recognize all loving relationships as blessed by God and will welcome all people to come to the communion table to share equally in God's love without patronizing or simply tolerating our differences.

Judy and Ray Harnly ~ Lancaster, PA

My reasons to worship include praising God, thanking God for grace and God's many blessings, and seeking guidance through partaking of the sacraments. To deny these aspects of worship on an equal basis to *any* of God's children—including GLBT persons—is an affront to God's magnificent creation in all of its infinite diversity. *Love* impels me to praise, *gratitude* compels me to thanksgiving, and *need* implores me to seek guidance and direction in dealing with my fellow beings. All this takes place in my life whether or not the church "allows" it. I already have that equality—the church just does not realize it yet.

Kenneth Bergey ~ Telford, PA

I believe that GLBT people are human beings created by God just like all the rest of us who live and breathe. It seems so simple. What a shame that there are so-called Christian leaders and lay people who have to be told that we are all equal in God's sight.

Leann Toews ~ Goessel, KS

We must ask: Is homosexuality of God's creation? Religious authorities wanted to exclude the followers of Jesus, even put them to death. Wise Gamaliel counseled that if their activity was privately chosen, it would pass away of its own accord, but if it was of God, "You might even be found opposing God" (Acts 5:33-39). I have experienced the Holy through the creativity and generosity of homosexuals. Once, when I was unemployed while recovering from a serious accident, a gay man offered to send money if I needed it—not a loan—a gift! Though not in my congregation, he was the church to me. I celebrate such a person within the Body of Christ.

Leland Wilson ~ Gold Canyon, AZ

A Christian friend once said to me, "I read the gospel and it tells me to love everybody and not to judge anybody. That keeps me busy for the rest of my life." I take that gospel mandate—straight from the lips of the Jesus I love and seek to follow—and add to it the realization that every person I meet teaches me something new about my life and my faith. When I think about the richness, wisdom, and blessing that my GLBT friends have brought me, my question becomes, "Doesn't the church know what it's missing?

Libby Smith ~ Sellersville, PA

Jesus welcomed all people from the entire spectrum of society to come to faith. Nowhere in Scripture are we admonished to judge or decide who is fit to receive God's love, forgiveness, and mercy. The diverse gifts and insights of GLBT people are vitally needed to carry out the programs of the church. Heterosexual couples will be challenged to strengthen their relationships as they observe same-sex unions forged under trying circumstances. An inclusive church will bear witness that we have all been redeemed, and as citizens of God's kingdom, we may equally partake of God's blessings.

Lloyd and Mary Jo Miller ~ South Bend, IN

In my opinion, the question of whether or not the GLBT community should be included in worshiping God in the church is ludicrous. As a Christian who happens to be lesbian, I claim the promises of our Lord Jesus. He never put qualifiers on those promises, and He does not deny them to anyone, including the GLBT community. John 3:16 says, "*Whosoever* believes in [Jesus]...[will] have everlasting life." We who believe in God are called to worship Him. "Enter into his gates with thanksgiving, and into his courts with praise..." (Psalm 100:4). "Let everything that hath breath praise the Lord" (Psalm 150:6). [Scripture from KJV]

Loreli H. Bauer ~ Perkasie, PA

We do not have a choice about many circumstances in our lives, but I believe we each have a choice about following Jesus. I have made commitments blessed by God to many GLBT people. Jesus himself purifies the church and presents her without blemish to God, so I do not have to do that. The Spirit breaks forth in all believers, united and different. I would rather risk welcoming believers than rejecting them. This walk in the church has brought some tears to me, but also much blessing. Jesus still leads on! And the church still has much work to do!

Loretta Baumgartner ~ Hesston, KS

As I consider with sadness the state of the so-called "everyone is welcome" in our Mennonite churches, I often think of the songs, stories, and themes we teach our children. We do get it right sometimes. We teach that God loves everyone; God welcomes everyone, and we are called to love God with all our being and our neighbors as ourselves. God must weep when we grow up and reject the Master's plan. We put up barriers, deny the simplicity of the gospel message, delineate conditions of welcome, and limit God's unconditional love. Where do we go wrong?

MaDonna Holsopple ~ Baltimore, MD

I have an intelligent Christian daughter who came out to us as lesbian sixteen years ago. Accepting this knowledge was not easy, but in discussions with other parents and my pastor, and through extensive reading on the subject, I came to understand what the Bible really says about homosexuality. I am thankful that my daughter is fortunate to live in a community where the Mennonite Church means it when it says, "We *welcome* and value each person as having been uniquely made in God's image." I pray that *all* our Mennonite churches will welcome *all* of God's children.

Marilyn H. Denlinger ~ Ronks, PA

Everyone is a child of God and equally loved by Him. That is why I believe the church should include and accept persons who are GLBT.

Marjorie Isaak ~ Sellersville, PA

As parents supporting our GLBT children, it was not a good feeling to be asked to stay outside the gates at a church conference. How must our children feel to be excluded from the church? The church's mission is reconciliation, not judgment! As a teenager, our son Robert was the Ontario MYF president. Later, he was asked to consider the ministry. An acquaintance told us that he reminded her of his great-grandfather, who was a Mennonite bishop in Michigan. Robert has the potential to be a great church leader, but he now teaches at a public high school. Is salvation not for everyone who has faith?

Mary and Roy Gascho ~ Kitchener, ON, Canada

The role of the church is to be loving, inclusive, and recognizing that there is that of God in everyone.

Mary L. and Richard N. Reichley ~ Harleysville, PA

My prayer is that the Christian church will move away from trying to "corral" sinners, and will instead create spacious pastures for all of us to experience God's grace in community. This involves modeling Jesus' ability to mingle and fellowship and search freely with all people—regardless. When anyone seeks membership, I believe that it should be a matter of leading between that one individual, the congregation, and God.

Mary Lou Cummings ~ Quakertown, PA

My spirituality has been influenced by both the Mennonite and Quaker faith traditions. However, the Quaker foundational tenet that God's Spirit, the "Inner Light," "that of God," exists within every human being shapes my belief that all people are created by God, loved for who they are, and gifted with the Divine Presence. I believe that regardless of gender, sexual affinity, or any other category, we are called to use our spiritual gifts for nurture, growth, and witness in whatever capacity we feel a spiritual leading. To deny inclusion in the full life of the church to GLBT people is to deny them the full expression of God's indwelling presence.

Mary Lou Hartzler ~ Lansdowne, PA

I believe the Bible teaches us to practice tolerance for *all people* by accepting them for who they are and treating them with respect. I grew up in a Mennonite and Brethren community and personally experienced the narrow, judgmental attitudes that have alienated many fine people from embracing any church. I pray that policies and feelings regarding GLBT people will change. Many people through the ages have been killed and maligned for their beliefs because of dogmatic interpretation of the Bible and people who are sure they are right and have an exclusive link to God. They are missing some of God's greatest blessings.

Mary Lou Richards ~ Harleysville, PA

Jesus accepted *all* people. He did not discriminate; nobody was left out. Hence, I believe:

– We, the church (including leaders), are not in a position to "play God" by determining who is Christian. Membership should be based on each individual's confession of faith.

– The Mennonite and Brethren churches have lost many excellent members, including pastors, due to the current policy of excluding GLBT folks. What a shame that my Christian brothers and sisters need to find their support and acceptance elsewhere. As a Christian, I refuse to be judgmental; consequently, I embrace GLBT people as members and leaders of the church.

Mary S. Kauffman ~ Harrisonburg, VA

I have been a student of the parables and aphorisms of Jesus for several years. The wisdom I find in these teachings leads me to see a man who is accepting of all people, especially folks who would be considered less than righteous in his day. He traveled with them, spoke with them, healed them and, most importantly, he ate with them. Many churches today exclude GLBT folks from a misguided biblical perspective. It demonstrates how these churches worship the idols of church unity, church doctrine, or church tradition and ignore the life and teachings of the sage from Nazareth.

Mike Short ~ Pleasant Hill, OH

We are in the biblical tradition where the religious community keeps trying to draw the boundaries and Jesus keeps stepping over those lines! Beyond the consternation of people when Jesus heals the bent-over woman on the Sabbath, Jesus pushes further, naming her as a "daughter of Abraham"—the one they saw as unfit (Luke 13:10-17). I hope for a church where people hear the good news that each is made in the image of God. I long for all to be received as "children of Abraham," especially those long shut out. It's tremendously good news that God is host of this banquet, and we are simply guests, servers, and door openers.   **Pam Dintaman ~ Lancaster, PA**

We believe that accepting GLBT people as fully participating members is a justice issue. The theme of justice is central in the Bible. God works in the world to meet the needs of all people who are oppressed. GLBT people have the same need for companionship as heterosexual people. We do not see how a loving same-sex couple committed to each other for life could adversely affect the heterosexual family. Our son and his partner have enriched our family for fifteen years.

"But we make God's love too narrow, by false limits of our own,
and we magnify God's strictness, with a zeal God will not own."
Paul and Martha Snyder ~ Kitchener, Ontario

I was brought up with the belief that all people are children of God and that God loves all his children. I was also taught that we are all different and that diversity in all aspects of life is to be respected.

Paula Zook Bachman ~ Boise, ID

Sexual orientation has nothing at all to do with ability in church leadership. Some of the most eloquent preachers, capable organizers, and effective church nurturers will inevitably be GLBT people. To deny them the space to use their gifts for the benefit of the church is a grave error. It cannot be expected that GLBT people will feel genuinely welcome in a setting in which they are asked not to express their gifts, including leadership in the church.

Peter Sensenig ~ Harrisonburg, VA

He spoke with a quiet intensity: "My church told me clearly that I was an abomination to the Lord. I didn't want to be an abomination. I prayed, I begged the Lord to deliver me from this. I sought counseling; I did all the right things. No deliverance came."

Having thus spoken—as part of a panel discussion at a Mennonite Christian college—he disappeared. However, his desperation still haunts the halls of EMU. Who will tell him that he was not delivered because his same-gender attraction was his own choice? How long will the church continue to blame the one we have victimized?

Ray E. Horst ~ Harrisonburg, VA

I believe the church is a community of God's people called to follow in Jesus' footsteps, to live as Jesus lived—a life of love, compassion, forgiveness, and caring for all. I want to be part of a church that welcomes everyone to its table—a people who honor diversity and practice love, who support each other as we walk our personal journeys of faith, true to who we are as unique beings. We are *all* God's children.

Rebecca Fast, London, ON, Canada

We welcome GLBT folks because "they" are people. Using labels turns people into objects. The Apostle Paul's words are compelling. "Welcome one another as Christ welcomed you, for the glory of God," and "All of you who were baptized into Christ have clothed yourselves with Christ. There is neither Jew nor Greek, there is neither slave nor free, there is not male and female; for you are all one in Christ Jesus." We were welcomed into Christ's body without regard to false standards. Anything the organized church adds as requirement is a denial of the Gospel. We desire to welcome any who choose Christ's way.   **Richard and Mary Lichty ~ Hatfield, PA**

I Timothy 4:4 – For everything God created is good...

Leviticus 18 and Romans 1 are used to condemn homosexual people today. Homosexual orientation as we know it was unknown to the writers of these

Scriptures. How could they have written about something that wouldn't be comprehensible until almost two thousand years later? Because sexual orientation is real, that means God established it. Just because he didn't prompt mankind to discover it until now doesn't mean it isn't good.

"You have heard it said ...but I say unto you" ...again.

Robert Henrikson ~ Harrisonburg, VA

My heart aches for GLBT people who grew up in the Mennonite Church and feel like second-class citizens because of the unkind words and messages from the church. I am sad for those who need to be silent and cannot share who they are in order to stay in the Mennonite Church. I am sad for those who feel they need to leave the Mennonite Church. These faithful individuals have much to teach us. Other denominations are gaining people who are wonderful teachers and ministers, and we cry that we have a leadership shortage. I long for the day when all GLBT people will be welcome in the Mennonite Church.

Rose Althouse Moyer ~ Harleysville, PA

The entire Gospel is about inclusiveness, caring for everyone and community. There are many direct instructions from the Word, such as, "See that you do not despise one of these little ones; for I tell you that in heaven their angels always behold the face of my Father who is in heaven" (Matthew 18: 10-11). For us, the church as an institution has always been narrow-minded—more concerned about keeping the status quo than really reaching out and ***doing*** Justice—more concerned about keeping its power and control over people than really discerning its mission by listening to people.

Rosie Hartzler and Dusty Baumer ~ Windham, ME

I have a dream that one day soon, all of God's children will be welcomed into the Mennonite Church. I have met many vibrant GLBT Christians who love the church and wish to be part of it. A number of them have outstanding leadership skills and are sensitive, caring individuals who have much to offer if given the opportunity to serve. I feel it is important to provide a "level playing field" with the same privileges for ***all*** members, including the choice to be married or to remain single. Then GLBT people would no longer be treated as second-class citizens. **Ruby Lehman ~ Harrisonburg, VA**

We believe GLBT people are created in the image of God, including their sexual nature and orientation. When God looked at his creation, he called it "good." Peter learned in a vision that what God had created should not be called unclean. Jesus clearly stated, "***Whoever*** believes in me has eternal life." His guidelines for relationships are to love God with our whole being and our neighbors as ourselves. Love and commitment to follow Christ's teachings should be the basis for inclusion in the church. Sexual orientation should not exclude anyone from full participation in the church.

Ruth and Jay Martin ~ Lancaster, PA

God said, "Let us make humankind in our image, according to our like-ness...So God created humankind...God saw everything that [God] had made and indeed it was very good" (Genesis 1:26ff). God has blessed us with a creation that is tremendously varied in all aspects: living creatures, plants, landscapes, people, color, size, shape. Why then is it so difficult to accept the fact that God also created variety in sexual orientation? (Variety in sexual orientation has been documented in animals. See booklets #5 and 7 in the *Welcome to Dialogue* series.) God pronounced all God's creation "very good." Dare we do otherwise?

Ruth Conrad Liechty ~ Goshen, IN

"Do you still love me?" was our daughter's first question after sharing with us that she was a lesbian. She knew we loved her, but would we still love her now that she had shared her secret? I didn't know the answers to all the other questions tumbling through my mind at that moment, but the answer to this one was unquestionably, "Yes!" Our daughter is sure of our love because she and her partner are welcome in our family gatherings and are treated with re-spect. They know that we support their committed relationship with joy. I wish that Karen and Sue could hear and feel the same answer from the church.   **Sarah Myers ~ Mount Joy, PA**

It is obvious in the Mennonite Church that agreement, even on important issues like non-violence, is not the basis of our unity. Real unity comes from being able to see the image of God in others (John 17:20-23). God probably created our differences so we could see, as Jesus did, different images of God—in Zacchaeus, in the thief on the cross, in a child. Seeing God where we didn't expect to see God deepens our understanding of God and changes us. Excluding people of different sexual orientations from the church, even though they make the same faith commitments as we do, stunts our under-standing of God.   **Stanley Bohn ~ Newton, KS**

I believe Queer people are included in God's Church. My "gaydar" lets me recognize another member of the queer community without being told. When I was still in the closet, people who had known me for years would tell me that they did not know anyone who was queer. I would bite my lip trying not to shout, "*You know me*!" "Gaydar" enables me to see gay people within the pages of the Bible and to hear Christ affirming their place in God's kingdom. I see Peter's acceptance of all God's creation as clean. God's Spirit assures me that God loves me.

Susan Reinhold ~ Mount Joy, PA

GLBT people are just as much a part of God's creation as are heterosexual people. There is nothing immoral about being GLB or T. Every individual is born with her/his own set of fingerprints, eye color, facial features, and sexual orientation. No one orientation is better or more true than another. Every human being has gifts to offer and needs to be met and, therefore, has the right to feel safe and accepted in God's community. As the song from my days as a youth in church goes, "*All* God's critters got a place in the choir...."

Suzanne Zook ~ Arvada, CO

During the time I served as an ordained minister in the Church of the Brethren, I often heard about a "leadership crisis." At the same time, the church turned away leaders who were called, and sometimes already ordained, simply because of their sexual orientation. What foolishness! I now serve in a UCC congregation that welcomes all people with open arms and celebrates whatever gifts they bring. GLBT people in our congregation are not second-class church members. Like all of us, they are God's children. The day all churches in all denominations recognize that fact will be a day of great rejoicing in heaven.

Sylvia Eagan ~ Portland, OR

The Mennonite Church needs the forgiveness of its gay and lesbian sons and daughters in order to bring healing to all those affected by the discriminatory and rejecting teachings of the church. Effective forgiveness that leads to reconciliation can happen only after the gay/lesbian community is fully welcomed in the church on an equal basis. The Mennonite Church is wounding itself spiritually through its inhospitality towards the GLBT community. Today God invites the church to reconstitute its redemption once again in the arms of those whom it has despised and rejected. Parents and friends work and pray to hasten that day.

Victor Fast ~ London, ON, Canada

As an educator, therapist, and pastor, I know friends whose orientation is toward the same sex. They are sensitive, creative, trustworthy, affectionate, and life-giving. Most are fruit-bearing disciples of Christ. Their witness convinces me that our orientations are neither chosen nor evil, but a part of that human giftedness for which all are responsible. I read the Bible through the life of Christ as I understand and know him through the Spirit. I find no basis for judging sexual orientation, but I hear Christ's high ethical standard of love. I choose the risk of including people whom our Lord may someday exclude over the risk of excluding those whom my Lord accepts.

Walter S. Friesen ~ Newton, KS

In this homophobic American environment, no one in his/her right mind would choose to identify as GLBT. It must be terrifying to discover one's sexual orientation as other than heterosexual. To realize that the truthful revelation of that identity might result in rejection by the most significant people in one's life raises the terrifying experience to life threatening levels.

Any response other than compassion by those who claim to care should be unthinkable for any decent human, but particularly for those who identify as followers of the Man of Sorrows.

Wilson Kratz ~ Telford, PA

We believe God is gracious and loving, and enters into a covenant relationship with us. In response to God's gracious initiative, we are called to live in relationships of covenant love with each other. We believe that the church should uphold the same standards of covenant love for all human sexual relationships, and that distinctions should not be made on the basis of sexual orientation. We believe that the church should support monogamous committed relationships based on mutuality for GLBT members as we do now for heterosexual members.

~ The Seekers Sunday School Class of the Bethel College Mennonite Church, North Newton, Kansas. (The first Sunday school class to become a member of the Supportive Congregations Network.)

Dan Baumgartner	**Ruth Linscheid**
Glen and Karen Ediger	**Dwight and LaVonne Platt**
Duane and Elizabeth Friesen	**Miner and Valetta Seymour**
Eleanor Kaufman	**Francis Toews**
Bonnie Krehbiel	**James and Lonabelle Yoder**

EPILOGUE

"[Jesus] came to what was his own, and his own people did not accept him" (John 1:11).

The greatest gift God has ever given was discarded as rubbish by the leaders of God's people whom God had called to be bearers of God's message of love and deliverance to all people. The gentle Jesus, when he was mocked and scorned, did not lash out in anger. In the anguish and pain of a slow and horrible death, he prayed that God would forgive the cruel, unfeeling people who were torturing him. This same Jesus was handed over to the Roman governor by the religious leaders of his day.

Why? Why did they demand the death of an innocent man? Why did they scorn the gift of God's anointed one? Was it because they could not bear to hear his words of truth that convicted them of the evil of their own hearts and threatened their positions of wealth and power?

They did not want that kind of messiah. They wanted a deliverer who would destroy their enemies and lead them to freedom from Roman rule. They wanted a messiah who would elevate them to even greater positions of wealth and power. They did not expect the anointed one to be born into the home of low class, ordinary parents.

In short, Jesus did not meet their expectations; his teachings infuriated them. He loved the company of the poor, the outcasts, the widows, and orphans. He even touched lepers and healed them! He did not interpret or follow the law as they prescribed it. He was not content to leave things as they had always been.

So, the religious leaders rejected him—they cast him out! And in all the ages since that day, the majority of people endowed with power have scorned, rejected, and trampled upon the poor and marginalized people of society. People with power make the rules for those beneath them in the social order without listening to the personal experiences of their lives.

While the crowds of common people who loved Jesus slept, their religious leaders pushed forward on their mission to destroy the one who had spoken words that powerfully convicted them. They dared not arrest Jesus by day because they feared that the crowds would rise up in protest, so they held the trial at night. It needed to be done quickly before the Jewish people got wind of what was happening.

When the common people woke up on Friday morning, Jesus was already on his final journey to the cross. It was too late for them to make their voices heard! The soldiers of Rome were obeying the orders of the Roman governor and were driving Jesus to the cross.

It was too late for the people to cry out for justice for the man who loved them so deeply. They gathered in great sorrow to follow him to Golgotha. The Gospel writer Luke recorded that "a great number of the people followed him, and among them were women who were beating their breasts and wailing for him" (Luke 23:27).

If you have read the true stories in this book, you have met a small sample of the great company of people who can attest to God's call to them to be shepherds of God's people or to exercise their gifts in other ways in the work of the kingdom of God.

These people are my friends—my brothers and sisters in God's family. I see them as God's good gifts discarded by the church. It hurts me much that my denomination—my church home for nearly eighty years— refuses to accept God's good gifts. My heart aches for our leaders who are blind to these good gifts of God. I am frustrated by those who see and know that GLBT individuals are good people but are not willing to speak up to defend them.

I do not understand how caring and loving people can refuse to listen to the life experiences of our own children—the children who have grown up in the church. We spend money and attend conferences and workshops to teach us how to be missional people, but we close the door to our own children. It doesn't make sense to me.

How long will we walk quietly by and allow sincere people of God to be sacrificed to the politics of the church? How can we continue to wound the sons and daughters of our church and turn them away?

On that day when we stand before our Creator, when there are no longer any "haves" and "have-nots"—on that day when our lives are laid bare before the One who knows every detail—what will our Maker say to us? I wonder if God might say, "I was gay and you did not welcome me, I was lesbian and you turned your back on me, I was bisexual and you said that I was 'evil,' I was transgender and you fired me."

~ *Roberta Showalter Kreider*

RESOURCES
Selected Anabaptist Writings

Eberly, William R. "Homosexual Acts or HOMOSEXUAL Persons." (www.voicesforanopenspirit.org/resources/humansexuality/eberly200208.php)

Friesen, Walter S. *A Personal Witness About Biblical Faith and Homsexuality.* Newton, KS: Walter S. Friesen, 2000. Email:wcfriesen@juno.com

Hershberger, Anne Krabill, editor. *Sexuality: God's Gift.* Scottdale, PA: Herald Press, 1999.

Johns, Loren. "Homosexuality and the Bible: A Case Study in the Use of the Bible for Ethics." (www.ambs.edu/LJohns/glbmenu.htm)

_____. "Statements of Mennonite Conferences, Boards, and Committees on Homosexuality (1985-2003)." (www.ambs.edu/LJohns/glbmenu.htm)

Kraus, C. Norman, editor. *To Continue the Dialogue: Biblical Interpretation and Homosexuality.* Telford, PA: Pandora Press U.S. (now Cascadia Publishing House), 2001.

Kreider, Roberta Showalter, editor. *From Wounded Hearts: Faith Stories of Lesbian, Gay, Bisexual, and Transgender People and Those Who Love Them.* (Second edition). Sellersville, PA: Roberta Showalter Kreider. Published in association with Strategic Press, Kulpsville, PA, 2003. (First edition published by Chi Rho Press, Inc., Gaithersburg, MD., 1998.)

_____. *Together in Love: Faith Stories of Gay, Lesbian, Bisexual, and Transgender Couples.* Sellersville, PA: Roberta Showalter Kreider. Published in association with Strategic Press, Kulpsville, PA, 2002.

Liechty, Ruth Conrad, series editor. *Welcome to Dialogue Series: A Search for Inclusiveness* (booklets), 2001. Series includes:
1. *Sharing Personal Convictions*
2. *Historical Perspectives*
3. *Discerning Church Membership, Part I*
4. *On Biblical Interpretation*

5. *Biological and Psychological Views*

6. *Discerning Church Membership, Part II*

7. *These, too, are Voices from God's Table, 2004.*
Order from Ruth Conrad Liechty
1568 Redbud Court, Goshen, IN 46526.

Schwartzentruber, Hubert. Chapter 6, "Worse Than Bullets: Homosexuality and Christian Faith." *Jesus in Back Alleys: The Story and Reflections of a Contemporary Prophet.* Telford, PA: DreamSeeker Books, an imprint of Pandora Press U.S. (now Cascadia Publishing House), 2002.

Other Resources

(Many other good resources are available. I can only list a few here.)

Bess, Howard H. *Pastor, I Am Gay.* Palmer, AK: Palmer Publishing Co., 1995.

Helminiak, Daniel A. *What the Bible Really Says about Homosexuality.* San Francisco: Alamo Square Press, 1994.

Holben, L.R. *What Christians Think About Homosexuality: Six Representative Views.* North Richland Hills, TX: Bibal Press, 1999.

Human Rights Campaign Foundation. *Finally Free: Personal Stories: How Love and Self-Acceptance Saved Us from "Ex-Gay" Ministries.* Washington, DC: HRC, 2000.

Morrison, Melanie. *The Grace of Coming Home: Spirituality, Sexuality, and the Struggle for Justice.* Cleveland: The Pilgrim Press, 1995.

Scanzoni, Letha and Virginia Ramey Mollenkott. *Is the Homosexual My Neighbor? A Positive Christian Response.* (Second edition) San Francisco: HarperSanFrancisco, a division of HarperCollins Publishers, 1978, 1994.

Truluck, Rembert S. *Steps to Recovery from Bible Abuse.* Gaithersburg, MD: Chi Rho Press, 2000.

Wallner, Mary Lou. *The Slow Miracle of Transformation.* Cabot, AR: Mary Lou Wallner, 2003. (www.teach-ministries.org)
E-mail: marylou@teach-ministries.org

Waun, Maurine C. *More Than Welcome: Learning to Embrace Gay, Lesbian, Bisexual, and Transgendered Persons in the Church.* St. Louis: Chalice Press, 1999.

White, Mel. *Stranger at the Gate. To Be Gay and Christian in America.* New York: Simon & Schuster, 1994.

Wink, Walter, editor. *Homosexuality and Christian Faith: Questions of Conscience for the Churches*. Minneapolis: Fortress Press, 1999.

Helpful Organizations

Brethren/Mennonite Council for Lesbian, Gay, Bisexual, and Transgender Interests
BMC, PO Box 6300, Minneapolis, MN 55406-0300.
Phone (612) 343-2060   Fax: (612) 343-2061
E-mail: bmc@bmclgbt.org   Web: www.bmclgbt.org

Connecting Families
Ruth Conrad Liechty, Contact Person
1568 Redbud Court, Goshen, IN 46526
E-mail: rliechty@juno.com

Evangelicals Concerned, Inc.
311 East 72nd Street, New York, NY 10021
E-mail: RBlair@ecinc.org

Gay, Lesbian, Straight Education Network
121 West 27th Street, Suite 804, New York, NY 10001
Phone: (212) 727-0135   Web: www.GLSEN.org
GLSEN is the largest national organization that brings together concerned citizens from all walks of life in order to end the destructive effects of anti-gay bias in K-12 schools across the country.

Human Rights Campaign Foundation
1640 Rhode Island Avenue, N.W., Washington, DC 20036
Phone: (202) 628-4160   E-mail: hrc@hrc.org
Web: www.hrc.org

IMPACT Communications
Dotti Berry, President   Phone: (360) 305-0909
4402 Carstan Loop, Blaine, WA 98230
E-mail: dotti@GLBTcoach.com   Web: www.GLBTcoach.com
Dottie is a diversity and sexuality educator and serves as a "coach" for the GLBT community.

Parents, Families and Friends of Lesbians and Gays (PFLAG)
(Now includes Bisexuals and Transgenders)
1726 M Street, N.W., Suite 400, Washington, DC 20036
Phone: (202) 467-8180   Fax: (202) 467-8194
E-mail: info@pflag.org   Web: www.pflag.org

Soulforce
  PO Box 3195, Lynchburg, VA 24503
  Phone (toll free): (877) 705-6393   Fax: (434) 384-9333
  E-mail: mel@soulforce.org   Web: www.soulforce.org
  Soulforce is an interfaith movement committed to ending spiritual violence perpetuated by religious policies and teachings against gay, lesbian, bisexual, and transgender people through nonviolent teachings of Gandhi and Martin Luther King, Jr.

The Shower of Stoles Project
Martha G. Juillerat, National Program Director
  57 Upton Avenue S., Minneapolis, MN 55405
  E-mail: stoleproj@aol.com   Web: www.showerofstoles.org
  The purpose of the Shower of Stoles is to offer a creative form of expression to illustrate the enormity of the denial of the calls of GLBT people for leadership in their faith communities. Check the website for a new video.

Universal Fellowship of Metropolitan Community Churches
  8704 Santa Monica Blvd., 2nd Floor, West Hollywood, CA 90069
  Phone: (310) 360-8640   E-mail: info@MCCchurch.org
  Web: www.MCCchurch.org

Voices for an Open Spirit (VOS)
  9 North Union Street, Elgin, IL 60123
  Phone: (847) 697-1371   Fax: (847) 697-7774
  E-mail: voicesforanopenspirit@hotmail.com
  Web: www.voicesforanopenspirit.org/
  A grassroots movement in the Church of the Brethren fostering openness and inclusion, building bridges, and seeking common ground.

God of grace and God of glory,
on Thy people pour Thy power;
crown Thine ancient church's story;
bring her bud to glorious flower.
Grant us wisdom, grant us courage,
for the facing of this hour,
for the facing of this hour.

Cure Thy children's warring madness;
bend our pride to Thy control.
Shame our wanton, selfish gladness,
rich in things and poor in soul.
Grant us wisdom, grant us courage,
lest we miss Thy kingdom's goal,
lest we miss Thy kingdom's goal.

Set our feet on lofty places;
gird our lives that they may be
armored with all Christ-like graces
in the quest to set all free.
Grant us wisdom, grant us courage,
keep our hope secure in Thee,
keep our hope secure in Thee.

Harry Emerson Fosdick, 1930 (Altered)

The Cost of Truth

❧

From Wounded Hearts

❧

Together in Love

To order, send a check or
money order to

Kreiders Books
24-B Green Top Road
Sellersville, PA 18960-1223

Phone: (215) 257-7322   E-mail: kreiders@netcarrier.com

Single copies: $24.00 (U.S. funds only)

Bulk rate: Six or more copies to one address
(mixed or matched)
$20.00 each (U.S. funds only)

Pennsylvania residents: Add 6% sales tax to all orders

All books **postpaid** within the United States
Additional postage required for foreign addresses

Printed in the United States
39616LVS00005B/142-153